PENGUIN BOOKS

THE TATAS, FREDDIE MERCURY AND OTHER BAWAS

Coomi Kapoor is a pioneer political journalist who was the first female chief reporter and bureau chief in Delhi. She has been in the profession for nearly five decades, and has worked with the *Indian Express, India Today, Sunday Mail, Indian Post, Illustrated Weekly of India* and *Motherland*. She is currently a consulting editor at *Indian Express*, where her popular column, 'Inside Track', appears regularly. Her earlier book, *The Emergency: A Personal History* (2015), was a bestseller.

PRAISE FOR THE BOOK

'Anecdotes and tidbits infuse life and vibrancy into the book . . . the volume is rich with painstaking research and unusual details . . . A treasure trove of moments from lost times'—Shabnam Minwala, *The Hindu*

'For colour, drama, endurance and originality, this tiny endogamous community is like the much-loved Parsi charity—truly a Time and Talents Club'—Sunil Sethi, *India Today*

'Veteran Indian journalist Coomi Kapoor has penned a definitive book about her community . . . an insight into the Indian Parsis, whose meritocracy outweighs their rapidly dwindling population'—Joydeep Sengupta, *Khaleej Times*

'The book offers its own well researched account of the great Parsi Battle Royale—Ratan Tata v. Cyrus Mistry and Nusli Wadia and the control for the house of Tatas. Kapoor in a coup of sorts was able to interview all three opponents'—Vaihayasi Pande Daniel, Rediff.com

'An insider's account, the writing flows well and is readable, the research is thorough'—Madhulika Liddle, *New Indian Express*

'A riveting account of some of the famous members of the Parsi community who have brought much accolades to India in the past century' —Reshmi Chakravorty, *Deccan Chronicle*

'Coomi Kapoor explores the history of the Parsi community through its prominent names and how they transformed cities with their entrepreneurial genius . . . The cast of characters in her book is as wide as it is varied' —Jane Borges, *Midday*

'It is a delightful easy read—well researched with many nuggets thrown in that even most Parsis would not be aware of. What sets this book apart from other works on the community is that Coomi has focused on the Parsis of the last century and included some of the newer and younger enterprising ones'—Niloufer Billimoria, *Tribune*

'Written in a racy entertaining style, it holds the readers' interest throughout. The book is largely a celebration of the material and cultural legacy of the community'—Bakhtiar Dadabhoy, *Parsiana*

PRAISE FOR *THE EMERGENCY: A PERSONAL HISTORY*

'Both so necessary and also such an evocative reminder. Combining a well-researched chronological historical account with personal anecdotal experiences of the impact on individual lives, her book recreates the 21 months of the Emergency and what it was like to live in India at that time'—Karan Thapar, *Hindustan Times*

'*The Emergency: A Personal History* is a riveting and necessary account of the elite politics of the Emergency, and the way it impinged upon one family . . . The strength of a personal history lies in human detail. The effortless, if understated, descriptions of an elite in a mode of complicity will leave you reeling . . .'—Pratap Bhanu Mehta, *Financial Express*

'Kapoor writes sensitively about that traumatic period when the government targeted both her husband Virendra and her flamboyant brother-in-law Subramanian Swamy, and she herself suffered much' —Sunanda K. Datta-Ray, *Telegraph*

'Both carefully researched and delightfully readable . . . Ms Kapoor is punctilious: her story has villains—the boorish Sanjay, the Machiavellian S.S. Ray—but few real heroes, just ordinary people in extraordinary circumstances'—Mihir S. Sharma, *Business Standard*

'If by now you are not convinced to read this book, then I can only quote Karl Marx (a much derided figure these days): History repeats itself, first as tragedy, then as farce'—Anil Padmanabhan, *Mint*

'Kapoor has done a grand job of reminding us how easily self-complacency and self-will can seep into our body politic. *The Emergency* should be required reading'—Sandhya Rao, *Hindu Business Line*

'Coomi Kapoor's immensely readable and engrossing retelling of the darkest 21 months of independent India is a reminder and a wake-up call even to those who still have vivid memories of Indira Gandhi's Emergency' —Shreekant Sambrani, *Business Standard*

THE TATAS, FREDDIE MERCURY & OTHER BAWAS

An Intimate History of the Parsis

Coomi Kapoor

PENGUIN BOOKS

An imprint of Penguin Random House

PENGUIN BOOKS

USA | Canada | UK | Ireland | Australia
New Zealand | India | South Africa | China

Penguin Books is part of the Penguin Random House group of companies
whose addresses can be found at global.penguinrandomhouse.com

Published by Penguin Random House India Pvt. Ltd
4th Floor, Capital Tower 1, MG Road,
Gurugram 122 002, Haryana, India

| Penguin
Random House
India

First published by Westland Non-Fiction, an imprint of Westland Publications
Private Limited, in 2021
This edition published in Penguin Books by Penguin Random House India 2023

ISBN 9780143459811

Typeset in Adobe Garamond Pro by Manipal Technologies Limited, Manipal
Printed at Replika Press Pvt. Ltd, India

www.penguin.co.in

*To my forefathers, who travelled far and fought
fiercely to preserve their faith and identity*

Contents

A section of the Tata Family Tree

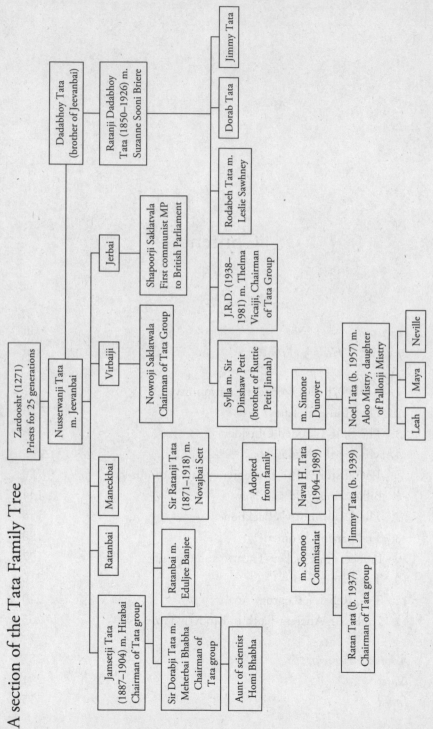

A section of the Wadia Family Tree

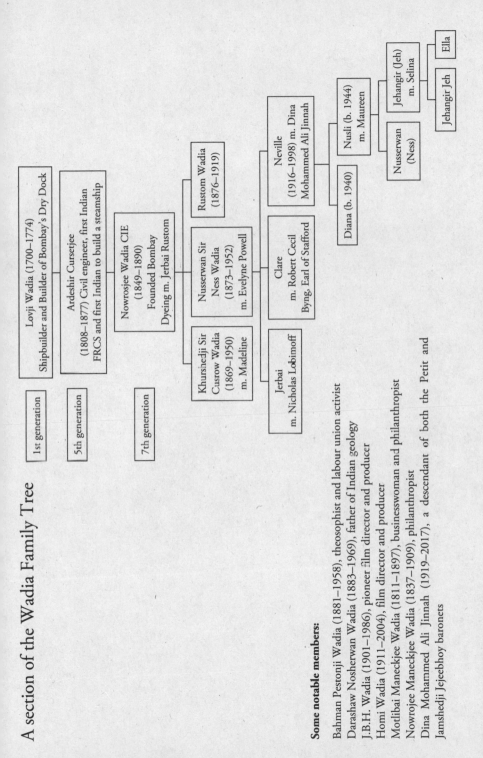

1st generation

Lovji Wadia (1700–1774)
Shipbuilder and Builder of Bombay's Dry Dock

5th generation

Ardeshir Cursetjee
(1808–1877) Civil engineer, first Indian
FRCS and first Indian to build a steamship

7th generation

Nowrosjee Wadia CIE
(1849–1890)
Founded Bombay
Dyeing m. Jerbai Rustom

Rustom Wadia
(1876–1919)

Khurshedji Sir
Cusrow Wadia
(1869–1950)
m. Madeline

Nusserwan Sir
Ness Wadia
(1873–1952)
m. Evelyne Powell

Jerbai
m. Nicholas Lobimoff

Clare
m. Robert Cecil
Byng, Earl of Stafford

Neville
(1916–1998) m. Dina
Mohammed Ali Jinnah

Diana (b. 1940)

Nusli (b. 1944)
m. Maureen

Nusserwan
(Ness)

Jehangir (Jeh)
m. Selina

Jehangir Jeh

Ella

Some notable members:

Bahman Pestonji Wadia (1881–1958), theosophist and labour union activist
Darashaw Nosherwan Wadia (1883–1969), father of Indian geology
J.B.H. Wadia (1901–1986), pioneer film director and producer
Homi Wadia (1911–2004), film director and producer
Motlibai Maneckjee Wadia (1811–1897), businesswoman and philanthropist
Nowrojee Maneckjee Wadia (1837–1909), philanthropist
Dina Mohammed Ali Jinnah (1919–2017), a descendant of both the Petit and
Jamshedji Jejeebhoy baronets

Foreword

This well-researched and informative book brings out in vivid colours the saga of a microscopic community to which the author and I are proud to belong. The book begins with a short history of the Parsis after they landed in India, and then goes on to a contemporary theme, which is the peremptory sacking of Cyrus Mistry by the board of Tata Sons as the executive chairman of Tata Sons. This is then followed by a chapter entitled 'The House of Tatas', which gives interesting details about the founder of the group, namely, Jamsetji Tata. The surname 'Tata' is believed to have been derived from Gujarati words which signify a hot temper. An interesting detail is that Jamsetji was born when his father was only seventeen years old. After the Parsis came to India, they adopted many of the ways of the majority community, including child marriages at that time. In fact, thanks to a child marriage between Sir Temulji Nariman and his wife at the tender age of five and three, respectively, they enjoyed a married life of eighty-six years, entering the *Guinness Book of World Records* for the longest-ever marriage, until they were recently pipped by two marriages which extended to ninety years each. Jamsetji's curiosity

and extensive travels led to the birth of the multifarious activities
of the House of Tata, which included the first world-class luxury
hotel built in 1903 in Bombay. Incidentally, my great-grandfather,
Sorabji Contractor, was the person who actually built this hotel
under a British architect who is alleged to have designed it the
wrong way around! Another interesting detail is Jamsetji's visit
to England in 1880, in which he attended a lecture by Thomas
Carlyle who observed, 'Those who control iron and steel will
in time come to control gold as well.' This led to many further
travels, including to the USA, and the setting up of the Tata Iron
and Steel Company.

Interesting details are given about the House of the Wadias,
the founders of Bombay's shipping industry, including the
signing of the Treaty of Nanking in 1842, whereby the Chinese
Emperor ceded the territory of Hong Kong to the British,
onboard a Wadia ship—the *HMS Cornwallis*. Another interesting
historical event is the composition of the American national
anthem by Francis Scott Key during the Anglo-American War
of 1812 onboard another Wadia vessel, the *HMS Minden*. The
other business houses of the Parsi community, the Shapoorji
Pallonji group and the Godrej group, are also described in vivid
and punctilious detail.

In a chapter entitled 'The Community's Backbone', the Parsi
professional is discussed. In the field of law, outstanding judges and
lawyers belonging to this community are set out in some detail.
The same goes for esteemed members of the Indian Civil Service,
great Parsi doctors and noted Parsi politicians. There is also an
interesting discussion of remarkable Parsi women, beginning with
Madame Bhikaiji Cama, who unfurled the first Indian flag in
Stuttgart; Mithan Jamshed Lam, who was the first Indian woman
to practise in the Bombay High Court; Homai Vyarawalla, the
Leni Riefenstahl of Indian photography; and an interesting
lady who bore the same name as Mohammed Ali Jinnah's wife,

Rati Petit, and went on to marry a German professor of philosophy who converted to Buddhism and took the name 'Lama Angarika Govinda', Rati taking the name of 'Li Gotami Govinda'. Beauty queens such as Persis Khambatta are also touched upon, as is the colourful Bapsy Pavry, who married the sixteenth Marquess of Winchester when he was ninety years old, under the mistaken belief that not only did he have an exalted title, but that he also had a huge amount of wealth which went with that title. The old Marquess is also supposed to have married Bapsy in the fond hope that she was an heiress—both proved to be wrong, leading to a separation within days of the marriage.

In another interesting chapter entitled 'The Iconic Four', a contentious issue is raised as to who could be regarded as the four most remarkable Parsis in post-independence India. Coomi names the scientist Homi Bhabha, Field Marshal Manekshaw and two outstanding musicians, Zubin Mehta and Freddie Mercury. Nani Palkhivala is thrown in as a possible fifth. Madame Bhikaiji Cama then makes a reappearance in the chapter entitled 'Two Rebels a Century Apart', together with Kobad Ghandy, who had faced a long stint in jail, being outlawed by the Government of India as a Maoist.

The book ends with a chapter entitled 'Coda: An Ancient Faith in Modern Times', outlining how the orthodox among the Parsis in India appear to have the upper hand in not accepting converts. Coomi, however, is hopeful that a religion that has survived for so long despite all odds, will somehow manage to survive in spite of the declining number of believers, the 'indomitable spirit' of the community not being easily snuffed out. This book is a must-read for whoever is interested in the trajectory of this microscopic community in India, and the amazing and remarkable success that it has achieved in this country and all over the world.

Justice R.F. Nariman

Justice Rohinton Fali Nariman was a judge of the Supreme Court of India, a scholar and an eminent authority on Zoroastrianism. He was trained as a priest at age twelve.

Prologue

A History of the Parsis

Very late in life, on a pilgrimage to the Parsi heritage sites—Sanjan, Navsari, Udvada and Surat—I was stumped when the gentleman escorting me inquired whether my ancestors were from Navsari or Surat. Only when I returned to Delhi and quizzed my sister did I learn more about my forefathers. I wondered how I could have been so incurious about my roots. As a child growing up in Bombay, I was conscious that we were rather different from most people around us. My paternal grandfather, Dinshah Kapadia, wore his Parsi identity on his sleeve, supremely convinced of the superiority of his race; an attitude that embarrassed us kids. My mother, Aloo Kapadia, dressed differently from my friends' mothers, usually in old-fashioned georgettes with embroidered borders. She moved largely in exclusively Parsi circles and most of her friends in Bombay were members of the charitable organisation, the Time & Talents Club. She was a high priest's daughter and prayed daily in front of a small urn of burning sandalwood sticks and incense, reading from a thick volume of Avesta prayers written in Gujarati.

This daily ritual of mumbling in front of the fire, prayer books open, was common to all the elders in the family.

If I grew up without much knowledge of my religion or community, it was because neither of my pragmatic parents had thought it necessary to steep my siblings and me in our Parsi heritage. Perhaps, too, my convent-educated elder siblings were self-conscious about how we sometimes stuck out because of our clothes, home, mannerisms and broken Hindi and so were dismissive of my mother's attempts at indoctrination.

We did, of course, learn by heart the basic prayers required for our navjote ceremony, even though the words in Avesta, the precursor of ancient Persian, were incomprehensible. The navjote is normally performed during childhood to confirm a Parsi child's entry into the faith by donning the muslin vest (sudreh) and tying the sacred girdle made of lambswool (kusti) and reciting the prayers with the priest. And we wore the sudreh and kusti as long as we lived in the parental home. Ethical values and honesty were constant themes in what our parents taught us. The whole family, decked out in new clothes, would pay a visit to the two big fire temples on Princess Street on Papeti, the day to remember the dead. (The major fire temples are called 'Atash Behram'—temples in which the sacred fire has been prepared with far more elaborate rituals, including a fire created by lightning.) On birthdays and auspicious occasions such as Navroz (the Parsi New Year), we prayed at the small agiary down the road. When I left Bombay to study in the United States, my mother acknowledged that it would be impractical to pack a pile of sudreh to wash and wear every day in a foreign land and sent me with just two in case I visited some place holy.

It turned out that my paternal family was originally from Surat and my mother's family from Navsari, something that would have been obvious had I bothered to take even a cursory interest in the family tree. My mother's father, Dastur Nosherwan

Jamasp Asa, was the high priest of the Deccan, Poona, as well
as of isolated cantonment areas in Madhya Pradesh, Rajasthan
and Uttar Pradesh. My mother used to claim proudly that her
family line could trace its ancestry back to Neryosangh Dhaval—
believed to be the priest who arrived with the first boatload of
Parsis in Sanjan. Many priestly families originated from Navsari,
which played a central role in the religious life of the Parsis for
some eight centuries. Records of the names of those young boys
who took the priestly exam to become navars (the first step to
being ordained as a Zoroastrian priest) are maintained, which is
how priestly ancestry can be traced. However, the family lore that
the Jamasp Asa line can actually be traced all the way back to
the first priest is a matter of faith rather than fact. There was a
priest, Neryosangh Dhaval, a scholar of Sanskrit in the eleventh or
twelfth century, who could possibly have been a forefather.

While my mother generally deferred to my father's more
dominating family, I now realise that her lineage was far more
impressive. One ancestor, Dastur Jamasp Asa, born in Navsari
in 1693 was an acclaimed scholar and priest. He studied Persian,
Sanskrit and astrology from a Hindu pandit, but he was also eager
to learn Zand/Pahlavi, which was taught to him by a visiting
priest from Iran, Dastur Velayati. When Dastur Velayati left
India, he pronounced Dastur Jamasp Asa the most perceptive of
his three priestly students and presented him with copies of two
Pahlavi texts.[1] Jamasp Asa's lineage was considered to hold the
third chair among the dasturs of Navsari. (The first chair was held
by descendants of Dastur Meherji Rana, the scholar-priest who
explained the religion to the Mughal emperor Akbar.)

A forward-thinking man, Jamasp Asa annoyed the leading
priests of his time by offering translations of religious texts to
Behedins. While Parsis are proud that they do not follow any
formal caste system and that there is no culturally sanctioned
discrimination, Behedins are laymen who cannot become priests.

Jamasp Asa believed that knowledgeable Behedins should be allowed to enter the priesthood—a premise so radical, it remains unacceptable to the community, with Behedins still frozen out of the Parsi clergy, although the offspring of the priestly classes are, of course, permitted to forego their traditional occupations and opt instead for ordinary jobs.

In 1843, a prosperous Parsi merchant who lived in Poona, Sorabji Patel, was allotted a large parcel of land in the environs of the old city. He decided his land would host Poona's first fire temple. The Bombay Parsi Punchayet (BPP) recommended a Navsari dastur from the Jamasp Asa line, and Dastur Jamaspji Edulji was selected to be the first dastur of the Patel fire temple. (His brother Jamshedji Jamaspji was an ancestor of the line of priests at the Anjuman Atash Behram in South Bombay.) On Dastur Edulji's death in 1846, his eldest son, Dastur Nosherwan Jamaspji, was installed as the high priest. Dastur Nosherwan was honoured by the British government and made a Khan Bahadur for his loyalty. He is remembered for his social contributions, including digging wells in Poona[2] (now Pune) for all to use during a drought. He was recognised as the senior priest of all Parsi communities in the Deccan and, in 1893, the Sardar Dastur Nosherwan School for Zoroastrian girls was founded in his memory. The school's pupils largely comprised girls from middle-class Parsi families and Zoroastrian prayers were chanted daily. A school for boys in Poona, named after his younger brother, Dastur Hoshang, opened in 1912, nearly twenty years after the girls' school. Both schools continue to flourish, though there are hardly any Parsi children who now attend.

Dastur Hoshang Jamaspji was one of the most illustrious members of the Poona Dastur line. A scholar who knew twelve languages, he had mastered the Zend-Avesta and Pahlavi alongside Sanskrit, Marathi, English, German, Hebrew and Latin. He earned his doctorate in 1890 from the University of Vienna and was a professor of Oriental languages at the Deccan College, Poona. Earlier, as assistant inam commissioner in the Berar Province, he helped the British East India Company by translating 'treasonous correspondence' during the 1857 uprising. From the Indian perspective, of course, Dastur Hoshang's actions were treasonous, a betrayal of the efforts of the first freedom fighters. His successor, Dastur Kaikobad, the son of Dastur Nosherwan's only son Dastur Adarbad, was also a scholar and reformist. He faced the wrath of orthodox Parsis when, in 1911, he and a kinsman, Dastur J. Jamasp Asa of Bombay, performed the navjote of the second daughter of Ratanji Dadabhoy Tata and his French wife Suzanne. In 1914, he went to Burma and officiated at the navjote of Bella, an adopted girl of non-Parsi stock, which provoked a court case in Burma that was taken up by the Privy Council in London. Faced with a barrage of criticism from the community and under pressure from the fire-temple trustees, Dastur Kaikobad promised not to undertake such ceremonies again. But his liberal attitude towards intermarriage and even conversion remained unchanged. Two years later, in 1916, he declared publicly that he had done no wrong in Burma. And at a conference of world religions in London in 1924, he read out a paper reiterating his views.[3] His elder son, my grandfather Dastur Nosherwan, died when I was very young so my recollections are based on sepia-tinted photographs of a handsome man with a flowing white beard, dressed in the white muslin robes and turban of a priest. The last of the line was my uncle Dastur Hormazdiar, who was pressured, on the untimely death of his father in 1949, into taking the position of high priest at a very young age. My jolly uncle, who was fascinated by planes and wanted to enlist in the air force, was temperamentally disinclined to be a priest. After his death nearly a decade ago, there was no one left from the Poona Jamasp Asa Dastur male lineage to carry on the tradition, and the prayers are now said by a panthaki (priest-in-charge) at the fire temple. My cousin Mehernawaz

Vakil continues to conscientiously oversee the functioning of the
temple, but as a woman, is not permitted to play any formal role.

Parsis no longer live in the vicinity of Pune's venerable Patel
fire temple. They all moved a long time ago to the cantonment
and other, newer parts of the town. Once the monsoon capital
of Bombay's rich Parsis and a scholarly centre, Pune has now
become an industrial and commercial hub. The temple stands
in splendid isolation, amidst the otherwise bustling Nana Peth,
a lower-middle-class Maharashtrian neighbourhood. The family
mansion, Dastur Hall, decorated in the opulent style of a British
country house, with imposing family portraits hung on the walls,
was torn down to make way for a housing colony. Dastur Hall was
home to a large joint family; apart from the high priest's family,
various members of the extended Dastur clan in Poona made
their homes there and contributed to expanding the building over
the years. Most did not become priests, even if they all studied
to be navars. They were professionals, usually working for the
British government or the Poona civic authorities. One became a
police officer. Accompanied by his cook, this dogged policeman
unsuccessfully pursued the general of the 1857 rebellion, Tatya
Tope, through the jungles of Madhya Pradesh, according to my
aunt Mithoo Coorlawala.[4] (Incidentally, a couple of years ago,
this aunt, a repository of family lore, celebrated her hundredth
birthday.)

Consanguineous marriage, between cousins, was the preferred
option in the Dastur family, so nearly everyone could trace their
ancestry back to Dastur Jamasp Asa multiple times. Such excessive
inbreeding affected the physical and mental health of some family
members. In my childhood, I recall one eccentric relation who
believed he was a bandmaster and always moved his arms up and
down, keeping time to the music in his head. My mother, Aloo
Dastur, was only the third female descendant of her family to not
marry a relative.

Khushroo Nariman, now popularly known as Vir Nariman, was the nephew of Dastur Hoshang and his wife Hirabai, and an exception in a family loyal to the British. Since Khushroo and his brother were orphaned early, they were brought up by their aunt and uncle at Dastur Hall. Nariman later studied law at Bombay University and joined the Indian National Congress. Unlike the earlier generation of Parsi Congress leaders, who were all moderates, Nariman was part of the radical faction and learnt his first political lessons from Bal Gangadhar Tilak. An elected municipal corporator, he launched a campaign against corruption in the reclamation of a part of Bombay's Back Bay, which was later named 'Nariman Point' in his honour. He exposed the shady transactions of the Bombay Development Directorate which was later dissolved. Thomas Harvey, superintendent engineer in the Directorate, sought to prosecute Nariman for defamation. It turned out that the chief presidency magistrate, Sir H.P. Dastur, who acquitted Nariman after a year-long trial keenly followed across the Bombay Presidency, was a close relative. Not that this was necessarily to Nariman's advantage. H.P. Dastur's detractors claimed that he had earned his knighthood by sending Congressmen to jail, including his kinsman Nariman, whom he sent to prison in 1930 for breaking the salt laws. As Nariman was president of the Bombay Congress Committee and a popular state leader, most people assumed that he would be appointed leader of the state Congress legislative party and the first chief minister of what at Independence had become Bombay State. But a relatively unknown politician, B.G. Kher, was selected instead and many Parsis were resentful. We grew up listening to our family conversations suggesting that Sardar Patel had scuttled Nariman's chances.

Another illustrious member of the Dastur family was Sir Jamshedji Kanga, my grandfather's cousin. Kanga, an icon of the Bombay High Court, mentored generations of the country's leading Parsi lawyers. Although the Jamasp Asa family and a few others were hereditary high priests, this was not typical of the community. Priests were expected to secure a position for themselves and were normally paid a meagre salary. Little has changed and, as a consequence, today few choose to enter the priesthood full-time. According to a recent survey in the fortnightly community magazine *Parsiana*, there are 148 agiaries across India, of which only 30 per cent are economically self-sufficient. Some fire temples in far-off places that no longer have a Parsi community to speak of have fallen into disuse and are in danger of being taken over by encroachers. Already, in the West, the Zoroastrian priesthood is a vocation, not a full-time job. Many priests in North America, for instance, are highly paid doctors, lawyers and management consultants. Even the Jamasp Asa descendant in charge of the Anjuman Atash Behram in Mumbai is a London-based oncologist and surgeon. He shuttles, improbably, between London and Mumbai to perform his duties at key religious ceremonies.

My father's family were Behedins and marriage with an Athornan would once have been unthinkable. My paternal grandfather, Professor Dinshah Kapadia, was a self-made man who rose from humble beginnings to become acting principal of Elphinstone College, and later principal of the prestigious Deccan College, Poona. Apart from the subject he taught, mathematics, he was an authority on Avesta and Pahlavi, the dead languages in which Zoroastrian prayers and scriptures are written. He painstakingly prepared a glossary of the Pahlavi Vendidad, Avesta words with their English translations. And although his eldest son, my father Jamshed, worked for the British government as a member of the Indian Civil Service, and another son, Homi, joined the Royal Navy, Dinshahji and his family were far more nationalistically inclined than the Dasturs. He was friendly with all the well-known Poona scholars, some of whom, such as Tilak and Gopal Krishna Gokhale, were stalwarts of the Freedom movement.

The Kapadias were solid middle class Parsis with conventional professions like doctors, lawyers, professors and engineers. But there were some rebels who sprouted from this unlikely soil. Take my father's cousin's daughter, Nelly. A student at the JJ School of Art, she was demoted for defiance and finally after a showdown with the principal walked out of the college, much to the horror of her family. But the extremely gifted Nelly got a scholarship to London and became a renowned weaver, textile designer and crafts activist, who experimented with Scandinavian modernism and Indian crafts traditions. She was a pioneer in the revival and the popularization of the Kalamkari. Nelly Sethna (her married name) passed away in 1992, but she wove a rich legacy by which she is still fondly remembered in the art world.

Dinshahji's arranged marriage to Nellie Divecha was across the Parsi social divide. My paternal grandmother's family, the Divechas, had lived in Bombay much longer than the Kapadias who had come to Bombay from Surat. An ancestor, Framji Pestonji Divecha, the 'head native servant' of the governor of Bombay at Parel, was granted the khot of the two villages of Mahul and Maravli in Salsette taluka in 1830 by the East India Company as a reward for his 'long, faithful and meritorious service'. (My father used to joke that 'head native servant' meant Framji was the butler; my great-aunt preferred to assume he was the governor's steward.) In his will, Framji decreed that the land was to be bequeathed to his children's children and could not be sold until then. A prolonged lawsuit followed to determine whether 'chhokra na chhokra', the Gujarati phrase, included girls since 'chhokra' could refer to both children, generally, as well as boys specifically. The Divechas faced other legal challenges; Parsis are a litigious lot. Suddenly, the easy-going family of my great-grandfather Pestonji Divecha, who basically lived off rental income from his land and the yields from his mango orchards, toddy trees and salt pans, was scared the lawsuits would lead to financial ruin. It was hastily decided that it might be best if the eldest daughter Navajbhai (Nellie) was married off to a promising, suitably educated Parsi man, even if he were not of the same income bracket or social standing as them. Her brother, Framji (Fali) Divecha, remained a bachelor. He fell in love with a beautiful Hungarian woman on one of his frequent trips abroad but could not marry her because his mother threatened to commit suicide if he dared to marry a 'juddin', a non-Zoroastrian. So he gave up his true love and frittered away much of what was left of the family fortune in a series of hare-brained schemes. The difference in backgrounds and interests between the two families is illustrated by a story my grandfather was fond of relating. Fali Divecha travelled to many parts of the world, from Peru in South America to deepest Africa, on a series of tramp steamers. Once aboard, Fali would take on the role of the ship's doctor on the strength of the licence he obtained for owning Wright and Company, a chemist's shop in Bombay. Before Fali's departure on one of his trips, Dinshahji introduced him to a friend, the physicist C.V. Raman, who would be travelling on the same boat. Fali Mama later complained to Dinshahji that his friend, who would go on to win a Nobel prize, was a bit dim. Raman had a similar observation to make about my great-uncle!

Eventually, the Divecha family saw off the various lawsuits and claims on their land. It was the lack of a dot on the word 'chokra' in Gujarati that came to their rescue. Since Fali Mama died a bachelor, his sister's children became part-shareholders of the Salsette estate, in the area now known as Trombay. In 1947, most of Mahul was acquired for a pittance by the central government under the Land Acquisition Act to set up the Bhabha Atomic Research Centre. Lawsuits over compensation went on for years, though the conclusion, with a paltry few extra paise thrown in per acre, was hardly worth the wait. By the mid-1970s, the state government acquired the rest of the land, which included large stretches of mangroves and mango orchards, under the Urban Land Ceiling Act. However, a few years later, the Maharashtra state government decided it was unable to pay for the land and it was returned to its owners. By then, squatters and slum landlords had taken possession of the vacant plots, and the lands were seemingly irretrievable. One person who tried to help the Divecha family trace its land tracts was threatened with a pistol by the land mafia and hastily backed out of offering any further assistance. Effectively, the family's considerable tracts of land had become illusory, a fate met by many Parsis whose holdings were now only nominally theirs.

My paternal grandfather Dinshahji's family had moved to Bombay from Surat. The surname Kapadia was assumed because his grandfather sold fabric and 'kapad' is the Gujarati word for cloth. Dinshahji's father, Dorabji, was a newspaper reporter who apparently never amounted to much, and Dinshahji looked more to his uncle, a doctor, for inspiration. A God-fearing, righteous man and the backbone of the Poona Parsi Punchayet, Dinshahji would roar with disapproval and shake his cane in fury if he heard of any Parsi marrying out of the faith and point proudly to his own offspring. The priestly branch of my family, in contrast, was far more tolerant of those who married outside the religion. A close relative joined the RAF, married an Englishwoman, changed his name from 'Hoshang' to 'Horace' and was fair-complexioned enough to pass for British. It was he, rather than his family in India, who wanted to cut off all contact.

Dinshahji's four children remained true to the faith, all of them marrying Parsis. All three sons were taught the Avesta. When his granddaughter, my sister Roxna, declared her intention to marry a Hindu, he was beside himself with horror and grief. In the style of a Victorian novel, the octogenarian wrote an agonised letter to my sister in tiny, spidery handwriting begging her not to take such a terrible, terrible step. It would, he wrote, leave her an outcast and bring disgrace to the whole family. He chided my parents for not ensuring that their children were introduced into the right Parsi company. It would have broken his heart had he survived to see that of his ten grandchildren, only three married Parsis. And of his fourteen married great-grandchildren, not a single one has a Parsi spouse, though there is a little hope since three are still unmarried. Over half of the younger generations of Dinshahji's descendants have left India to settle in the US, Canada and the United Kingdom. They now have only the vaguest and slimmest of connections to the religion and culture that their ancestors fought so hard to preserve over the centuries.

Brought up with Dinshahji's dire warnings ringing in my ears, and having heard my mother's stories of the disgrace the family faced because her grandfather had presided over the navjote ceremony of Bela, I accepted unquestioningly that once I had married out, I had become a 'parjat', an outcaste. My parents, while they may have disapproved of intermarriage, were liberal enough to accept that times had changed. My mother's greatest fear was, 'What will people say?' It is for this reason that, at our mother's funeral, my sister had insisted that the grandchildren sit outside in the general enclosure for visitors at Doongerwadi and not in the prayer hall with the family when the ritual Parsi prayers were recited, much to the fury of my daughters and niece, since none of the relations present had voiced any objection.

* * *

Despite the commonness of intermarriage in recent times, and despite having lived in India for centuries, the Parsis continue to maintain a distinctive identity, religion and culture—the result of what had been an overwhelmingly endogamous community. To some extent, even their looks tend to set them apart. Parsis are relatively fairer than the average Indian and hooked noses are a common feature. Decades ago, Parsi women draped their saris in a way that became characteristic of the community and the men always covered their heads—either with a long, stiff, lacquered black pagree or a black prayer cap. Today, like everyone else, Parsis wear traditional clothes only on ceremonial occasions. In any case, Parsis adopted Western-style dress before most of their contemporaries in India.

Followers of the prophet Zarathustra—who is believed to have been born in Central Asia and lived sometime between 1500 BCE and 2000 BCE—Parsis practise Zoroastrianism, considered by many the world's oldest monotheistic religion—older than Judaism, Christianity and Islam. Zoroastrianism exercised a profound influence on Christianity and Judaism, particularly on such issues as heaven, hell and the Day of Judgment. Zoroastrian scriptures preach the constant struggle between truth and falsehood.

Parsis see themselves as inheritors of the glorious traditions of two great ancient Persian empires, the Achaeminid (550–330 BCE) and the Sassanid (224–651 CE). The ruins of Persepolis, standing majestically atop a hill, an architectural marvel of the ancient world, are a legacy of the mighty Persian empire founded by Cyrus the Great and strengthened by Darius I. A replica of the 'Cylinder of Cyrus' from 539 BCE is preserved in the United Nations building in New York and is acknowledged as the world's first bill of human rights as per scholars like Fali Nariman. Unusually for a king, the clay cylinder, also known as the 'Edict of Cyrus', does not boast of conquests but instead records what the king had done for the well-being of the people he had conquered.[5]

The Bible contains several mentions of Cyrus: he is the king of Persia who conquered Babylon and set free the Jews who had lived in captivity for seventy years, allowing them to return to

Jerusalem. His successor, Darius I, honoured Cyrus's wishes by rebuilding destroyed Jewish temples. The Old Testament in the Book of Ezra refers to Cyrus as 'Anointed of the Lord', a term normally reserved for Jewish prophets. Other Zoroastrians find mention in the New Testament. The magi, or wise men, from the East who brought gifts for the infant Jesus were Zoroastrian priests who specialised in astrology and the occult. The word 'magi', which today also means sorcerer, is derived from the Old Persian word 'maguš'. The magi were following a star in pursuit of a thousand-year-old prophecy that a saviour would be born of a virgin. Zarathustra is mentioned in ancient Greek and Roman literature, including the writings of Plato, albeit not as a prophet but a philosopher.[6]

Alexander the Great ('the accursed Iskandar', as Parsis refer to him[7]) defeated the Persian empire in 330 BCE, and his drunken army burnt down most of Persepolis, including the famous library with its extraordinary store of ancient religious texts. This is why details of Zoroastrian practices and tenets are shrouded in mystery. The French scholar James Darmesteter wrote in 1880, in his *Introduction to the Zend Avesta, Vol. I* that 'No other great belief in the world ever left such poor and meagre monuments of its past splendour.' Zarathustra's teachings, as detailed in the holy texts known as the 'Gathas', were preserved orally for centuries and transcribed by priests only during the Sassanian era. The Sassanid Empire (224–651 CE) was recognised as a major world power, as was its rival, the Roman-Byzantine Empire. Founded by Ardashir I, the Sassanids influenced the art and culture of both Europe and Asia in medieval times. Under a succession of Sassanid kings, Zoroastrianism was the state religion. The empire collapsed when Persia came under Arab control after the Battle of Nahavand around the year 642 CE as maintained by several historians

With the arrival of the Arabs, the Persians who resisted conversion to Islam were persecuted. Some fled to the mountains of Khorasan on the border of Afghanistan and the Persian empire, while others moved to remote areas like Yazd and Kerman, where they continued to follow their faith despite persecution and discrimination. A small group that lived in Khorasan for over a hundred years moved to the city of Hormuz in the Persian Gulf. But in the fifteen years that followed, they found no peace and decided to sail to India, a country that had ancient trade links with Persia. They landed at Div, an island on the west coast of India, and two decades later, sailed to the mainland. Parsis arrived in India around the eighth century, if one accepts the account in *Kisseh-i-Sanjan*, written in the sixteenth century by the Parsi priest Bahman Kaikobad Sanjana. The story goes that the Persian migrants, exhausted after fighting through a fierce storm, landed in Sanjan, a port in Gujarat. They were taken to meet the Hindu king, Jadi Rana, whom their spokesperson, a priest, asked for asylum.[8] The Gujarati king, impressed by the priest who recited Sanskrit verses (Sanskrit and Avesta were parallel languages, with many words in common), permitted the refugees to remain if they adhered to five conditions. The stipulations were: that they would not bear arms; they would teach the Hindu Brahmin priests the Persian religion; their women would wear the local dress; they would marry after sunset; and they would work in the fields and not expect charity. According to former Supreme Court justice Rohinton Nariman, the Hindu king's strictures, at least as reported in the *Kisseh*, did not refer to any bar on converting the local populace to Zoroastrianism. This controversial clause was only introduced into Zoroastrian texts at a later date.[9]

The local people referred to the new arrivals as Parsis since they came from the Pars region in Iran.[10] (Later, they also came to be affectionately termed 'Bawas' in Gujarati.) The story of the meeting between Jadi Rana and the Persian migrants has been passed down the generations for centuries. The authenticity of the *Kisseh-i-Sanjan* account is, however, disputed. Some historians maintain that Zoroastrians may have settled in India at different times over the centuries rather than arriving as a single group.

A popular community legend tells how Jadi Rana was reluctant at first to accept the Parsis, telling them that his kingdom was full and there was no place for refugees. The priest then asked him for a bowl filled to the brim with milk. He mixed some sugar in the milk to make the point that Parsis would sweeten the environment without disturbing its equilibrium. Few would dispute that the Parsis have indeed enriched the environment of their adopted homeland, especially over the last two and a half centuries. Parsis can boast among their ranks some of the best known names in modern Indian history. During British colonial rule, Parsis were at the forefront of education and business. Mahatma Gandhi remarked that 'In numbers the Parsis are beneath contempt, in contributions beyond compare.'

Dadabhai Naoroji, affectionately termed 'the grand old man of India', was one of the founding leaders of the Congress party and one of the original spokespersons of the Swadeshi movement. He was also the first Asian to be elected to the British parliament. Bhikhaiji Cama was an ardent woman revolutionary and an essential figure in the Indian independence movement. She unfurled the precursor of the Indian flag at a conference in Germany almost forty years before the country won its independence. Ardeshir Godrej was a fierce nationalist and a stubborn, eccentric, highly principled inventor whose best known innovations included indigenous locks and vegetable oil soap. The brilliant scientist Homi Bhabha was the father of India's nuclear programme. And another prominent Parsi, Sam Manekshaw, was the first Indian army chief to be elevated to the rank of field marshal after leading India to its most decisive military victory ever—the 1971 war against Pakistan which led to the formation of Bangladesh. Feroze Gandhi was an independent-thinking, crusading parliamentarian who married Indira Nehru. He fathered India's pre-eminent political dynasty, though the Nehru-Gandhis cannily changed the spelling from the anglicised 'Ghandy' to that favoured by the Mahatma and opted to stick with their mother's Hindu faith rather than their father's Zoroastrianism. Incidentally, the descendants of Mohammed Ali Jinnah, the founder of Pakistan, are Parsis who make their home in India. Nusli Wadia is Jinnah's only grandson. Zubin Mehta, one of the twentieth century's most renowned conductors of Western classical music, is a Parsi. As was Farrokh Bulsara, though he did not advertise his Parsi origins, preferring to go by 'Freddie Mercury', the iconic lead singer of the rock band Queen. And, as the world reeled from the coronavirus, it was a pair of Parsis, Cyrus Poonawalla and his son Adar, to whom we turned in hope as the world's largest producers of vaccines.

There are well-known, admired Parsis in fields as diverse as law, finance, medicine, social work, fine arts, cinema and sports. That so many from the community have shone and found a place in the annals of contemporary Indian history is all the more remarkable when weighed against their numbers. Today, there are an estimated 50,000 Parsis (the 2011 census put it at 57,000, but that number has declined since) in a country of over 1.3 billion people. Since the Parsi population has been declining at a rate of around 10 to 12 per cent each decade, demographers estimate that it will soon be down to 23,000, putting it in the category of a vanishing tribe. (The Parsi representative on the Minorities Commission, Kersi Deboo, questions the accuracy of the numbers from the 2011 Census as census workers in most of India ignorant of the term 'Parsi' simply lumped a number of Parsis outside Bombay in the 'other'' category.)[11]

Author Amitav Ghosh noted that 'Many, if not most, of the institutions and practices which define modern India can be traced back to Parsi origins.'[12] The Bollywood film industry too evolved from Parsi theatre, and the first Indian cricket team was formed in 1848 by Parsi members of the Orient Cricket Club. A few years later, the Parsi Cricket Club beat England during their 1889–90 tour to India—a historic feat.[13]

The Parsi legacy is so inextricable from contemporary Indian history, that much is either forgotten or unremarked upon. For instance, few are aware of the pioneering role played by a Parsi businessman in the growth of India's dairy industry, established in the 1920s in Anand in Gujarat.[14] Most Indians too are ignorant of the fact that the chikoo, native to Central America, was introduced to India by the Parsi textile magnate Sir Dinshaw Petit. The first indigenous biscuit, the 'surti batasa' or butter biscuit, was created by Faramji Pestonji Dotivala, who was experimenting with stale bread from a bakery bequeathed to him by the Dutch after they left Surat. The Parsi soda-manufacturing firm, Pallonji's, predated Coca-Cola and Pepsi and old-fashioned, uniquely Parsi beverages, such as raspberry soda and bottled mango juice, are still served at Parsi weddings.[15] The ability to borrow and amalgamate is also evident in the innovations of Parsi food, perhaps one of the oldest examples of fusion cuisine. When they settled on the west coast of India, the Parsis combined the flavours of Persia, where fruit and nuts are common embellishments in savoury dishes, with the spices of Gujarat, Maharashtra and Goa. They also borrowed elements from the cuisines of the British and Portuguese and occasionally from the French. Dhansak, that quintessentially Parsi preparation, originally conceived to be served at funerals, likely evolved from a Persian dish transformed through the use of Indian spices, dals and vegetables.

Serving authentic Parsi food along with their trademark biscuits, buns and cakes and special Iranian tea for over a century, the iconic Irani cafés, with their colonial-era furniture, once dotted old Bombay. The cafés were started by hardworking Zoroastrian Iranians who migrated to India in the late-nineteenth and early-twentieth century. But over the last few decades, these establishments have been dwindling rapidly. From a reported

350 restaurants in the 1950s there are now less than two dozen, and the Irani café culture is on the verge of extinction, with the younger generation disinterested in the family business.

* * *

In the beginning, Parsis lived mostly in Gujarat, in relative anonymity. They tended orchards and engaged in agriculture, embroidery and craft-making, since they had a natural aptitude for these vocations. In 1578, when the mighty Mughal emperor Akbar summoned a gathering of religious leaders at his court with the intention of evolving a religious doctrine, known as Din-i-Illahi, that would incorporate the best of all the faiths practiced within his empire. A scholarly Zoroastrian priest from Navsari, Dastur Meherjee Rana, was invited to this forum and Akbar was impressed by some of the tenets of Zoroastrianism. But it was with the arrival of European traders in India, sometime in the late-sixteenth century, that there was a dramatic rise in the fortunes of the Parsis. Displaying ingenuity and enterprise, Parsis were quick to pick up the languages and knowledge of the West, and to adapt to European skills, customs and practices. They became the brokers, and at times moneylenders, for the Europeans.

Parsi maritime traders, operating from ports in Gujarat such as Surat and Cambay, were active before the development of Bombay, now Mumbai, but it was with the establishment of the premier port in western India that the community really came into its own. Parsi families began migrating from Gujarat to Bombay around the period when the Portuguese king gifted the island to England in 1688 as part of his daughter Catherine's dowry when she married Charles II. In 1736, Lovji Wadia, belonging to a family of renowned shipbuilders in Surat, was persuaded by the East India company to move to Bombay and construct a dry dock.

He was an ancestor of Nusli Wadia, the billionaire businessman
and chairman of the Wadia group. Bombay became the main
hub for the Parsis, and they played a dominant role in the city's
social and economic life. As the academic Shernaz Cama, director
of the Parzor project, a UNESCO-approved effort to preserve
Parsi heritage, once told me: 'Everyone thinks the Parsis came
to Bombay and thrived but one should remember that Bombay
before the Parsis migrated there was just a series of fishing villages
on adjacent islands. If you see the numerous statutes of eminent
Parsis in the old parts of the city, you realise that most are of
people who did well in other places before migrating to what
became India's commercial capital.'[16]

The Parsis are actually far older residents of Mumbai than
the Maratha settlers as believed by many—something the Shiv
Sena forgot as they went about claiming that Marathas had a
special claim to jobs in India's commercial capital compared to
interlopers from other parts of the country. The first Parsi fire
temple was built in Bombay as early as 1673 in the Fort area.
Parsis were the dominant Indian community in Bombay until,
perhaps, 1832, when a mob of 200 Parsis (dog lovers) attacked
policemen who were rounding up stray dogs. The British
authorities subsequently decided to diversify the population and
actively encouraged other communities to migrate to Bombay.[17]
By the mid-eighteenth century, Parsis were one of the most
important mercantile communities in western India. Trade with
China had transformed Parsis from mere hawkers to merchant
princes who established great fortunes.[18] The phrase 'trade with
China' euphemised what was mostly the export of opium, which
had been officially banned for domestic consumption by the
Chinese authorities. Parsi traders obtained opium from India to
sell to Chinese smugglers and in return, imported Chinese goods
such as tea, silks, copper and gold. The Jivanji brothers were
the first Parsis to travel to China in 1756 and establish a firm in

Canton. They later took the name 'Readymoney' to indicate their affluence and willingness to lend money.

A Parsi surname is usually indicative of a person's background. Unlike Hindu surnames, which often denote caste, Parsi surnames usually indicate a place of origin or occupation. For example, Soonawalas were goldsmiths, Hiramanecks were jewellers and Presswalas worked in the printing presses. Some surnames were even more literal. A Reporter worked as a newspaper reporter, a Master was inevitably a schoolmaster, a Contractor was a mistry or mason, a Daruwala sold liquor (a Ginwala more specifically sold gin; similarly precisely descriptive surnames include Rumwala, Toddywala and Sodawaterbottleopenerwala), a Palkhiwala was a maker of chariots, a Clubwala worked at a club, a Canteenwala worked at a canteen, a Doctor was a doctor, an Engineer an engineer, a Vakil was a lawyer, a Kapadia was a cloth merchant and a Dastur was a priest. If your name did not reveal your occupation, it would reveal where you came from: Bombaywala, Poonawala, Bharucha (from Bharuch in Gujarat), Khambatta (from Khambhat, or Cambay), Divecha (from Div) and Irani (a Johnny-come-lately migrant from Iran). A few surnames specified the region with which the family did business: Frenchman, Velati (England), Chinoy (China), Hongkongwala or Adenwala, for instance.

By the 1830s, several Parsi families, including the Sethnas, Banajis, Patels, Camas and Tatas had opened businesses in China.[19] Jamsetjee Jejeebhoy, who started life in India selling old bottles (his maternal side's surname was Batlivala), became the Parsi trader with the most extensive ties to China. His wealth and reputation meant he became the first Indian baronet, the first Indian juror and a director of the first savings bank in Bombay, opened in 1835.[20] His philanthropy was legendary and his charitable contributions were not limited to the Parsi community alone but to society in general. Wealthy Parsis are responsible for many of the heritage buildings, statues and structures that are landmarks of the older parts of Bombay, whether it is the ornate Flora Fountain, once the city's centre, or Bhikha Behram, the sacred well located in the middle of a bustling city footpath or the stately Bombay University convocation hall with its gothic facade. Many of South Bombay's main arteries—Dadabhai Naoroji Road, Madame Cama Road and Nariman Point—are named after Parsis, as are the imposing, century-old commercial buildings on Dadabhai Naoroji Road, the heritage mile of Bombay, and many of the city's iconic institutions such as the Sir J.J. School of Art, the Sir J.J. Hospital, the Petit Library and the Jehangir Art Gallery.

Cynics say the opium business was the so-called ugly secret behind Parsi wealth and charity. And while it's true that the China trade played a major role in the amassing of several Parsi fortunes, it was essentially education and early entry into industrialisation under British colonial rule that was the key to the community's prosperity. Parsis were also suppliers, grocers and wine merchants to the British army and Indian railways which is why, even today, one finds stray Parsi families settled in remote cantonment towns and railway junctions. It is because of this close business relationship that Parsis are often spoken of as toadies of the British government, and their achievements attributed to the patronage of colonial rulers. The majority of the community was indeed loyal to the British crown and far more anglicised than other Indians. After the Indian rebellion of 1857, for instance, the BPP organised a meeting to congratulate the Raj for putting down the 'mutiny'. Before Independence, affluent Parsis often displayed pictures of British royalty in their Victorian-style drawing rooms replete with bric-a-brac, chandeliers and carved furniture. Sir Mancherjee Bhownaggree, the second Parsi (and second Indian) to become a member of Parliament in London was nicknamed Sir 'Bow and Agree' because of the manner in which he was perceived to curry favour with his British masters.

But very many Parsis were also freedom fighters and active supporters of the Swadeshi movement, including Dadabhai Naoroji (the first Indian MP in Britain, and nothing at all like Sir 'Bow and Agree'), Madame Cama, Sir Pherozeshah Mehta and Khurshed Nariman. Parsis also made major contributions to the development of the Gujarati language and literature and a nationalist press. One of the earliest vernacular newspapers in India was the *Mumbai Samachar*, founded by Fardunji Marzban in 1822; it is still in circulation. A few days before India became independent on 15 August 1947, a Parsi National Conference was held in Bombay. The speakers, including Sir Homi Mody and Sir Ardeshir Shroff, stressed that the Parsis' place in India's future should be secured on the grounds of merit and talent.[21] They rejected an offer from the Congress party for a special reservation in Parliament, similar to the one bestowed on the Anglo-Indian community.

Just as the Parsis thrived under British rule, they also flourished in independent India. Unlike some minorities, the Parsis never faced discrimination; rather, they are looked upon with admiration and respect. The late Prime Minister Indira Gandhi had a special affection for the Parsis and so does Prime Minister Narendra Modi. Kersi Deboo, vice chairman of the National Commission for Minorities recalls an incident in 2011 when Modi was chief minister of Gujarat to illustrate the point. When he and other members of Gujarat's Minorities Finance and Development Corporation called on Modi, his fellow minority members carried bouquets to greet the chief minister, he came armed with four thick volumes of the *History of the Parsis*. Modi remarked in awe, "Such a small community and what a history." As Chief Minister Modi ensured that Udvada, the holy pilgrimage destination of the Parsis, was given the status of a heritage site.

Today, Parsis remain wealthier than probably all other Indian communities. Some years ago, when the BPP was asked by a court about the criteria for allotting subsidised houses to the community's poor, it responded that any Parsi with an income of less than Rs 90,000 a month is considered poor. This when the average monthly income is estimated to be around Rs 13,000 in India. The statement caused a flutter in the press though the late Muncherjee Cama, a former punchayet trustee, insists that the press took the figures out of context and that they were calculated with property taxes and other local taxes in mind.[22] Another telling indicator of Parsi wealth is a report from Mumbai's Slum Rehabilitation Authority survey in 2015, which suggested that nine private individuals or trusts owned 6,600 acres in Greater Mumbai. Of the city's nine biggest landlords, six are Parsi trusts. But here again, says Cama, who administers a major Parsi trust, these landholdings are on paper, with squatters occupying land effectively controlled by the land mafia. And if the squatters aren't in control, he adds, much of the land is tied up in legal disputes.

Of course, broadly speaking, it is beyond dispute that the Parsis amassed great wealth. It is equally true that Parsis have redistributed plenty of that wealth through philanthropy. Even among Parsis, with their extensive legacy of progressive philanthropy, the Tatas' contributions were exceptional. For Jamsetji Tata, the visionary who founded the family firm in 1868, profit was not the ultimate goal. He and his sons, Dorabji and Ratanji, ploughed their money back into institutions of excellence that the government had either neglected to or failed to provide. These path-breaking institutions include the Tata Institute of Sciences (1911), the Tata Institute of Social Sciences (1936), the Tata Memorial Centre for Cancer Research and Treatment (1941) and the Tata Institute of Fundamental Research (1945). The tradition continued in the 1980s with the establishment of the Tata Theatre and National Centre for the Performing Arts. Jamsetji is a revered figure, and not just in the Parsi community. His statues, with flowing beard and characteristic Parsi pheta (a traditional tall, black, lacquered hat), have been erected in many parts of the country, from Jamshedpur, the township in eastern India founded in his memory, to Mumbai, where the group's headquarters are located. The company has an equally progressive approach to employee welfare. Suhel Seth, the prominent public relations professional, columnist and talking head, has been closely associated with the Tata group for much of his life and points out that as employers, they have always been ahead of the curve. The Tatas, he says, were among the first to introduce a five-day week and its policies on maternity leave, provident funds and free medical insurance set the standard for enlightened employers, both in India and further afield.[23] In a country where corruption in business dealings has been a way of life, the ethical standards of the Tatas have always set them apart.

For decades, the Tatas reigned supreme as not just the country's largest industrial group, but its most innovative, diverse and respected. The company's story is closely entwined with that of the Parsi community; in a sense, they are the community's crown jewels. Which is why it came as such a blow to Parsis when, on 24 October 2016, Bombay House, the Tata's historic headquarters, was plunged into the biggest crisis in its long history. The tremors and aftershocks of a no-holds-barred battle for control of this unique symbol of Parsi prosperity and progressiveness are still being felt.

1

Battle Which Divided a Community

It was a confrontation that set off tremors at the Bombay Stock Exchange, dominated the front pages of Indian newspapers for days and even made headlines abroad. On 24 October 2016, Ratan Naval Tata, seventy-eight at the time—the patriarch who controls the Tata Trusts, one of the world's largest philanthropic institutions—peremptorily sacked Cyrus Mistry, chairperson of the Tata group, with less than an hour's notice.

The Tata group was then India's largest corporate house, with an annual turnover of well over US$100 billion, and its logo is probably the most recognised and respected in the country. For generations, Indian steel was synonymous with the Tatas; Indian truck drivers used to paint the slogan 'OK Tata' on the rear of their vehicles to indicate that it was a Tata truck, and hence trustworthy; Tata salt is a staple in Indian middle-class homes; and the Tatas' Taj Mahal Hotel in Bombay has long been the gold standard for the country's hotels. Tata also has a huge global footprint: it manufactures Jaguar and Land Rover cars; it is a major player in Europe's steel industry and owns the Anglo-Dutch firm Corus Steel; its international hotel chain includes the historic

Pierre Hotel in New York City; it sells Tetley tea worldwide; and Tata Consultancy Services (TCS) provides software solutions for leading companies across the world.

It was to head up this vast business that, in 2012, Cyrus Mistry, thirty years Ratan Tata's junior, had been handpicked to succeed RNT (to use the sobriquet favoured by Tata employees) in the chair. Only, Cyrus was no ordinary hired gun. His family owned 18.37 per cent of Tata Sons, the closely controlled company that controls the vast Tata empire, with some 100 operating companies, including twenty-eight publicly listed companies spread over six continents. So wealthy are the Mistrys that when Cyrus's aged father, Pallonji took Irish citizenship late in his life, he was believed to have instantly become the richest man in that country. His sons, Shapoor and Cyrus, have been regularly featured in magazine lists of the wealthiest Indians.

But the Tata Trusts is in a dominant position over the Mistrys since it owns 66 per cent of the total shares of Tata Sons, and Ratan, while stepping down from stewardship of the group in 2012, at the age of seventy-five, retained his position as chairperson of the family's charitable trusts. The group's two main trusts, the Sir Ratan Tata and the Sir Dorab Tata trusts, were set up by the two sons of the group's legendary founder Jamsetji Tata. These eponymous trusts are, ultimately, the real power brokers. In the wake of Cyrus's peremptory sacking, the Mistry investment companies filed suit before the National Company Law Tribunal (NCLT), a quasi-judicial body that deals with corporate grievances in India. The long-running dispute finally came before the Supreme Court for adjudication.

Adding to the drama of this high-stakes corporate boardroom stand-off, Nusli Wadia—the blue-blooded chairperson of the Bombay Dyeing Group, one of India's oldest companies, and a director on three major Tata company boards for four decades—jumped into the fray. To the astonishment of both the Parsi community and the wider business world, Wadia sided openly with Cyrus against Ratan, his friend and long-time business ally. Ratan's predecessor J.R.D. Tata had looked upon the personable Nusli as the son he'd never had and was even keen to induct him to the Tata Sons board. Nusli often acted as a troubleshooter and sounding board for both J.R.D. and Ratan. Despite his long and close association with the Tatas, he always maintained he was 'a Wadia, not a Tata',[1] preferring to be king of his own castle.

Seven years younger than Ratan, Nusli earned his spurs earlier in life. His long feud with the late Dhirubhai Ambani, who rose from a petty trader to become the richest man in India is part of corporate folklore. (In 1989, Nusli's bitter battle with Ambani played a major role in the fall of Rajiv Gandhi's government.) Nusli is known as India's corporate samurai because of his propensity to become involved in high-powered corporate disputes and his willingness to fight others' battles. After being unceremoniously dumped from three Tata company boards along with Cyrus, Nusli filed criminal and civil defamation suits amounting to Rs 3,000 crore against Tata representatives for alleging in public statements to shareholders that he was acting in tandem with Cyrus against the interests of the Tatas. His plea was that, as an independent director, he had a duty to protect the rights of the shareholders, which is what he was doing when he protested Cyrus's removal. In 2020, Nusli scored a moral victory when, in the Supreme Court, Ratan issued a conciliatory statement that he had no intention to defame Nusli. And in turn, Nusli withdrew his suit.

* * *

Most shell-shocked of all, and divided on the issue of the Tata–Mistry–Wadia confrontation, is the country's minuscule, closely knit Parsi community. All three adversaries are Parsis. And a community that was used to making the news for its varied and impressive achievements, found itself in the spotlight for all the wrong reasons. Many Parsis thought that the feuding plutocrats, by washing their dirty linen in public, had stained the iconic group's unblemished 150-year-old reputation in India for its excellence and ethical probity.

At Mumbai's most exclusive club, the venerable Willingdon, a favourite haunt of upper-class Parsis, the Tata crisis dominated the conversation. Many of the aggrieved Parsis were also Tata shareholders and the showdown pinched them where perhaps it hurt most—their pockets. Initially, Cyrus enjoyed widespread sympathy for the brutal and public nature of his removal. But this sympathy was soon tempered by annoyance at Cyrus's indiscretion, in revealing sensitive information that could impact share prices, harming even the value of his own family's substantial stake. Some Parsis fear that the outcome of this bitter boardroom battle is that Parsis may have lost control of India's premier business house with deep roots in the community. Parsis universally agree that the differences between Ratan and Cyrus, however grave, could and should have been handled more gracefully. Unfortunately, the pragmatic Pallonji Mistry was ageing and incommunicado. The most tantalising question was why Ratan did not simply wait five short months and let Cyrus go quietly in April 2017, when the Tata chairperson's contract came up for renewal. Instead, the humiliating ouster had sent the firms listed on the stock exchange crashing by some 10 per cent.[2] This was certainly not the Tata way. The company has a tradition of not firing any employee except under the gravest of provocations.

Conspiracy theorists had a field day. One camp claimed that Cyrus was shunted out post-haste by Ratan because Cyrus was too eager to assert his independence and sought to undo some of Ratan's decisions. Another whispered that Cyrus was plotting to take control of the group, and that his family had had a covetous eye on it for over half a century. Cyrus was accused of trying to wind up some of RNT's more ambitious schemes, which had brought greater prominence to the Tata name, though at a huge financial cost. There was much speculation about why Nusli, who had no stake in the matter, had stepped into the ring and had so openly taken sides.

Indians at large were surprised that a popular minority community known as upright, gentlemanly, peaceful and law-abiding should engage in such an unseemly public spat. But, as Vicaiji Taraporevala, a senior Parsi advocate with half a century's experience, once told me Parsis have 'a history of litigation', that 'countless Parsi families have fought excessively over trifles.' There is, he said, 'a tradition that when two Parsis fight they never settle.'[3] In the early twentieth century, the Bombay High Court was flooded with cases in which both litigants were Parsis, as were the lawyers representing them. Fali Nariman, one of the country's most respected lawyers and a Parsi, concedes that 'Parsis are bad losers and seldom shy away from a court battle.'[4] Lawyer Berjis Desai wrote, 'In the Parsi DNA, there is an as yet unidentified litigation gene which is transmitted from one generation to the next.'[5]

Perhaps such litigiousness is the result of Parsis' strong belief in the virtue of truth and their own righteousness. This basic mantra of the Parsi religion, Zoroastrianism, is reflected in its first prayer *Ashem Vohu*, which stresses the importance of these two qualities, truth and righteousness, above all else. In the present imbroglio, too, all three principal players are convinced of the justness of their cause.

Parsis have a well-deserved reputation for integrity. The Maharaja of Baroda, Sayajirao Gaekwad, once remarked, 'The word of a Parsi is as sound for me as my own kingdom's currency.' An English judge in the British-era Privy Council, when assessing the worth of the testimony of a witness, felt that it should be noted that he was a Parsi and due cognisance be taken of this fact, Nariman once noted in a lecture.[6]

* * *

Cyrus's dismissal as chairperson of Tata Sons was shocking in its suddenness. He was informed of the decision less than an hour before the board meeting. His dismissal was not listed on the meeting's agenda. Cyrus just about had the time to text his wife to tell her that he was about to be fired. Further humiliation followed. He was asked to clear his office out that same day. When he realised that government-controlled financial institutions with large shareholdings in the group, such as Life Insurance Corporation, the Unit Trust of India and other mutual funds, were going to abstain rather than back him, Cyrus knew he was fighting a losing cause. He resigned from the boards of all the Tata companies he still headed.

While Ratan appeared to have won the battle to dismiss Cyrus, the war was not quite over. Ratan must have been discomfited to find that several independent directors on company boards as well as respected names in the world of business backed Cyrus. Thanks to probing questions from the pro-Cyrus camp, the Tata Trusts' role in the running of the group is now in the spotlight. For their charitable activities, the trusts, formed in the early twentieth century, were granted special dispensations by successive governments both in terms of income tax exemptions and the right to investments in corporate entities. Now, Cyrus has raised uncomfortable questions about whether charitable trusts can be used to control a major business empire, rather than fulfil the purpose for which they were originally set up.

Still despite Cyrus's efforts, Ratan ruthlessly took back total control of the group and Cyrus was convincingly ousted. By February 2017, Cyrus was removed as even an ordinary director from the Tata Sons board, a position held by his family for thirty-six years. In September 2017, the board voted to become a private company, which meant that Cyrus's family company, the Shapoorji Pallonji (SP) group, with its minority stake, would not be able to sell its shares without the board's approval. The rule, if upheld, ensures that the equity of the Mistry brothers would be, for all practical purposes, locked up and they would not have a chance to monetise it. (The recent Supreme Court ruling has upheld the decision of the Registrar of Companies to convert Tata Sons into a private company.) Equally disturbing for the Mistrys is the newly introduced Article 75 of the Tata Sons Articles of Association. Reports in the media such as the *Hindu Business Line* confirm that the article stipulates that shareholders can be compelled to sell their shares if more than 75 per cent of the shareholders present at any meeting demand that they do so.

Within four months of Cyrus's ouster, Ratan had appointed fifty three-year-old Nararajan Chandrasekaran, CEO of TCS, the group's unquestioned cash cow, as the group's chairperson. The move was swift and smooth. Ratan, who had taken over as interim chairperson, once again assumed the role of chairperson emeritus of the Tata Sons board. Though technically, there was a three-member selection committee, few doubted that the choice had been left to Ratan. As head of India's largest software exporter, Chandra, as he is popularly known, pushed TCS to new heights. Under his watch, TCS revenues jumped more than threefold. A computer engineer who has spent his entire career with the Tatas, Chandra, unlike his plutocratic predecessors, rose from humble beginnings in a small town in Tamil Nadu. He walked 3 kilometres each day to attend his Tamil-medium school. Chandra, an enthusiastic marathon runner, is a Tamil Brahmin, as are most top executives at TCS, which is sometimes jokingly referred to as the Tamil Coffee Sangam. Inevitably, there were snide comments about Tamil Brahmins replacing Parsis at

Tata. The 'Tam Brahms', as they are casually referred to by others (and even, sometimes, themselves), are characterised as clannish and close-knit, much like the Parsis. 'They are brilliant with figures, frugal and orthodox, and have been compared to Jews,' says Chitra Subramaniam, a leading investigative journalist and herself a Tamil Brahmin.[7] 'But unlike the Jews and Parsis,' she adds, 'Tam Brahms usually make money for others. They prefer job security to striking out on their own.' While the Tam Brahm computer wizards of TCS, often vegetarian and teetotalers, would easily service complex software solutions, they were awkward in their social interactions, particularly with foreign clients. In contrast, steeped in Western culture, Parsis excelled at tying up business deals over five-star meals and glasses of wine.

Parsis bemoan the appointment of the first non-Parsi chairperson at the Tata group as heralding the end of an era and sounding the death knell of a cherished community institution. After all, the group had been founded by Jamsetji, who came from a long line of Zoroastrian priests in the holy town of Navsari. His father, Nusserwanji Tata, was the first to give up the family's liturgical profession to try his hand at business. The crest of the Tata group, designed by the founder himself, adorns the foyer of the head office and carries the legend 'Humata, Hukhta, Hvarshta'. These words in Avesta encapsulate the basic Zoroastrian creed: Good Thoughts, Good Words and Good Deeds. In the early years, many of the employees and a sizeable chunk of the shareholders in blue-chip Tata firms were Parsis. Many Tata employees were shareholders too because they believed that money invested in the group was safer than in a bank. Up until the era of Ratan's beloved predecessor, Jehangir Ratan Tata (known universally as JRD), the board consisted almost entirely of Parsis, with directors frequently breaking into Gujarati and cracking quintessentially bawdy Parsi jokes with each other, says Maneck Davar, a journalist and entrepreneur familiar with the group.[8] In fact, out of the approximately 400,000 shares in the unlisted Tata Sons company, only one was ever owned by a non-Parsi, the erstwhile raja of Chhota Udaipur in eastern Gujarat.

Respected for picking his top executives shrewdly, JRD wooed the cream of Indian talent, though many of the eminent names he recruited still happened to be Parsis. Back then, even ordinary Parsis knew that if they were adequately qualified, there was a job for life waiting for them at Tatas. Either because Parsi numbers are declining sharply, or because bright Parsis are making other choices, including migrating abroad, the community no longer dominates the Tata group as it once did. The colourful, outspoken, individualistic Parsi pool of talent, which long guided the fortunes of the company, has been replaced by more conformist, faceless professionals. Public relations consultant Suhel Seth, who has been associated with the Tatas for decades, recalls that 'in the old days the people who controlled the group were fun-loving, garrulous, larger than life. At that time there was no death by analysis.'[9]

More than the appointment of a non-Parsi head of the group, what disturbs the community is that trustees of the charities have slowly been replaced by outsiders under Ratan's watch. After Cyrus's ouster, the number of Parsi trustees declined even further. Respected names, such as leading lawyer and former advocate general of Maharashtra, Darius Khambata, resigned on the grounds that he had no time to fulfil his duties. Meanwhile, Keki Dadiseth, former chairperson and a global executive director of Unilever, was not renominated as a trustee in 2017 when his term came to an end. Significantly, Dadiseth, as an independent director on the board of the Indian Hotels Corporation Limited, had backed Cyrus. Until as late as 2019, Ratan's half-brother, Noel, was not appointed as a trustee on any of the major Tata trusts. The omission was glaring. Ratan had once claimed that his half-brother lacked the experience and exposure needed to be chairperson, but most financial journalists agree that Noel has performed successfully in the Tata businesses in which he was involved, largely to do with retail marketing. It was only when Ratan's long-time financial advisor, Noshir Soonawala stepped down, at the age of eighty-four, and reportedly called on Ratan to induct Noel that Ratan's half-brother was appointed in his place. True, another Parsi, philanthropist Jehangir Jehangir, the fourth Sir Cowasji Jehangir baronet, was also inducted to the trusts, but the key positions of vice chairpersons went to non-Parsis, former bureaucrat Vijay Singh and south Indian industrialist Venu Srinivasan, neither of whom has had a long association with the group.

Until 2019, there was another Tamil Brahmin who seemed likely to play a decisive role in the future of the group—R. Venkataramanan. Still in his forties, he was Ratan's executive assistant until the latter retired, and reportedly continues to exert considerable influence on the ageing Tata scion. Venkataramanan, who goes by 'Venkat', was appointed as the managing trustee of all the group's key trusts and was one of only three lifetime trustees, along with Ratan and Krishna Kumar. (Others' trustees are appointed for fixed tenures.) However, in 2019, Venkat had to step down as managing trustee when, following Cyrus's complaint, the income tax department investigated him and discovered that he had a highly inflated salary for a trust employee, and that there was an ongoing CBI case against him. The trusts are no longer run by a single managing trustee but by a committee formed under the board.[10]

Within months of his removal, Cyrus and his elder brother Shapoor had filed a case before the NCLT. They argued that Cyrus's dismissal was illegal and that the subsequent actions of the Tata group amounted to suppression of minority shareholders. The ding-dong legal battle stretched over several years. First, it went to the National Company Law Tribunal (NCLT) where the Mistry case was rejected outright. But the appellate tribunal took a diametrically opposite position, upholding almost all of Mistry's charges. and finally the Supreme Court in 2021 ruled decisively in favour of the Tatas. Cyrus does not see his fight for justice as a corporate battle. 'I can lick my wounds and put that behind us. That phase is over. But we have to do whatever is necessary to protect our 18.37 per cent stake in Tata Sons.' Cyrus talks of ensuring that the values of the firm's founder are respected. 'This is about governance—it's not about me, it's not about position.'[11]

It is believed that Ratan was furious that Cyrus, whom he viewed as an outsider and interloper, should dare to stake claim to Jamsetji's sacred legacy. As with Cyrus, Ratan's supporters too frame the battle as one to preserve certain values and ethics. They, snobbishly, accuse Cyrus of having being 'an accountant', whereas the Tatas are 'entrepreneurs'. Some question why the billionaire Cyrus, with his own thriving family construction business, would want to step into a messy and thankless battle to reform someone else's company—one in which he did not have majority control. As a leading businessman, who wished to remain anonymous, said, 'Cyrus should have realised that Ratan is the boss because he controls the trusts. If he was not getting on with Ratan, he should have simply left.' The respected business journalist, Sucheta Dalal, who has closely followed the dispute, disagrees. She thinks Cyrus did not have much choice. 'It was a battle for his reputation,' she said. 'He needed to tell the world that he was doing the right thing. He was following all the rules and doing what he thought was best for the company.'[12]

* * *

For an insight into the dispute, one needs to step back a little and revisit the history of the three remarkable families whose heirs are presently at war with each other.

They have old and complex relationships with each other that have at various times been both congenial and contentious. In the case of the Mistrys and Tatas, the association goes back nearly a century. Cyrus's colourful grandfather, Shapoorji Pallonji, a pioneer in the construction business, was the preferred contractor for Tata projects. He was the contractor for the Tata headquarters, the four-storey Edwardian building, Bombay House, built in 1924 and designed by the Scottish architect George Willet. The Mistrys say their business association with the Tatas began in 1927 as Shapoorji acquired, from F.E. Dinshaw's estate, the company F.E. Dinshaw Limited which had dealings with the Tatas since 1927. This firm was later incorporated into the Mistrys' investment firm, Sterling Investment.

Despite his sizeable shareholding, it was only in June 1980, that Cyrus's father, the construction magnate Pallonji Mistry, was appointed a director on the board of Tata Sons. He consciously took a backseat on the board, remaining so silent a presence that he was nicknamed the 'Phantom of Bombay House'. In a twist of fate or perhaps some shrewd matchmaking, Noel Tata married Aloo Mistry, Pallonji's daughter and Cyrus's sister. When Ratan was looking for a successor, many assumed that Noel, one of the last surviving male members of the Tata family, was the obvious choice. Instead, Ratan picked Cyrus, who was not in the race but was, in fact, part of the selection committee. This despite the fact that the relationship between Pallonji Mistry and Ratan was formal and rather distant. According to a friend of Pallonji's, the latter once confided that Ratan rarely spoke to him.

The Tatas and the Wadias go back much further. The Wadias, Tatas and Petits (Nusli's mother's family) dominated Bombay's textile industry in the mid-nineteenth century. J.R.D. Tata's elder sister, Sylla, married into the Petit family (her husband was Fali Petit, Nusli's grandmother, Ruttie's brother). JRD always had a special fondness for Nusli and treated him like a son. Nusli's mother Dina and Ratan's mother Soonoo were 'like sisters', Nusli admits.[14] The two men were uncrowned princes of the community—handsome, charming, heirs to great legacies. They had another bond in common; they were the products of broken homes. Both were on the boards for each other's companies for decades. Nusli, initially more in touch with the political world, sometimes acted on behalf of Ratan and the Tatas in New Delhi. But those close to the two men say the fallout between these former fast friends had been building over the last few years.

One source of contention, according to media reports such as ones in *Mint* and other business reports, was Ratan's determination to fulfil JRD's thwarted dream of returning to the airline business. When the Tatas floated Vistara in collaboration with Singapore Airlines, Nusli saw it as treachery. He had launched his own airline, GoAir, earlier, to be run by his son Jeh, named after J.R.D. Tata's Vistara would be a direct competitor. A fascination for planes seems to run in the Tata genes. JRD was the first Indian to qualify for a pilot's licence. His sister Sylla was the first woman pilot of Indian origin. JRD founded India's first airline, Tata Airlines, in 1932, which eventually became Air India and was nationalised by the government. An aunt recalls that Ratan was drawn to aeroplanes even as a small child. He would rush out of the house to get a look whenever an aircraft flew overhead, and as a boy, he could recognise the make of most any plane.[15] As a student at Cornell University, Ratan revealed in an interview, he had earned pocket money doing odd jobs just so that he could take flying lessons. So enduring was this love for planes that at the age of sixty-nine, Ratan flew an F-16 Falcon.

The histories of the Tata, Wadia and Mistry families are integral parts of the saga of the Bombay Parsis. Each one of these venerable Parsi clans left a distinct impress on the city—the Tatas and Wadias as industrial pioneers, and the Mistrys as builders of major city landmarks. And because the Bombay Parsis are a tiny, endogamous community, their dizzying familial ties tend to be too complicated and confusing for outsiders to fully grasp. In the last generation, old-timers recall that JRD and Naval Tata, Ratan's father, barely spoke to each other though they were on the same boards for half a century. Naval and Pallonji Mistry were good friends, banding together to prevent JRD from making Nusli Wadia a member of the Tata Sons board. Nonetheless, Ratan and Nusli developed a close friendship when they entered their respective family businesses. While in recent years, Nusli has abandoned his old friend Ratan to frequently defend Cyrus, the son of the man who prevented Nusli from being appointed to the Tata Sons board.

Today, Mehli Mistry, Cyrus's first cousin on his mother's side and a second cousin on his father's side, has aligned with Ratan. Cyrus accuses Mehli of conspiring to remove him as the Tata chairperson while Mehli holds Cyrus responsible for ending his lucrative barging contracts with Tata Power after Cyrus took over as chairperson of Tata Sons. The Tata family would appear to be divided too. Noel Tata and his mother, Simone (Ratan's stepmother), both voted to remove Cyrus from his leadership role. But Jimmy Tata, RNT's reclusive and somewhat maverick younger brother, a regular at the Willingdon Club swimming pool and a trustee of the main Tata trusts, abstained, as did some other Tata relatives, descendants of the Saklatwalas, who own a very minor shareholding. It is, as someone once put it to me, a Parsi family saga fit for a novel.

Apart from their importance as pillars of Parsi business success, the Tatas and the Petits shaped the community's position on a key question: is conversion possible in the Zoroastrian religion? In the landmark case *Petit vs Jeejeebhoy* (1908), the Bombay High Court ruled on who qualifies as a Parsi Zoroastrian, an issue which even now excites strong feelings within the community as it did back then. The judgement held that a person born in another faith who had subsequently converted to Zoroastrianism was not entitled to the benefits of the religious institutions and funds that belonged to the community in India. Only a descendant of the original migrants from Iran could pray at a fire temple or have their body disposed of, according to traditional Zoroastrian funerary rites, in a dakhma (a sequestered garden with wells where corpses are left for scavenging birds such as vultures). Baronet Dinshaw Petit and other liberal Parsis, including R.D. Tata, JRD's father, were plaintiffs in the suit that wanted to establish the status of R.D. Tata's wife Suzanne, renamed 'Sooni'. A Frenchwoman by birth, Sooni claimed she had become a Zoroastrian since two priests agreed to perform her navjote or initiation ceremony. The Bombay High Court's judgement ruled against the plaintiffs, who sought to legitimise Sooni's conversion.

Ratan's mother Sooni left her first husband, Naval Tata, when her son was ten and Jimmy even younger. She remarried and her new husband was Sir Jamsetjee Jejeebhoy, the sixth baronet, a descendant of the original nineteenth-century merchant prince of Bombay. Soonoo's second husband's father, as head of the BPP, was the main defendant in the suit that sought to reject Suzanne Tata's claim to be recognised as a Parsi. Ratan Tata's mother's remarriage also had repercussions in the Parsi punchayet, which administers the community's properties and institutions. Lady Navajbai Tata was so incensed by her daughter-in-law's desertion that, though she was the only woman representative on the punchayet, she refused to sit on the same committee as Sir Jamsetjee Jejeebhoy. Since he refused to step down, she declared that she would, says Adi Jehangir, brother of the fourth Cowasji Jehangir baronet.[16]

Parsi history is a tangled web indeed.

2

The House of Tatas

Almost everyone who meets Ratan Naval Tata is bowled over by his charisma. Unpretentious and charming, and carrying the aura of the Tata name, RNT has been hailed as a brilliant, innovative leader who transformed the Tata group from India's largest industrial house into a global empire. He is known to be attentive to detail and obsessive about quality control. According to his colleagues, he rarely took more than forty-eight hours to make any decision, no matter how major.[1] Sometimes that speed and decisiveness can shade into impulsiveness, like when he dramatically upped his bid for the loss-making European Corus Steel group in 2007 to win a bidding war against the Brazilian giant CSN. The big picture, though, is that in over two decades under RNT's leadership, the value of the Tata empire expanded enormously, and now more than 50 per cent of the group's revenue comes from outside India. Few dispute Ratan's vision or his obsessive commitment to the Tata group. Stubbornness, the people who know him say, is Ratan's defining characteristic. 'If you put a gun to his head, he will say "Shoot me, I will not move out of the way,"' says Suhel Seth.[2]

RNT is seen as something of a loner who lavishes his affection on dogs. When he was Tata chairperson, strays habitually wandered into the lobby of Bombay House. But human beings were permitted entry only if they were a staff member or had an appointment. Seth recalls that, in February 2018, Prince Charles was to present Ratan Tata a Lifetime Achievement Award for innovation in philanthropy at Buckingham Palace, but RNT cried off at the last minute because one of his dogs was ill. The prince understood Ratan's love for his pet and, according to Seth, said approvingly of Ratan, 'That's a man.'[3] The affection Ratan lavishes on canine friends perhaps compensates for the fact that he has no nuclear family. R. Venkataramanan, Ratan's former executive assistant, when asked about his reported proximity to his boss, said, 'Not many know Mr Tata. There are two who are very close to him. They are Tito and Tango, his German Shepherds. Nobody else can come remotely close.'[4]

'Ratan is a very complex character,' says Nusli Wadia about his long-time friend, 'I don't think anyone has ever fathomed him. I think I'm as close as you can get. But even I have not fathomed him. He is very deep, but can be very petty, being easily influenced by the wrong type of people.' He adds that, despite their proximity, 'Ratan and I never got very personal. He is a total loner.' Ratan does not dispute that he values his privacy. 'I may not be very sociable but I am not anti-social,'[5] he explained to me.

A friend of his youth recalls that, in his early years in the Tata group, Ratan felt his surname was a burden. In the US, he had been at ease because his fellow students had no inkling of his privileged background. 'My father did not believe in breaking the law,' Ratan has said about his college years. 'And in those days a student was permitted only the amount approved by the RBI, which was meagre. There were times when money ran out before the month ended. Sometimes I had to borrow money from friends to get me past the next few days. I also did sundry odd jobs, even washing dishes, to supplement my income. That way I could do the things I wanted to—like taking flying lessons.'[6] After graduating from Cornell University in architecture and engineering, he was anxious to work in the US, unconstrained by judgement based on his family's legacy. For the seven years he lived there, Ratan had a good job in Los Angeles, a swanky apartment with a swimming pool and an unencumbered lifestyle.[7] However, his ageing grandmother, Lady Navajbai Tata, widow of Jamsetji's younger son, had other plans for him. She was the last survivor of her generation in the Tata family. Navajbai was also the first woman to join the board of Tata Sons, back in 1918, after the premature death of her husband, Sir Ratanji Tata. She had brought up Ratan and his younger brother Jimmy ever since their mother, Soonoo, née Commissariat, left their father, Naval. Ratan was only ten then and caught in the middle of an ugly separation and bitter divorce. It was only when he returned from the US that Ratan became close to his mother and his two half-sisters.

Naval later married a Swiss national, Simone Dunoyer. She was the protocol officer who ensured Naval was given VIP treatment every time he passed through the Geneva airport for an International Labour Organisation (ILO) meeting. Simone turned out to have a head for business and was the brain behind Lakmé, the Tata group's popular cosmetic brand. When he returned to India, it is possible that Ratan may have felt ignored in the family home. His father had a new family, which included his half-brother—christened Noel, since he was born on Christmas Day. Noel was twenty years younger, and perhaps Ratan resented the newcomer's presence. The relationship between Ratan and his stepmother is believed to be rather distant. According to the Tata grapevine, as chairperson of the company years later, Ratan would sell Lakmé off without taking Simone into confidence.

Ratan remembers his father fondly, but as 'a disciplinarian.' His father, Ratan told me, had high standards: 'It was not that my brother and I got caned but he expected a certain decorum from us. We were never allowed to flaunt our wealth.'[8] The relationship between Ratan's father, Naval and JRD, the chairperson of Tata group, was somewhat strained. Though both men were the same age, it was not until 1941 that Naval was finally made a member of the board of Tata Sons at Navajbai's urging. Though JRD and Naval were together directors of the group for nearly half a century, it was an open secret that they barely spoke to each other, mostly making do with the exchange of terse notes. Their temperaments and interests were very different. JRD was reserved, shy and had a short fuse; Naval was gregarious, indiscreet, a raconteur of racy stories. He was contemptuous of stuffy gatherings and more forgiving of human frailties than JRD. The latter had little faith in Naval's abilities. Naval mostly worked with the Tata electric and power companies. He was deeply interested in management and labour issues in India, and was an active member of the ILO. Naval had also been chairperson of the Indian Hockey Federation, during which period the Indian team won three gold medals at the Olympics. In 1971, he stood for election to parliament, despite JRD's strong disapproval, from the South Bombay seat as an independent candidate. He took on the fiery union leader and socialist George Fernandes and the unknown Congress candidate N.N. Kailas. Naval lost to Kailas but put up a creditable fight in a year when the Congress, led by Indira Gandhi, swept the polls.

Important as Ratan's father was, it was Ratan's grandmother who was arguably the main anchor in his life in his possibly lonely childhood. When Navajbai fell seriously ill, she asked specifically for Ratan, and he dropped everything to return to India. She survived that particular crisis and many crises after. 'She was a wonderful person,' Ratan recalls. 'Her social life was very full and she met many celebrities when her husband was alive. After he died, she was the correct widow who took on the role of a philanthropist.'[9] Navajbai had ingrained in her grandson an understanding of the unique legacy of the Tata name, the extraordinary history of the group and its path-breaking humanitarian services. She expected him to carry on the tradition. While his grandmother may have had full faith in Ratan, the top men in the company at that time—including chairperson and distant relative, JRD—did not view him as the heir to the empire. If anything, when Ratan joined the group, the knives were out for him. He was posted in Jamshedpur for six years, assigned to the shop floor and moved from one department to another, without any job title or clear-cut duties. This was followed by a series of tough assignments, such as overseeing the floundering Empress Mills and later, NELCO, a struggling electronics company. The harsh treatment of these early years left scars, and Ratan is not a man to forgive or forget easily. 'I thought they were testing me to see how long I would stay or if I would throw in the towel,' Ratan says candidly. Did the 'they' refer to Parsis in general in the company, who could have viewed him as potential competition? Ratan says that it was basically JRD and Sumant Moolgaokar who were responsible: 'They were not hostile, but they made sure that things were not pleasant.'[10] JRD's long, much-talked-about cold war with Naval may have been one reason for the uncharacteristically harsh treatment of Ratan. RNT though, prefers to look on the bright side. The runaround he was given and his hand in turning around NELCO was invaluable experience and, he says, in retrospect, a boon from which he was able to extract maximum benefit.

Business journalists and Ratan's friends from the old days remember him as an affable man with no airs; decent, fair and fun-loving. He was completely accessible, picking up the phone himself rather than using a secretary as an intermediary. He lived in the dealers' hostel and walked to the plant to report at six every morning. But over the years, he inevitably became more distant.

Mukund Rajan, who worked closely with RNT as his executive assistant for many years and was a director on the boards of several Tata companies, wrote in his memoirs that RNT became 'a senior statesman with a larger-than-life figure. Most of his colleagues came to be intimidated by his personality and stature.'[11]

Still, compared to most other Indian billionaires, Ratan's lifestyle is restrained, even modest. A business consultant, who met Ratan for the first time in 2016, was surprised that there were 'no ten channels of secretaries. I rang the bell and a mundu [serving boy] opened the door, no liveried servants or anything. Dogs wandered around. It was extreme sophistication and extreme simplicity.' The compact, whitewashed villa, overlooking the sea at Colaba, and designed by Ratan himself, refects his wealth and status but is tasteful, unlike the over-the-top razzle-dazzle of Antilla, Mukesh Ambani's twenty-seven-storey residence on Cumballa Hill. 'RNT gives you the impression of such old-world integrity,' the consultant adds, 'and his manners are so extraordinary, you feel a bit overwhelmed.' Satinder Lambah, a retired senior diplomat, told me that, in his experience, Ratan was one of the few top Indian businessmen who replied promptly and courteously to any letter addressed to him, answering each question in detail.[12] Others who have had business dealings with Ratan are similarly impressed by his politeness, attentiveness and ability to ask the right questions.

He is, of course, an astute businessman. Since retirement, Ratan's private fortune has increased substantially, as he began investing in promising start-ups. But none of this success and privilege has made Ratan less tense. Mukund Rajan believes that the problems of the Tatas post-2008, as it seemed the group had overstretched itself with the several billion dollars it had spent making questionable international acquisitions, took their toll on RNT, who thought he was being given a particularly rough ride by the media. There was a perception of victimisation by the media which never left him.[13] Who can be sure what precisely Ratan, who keeps his cards so close to his chest, felt but it's easy to believe that his anxieties and touchiness likely stemmed from his drive to fill the very large shoes left by his predecessors, starting with the group's visionary founder, Jamsetji Nusserwanji Tata.

* * *

Born in 1839, Jamsetji was the most far-sighted and multidimensional Indian businessman of his generation. He wanted to bring about a Western-style industrial revolution in India, then under British colonial rule. Three of Jamsetji's major dreams for his country—a steel plant, a hydropower plant and an institute of higher education in science and technology—fructified only after his death.

The man who founded the Tata group, Jamsetji was one of five children, the only boy among four girls. (Piloo Nanavutty, author of *The Parsis*, says that the surname 'Tata' is believed to have been derived from the Gujarati words 'tamta' or 'tikha', signifying someone who is peppery, hot-tempered. And most Tata chairpersons were indeed known for their tempers.[14]) He was born in his mother's family home: a neat, low-roofed, single-storey building in a tiny lane in Dasturvad (priests' quarters), Navsari. His father was only seventeen years old when Jamsetji was born. The house, which the Tatas have preserved as a museum, is near the family home of another eminent Parsi and close friend of Jamsetji's—Pherozeshah Mehta, a politician and lawyer who played a seminal role in municipal governance as chairman of the Bombay Municipal Corporation.

Jamsetji often expressed gratitude that his father, Nusserwanji Tata, gave him a great start in life, by way of a solid education and a sizeable inheritance. As a youth, Jamsetji went through the rigours of learning the prayers and austere rituals required of a navar. When he was fourteen, his father summoned him to Bombay for further studies. Soon after, he was enrolled in the college section of the Elphinstone Institution in Bombay. This was around the same time as the Indian uprising of 1857; the uprising had the effect of tightening British control over India and the highly intelligent Jamsetji had the advantage of a liberal, Western education, a major asset in what was becoming British India.

Nusserwanji, who was descended from a long line of priests in Navsari, was the first in the family to try his hand at trade. He moved to Bombay and built up a small business in commodities. Like many Parsi businessmen of that era, he could not resist the lure of trade with China, which is why an unkind story sometimes rears its head that the House of the Tatas was built on money made from dealing in opium. Nusserwanji had sent his son Jamsetji to China at one stage to set up offices in Hong Kong and Shanghai. In fact, Nusserwanji lost most of the profits from his China links when one of his partners, Premchand Roychand, became bankrupt. Nusserwanji recouped his fortune when he, along with a syndicate of merchants, won the contract to supply a year's worth of provisions for General Robert Napier's march on Abyssinia to rescue captured British subjects, as recounted in Bakhtiar Dadabhoy's profiles of prominent Parsis, *Sugar in Milk*.

Like his father, Jamsetji travelled extensively. His mansion, Esplanade House, was filled with curios, objets d'art and books. Jamsetji hosted many of the who's who of the time when they visited India.

After Nusserwanji's trading company went bust, Jamsetji spent four years in England settling his father's debts. During this period, Jamsetji visited Lancashire frequently to acquire first-hand knowledge about the manufacture of cotton. After Nusserwanji wound up his export–import business and retired, Jamsetji decided to try his luck in the cotton business. Unlike the Indian railways, or the coal and jute industries, which were financed and managed primarily by the British, the cotton industry originated through the initiative of Indian—primarily Parsi—entrepreneurs. In 1869, Jamsetji purchased a defunct oil pressing mill in Chinchpoogly, in the heart of Bombay, and turned it into a cotton mill, which he named 'Alexandra Mill'. After this venture succeeded, he perceived the advantages of selecting a site where power and raw material were easily available. His second acquisition was the Empress Mill in Nagpur, in central India, which was inaugurated in 1877. Next, Jamsetji acquired a jinxed mill in Bombay which regularly made losses. He renamed it 'Swadeshi Mills'—a break from his Anglophone naming convention. Eventually, Jamsetji managed to turn around even this unlucky mill. He had, by this time, become a supporter of the Swadeshi movement, and was present at the first session of the Indian National Congress in Bombay in 1885; he remained a generous donor to the party and a member for the rest of his life.[15]

The mills were not Jamsetji's only business interest. He also became one of the wealthiest landowners in Bombay and, in 1903, built the first world-class luxury hotel in the country. Until then, the better Indian hotels had a 'whites only' admission policy. The striking Taj Mahal Hotel, with its red-tiled Florentine gothic dome and Indo-Saracenic arches, was the first sight to greet visitors arriving at the Bombay harbour at Apollo Bunder. The Taj was built even before the landmark Gateway of India arch which was completed in 1924.

The hotel has, since its inauguration, hosted many celebrities from all over the world: from various maharajas and maharanis to Prince Charles, to the likes of George Bernard Shaw, Douglas Fairbanks, Jacqueline Onassis, Barack Obama and Hilary Clinton. The staff was tutored to extend true 'Oriental' hospitality. Even when the terrorist group Lashkar-e-Taiba seized the hotel during the 26/11 attacks in 2008, the behaviour of the staff reflected the spirit of service that was ingrained in the institution from Jamsetji's time. For two nights and three days, while the hotel was occupied by terrorists armed with automatic weapons and the hotel's iconic dome burned, the employees chose not to escape when they had the chance but stayed behind to help the guests trapped inside. Students at the Harvard Business School undertook a case study to figure out what motivated the staff to display such exemplary devotion to duty.

Jamsetji's progressive ideas had numerous outlets. He was the first in the city to electrify his home and equip it with the latest in European plumbing. To start a silkworm farm in Mysore, he borrowed Japanese technology. He tried to establish an Indian shipping company in collaboration with a Japanese line as a rival to the P&O monopoly. But P&O stymied his efforts by cutting its prices. Jamsetji had an encyclopaedic knowledge of a wide variety of subjects, which sometimes awed experts who had not expected him to be so well versed in their specialisations.

During a visit to England in 1880, Jamsetji attended a lecture by Thomas Carlyle. The celebrated essayist and social critic observed that 'Those who control iron and steel will in time come to control the gold as well.' His words struck a chord with Jamsetji. He was passionate about opening a steel mill, an ambition that many mocked. The chief commissioner of the Great Indian Peninsular Railways, Sir Frederick Upcott, who had been consulted about the possibility of purchasing steel rails from a potential Tata plant, scoffed at the idea, saying that he would eat every pound of steel rail the Tatas succeeded in making. Undeterred, Jamsetji travelled to the US to hire a leading geologist to locate the most suitable site for mining iron ore in India.

His son, Dorabji, was charged with zeroing in on a suitable site. After many setbacks, just as Dorabji was ready to throw in the towel, he discovered, quite by chance, a geological map at Durg near Nagpur, which indicated rich deposits of iron ore.

His team scoured the region and pinpointed a suitable site in Mayurbhanj with all the necessary requirements—iron ore, coal and limestone—and ideally situated at the confluence of two rivers. The maharaja of Mayurbhanj leased an area of 20 square miles to the Tatas. A town came up at the small village of Sakchi (now in Jharkhand). Years before the steel factory became a reality, Jamsetji had a clear vision for the township that would be built around the steel plant. In a letter to Dorabji, he outlined the requirements: 'Wide streets with shady trees, every other of the quick-growing variety.' He wanted space for lawns, gardens, football and hockey fields, parks and places of worship for all communities. He also mentioned the need for a hospital.[16] Sakchi was renamed 'Jamshedpur' by the viceroy in January 1919 and it is a testament to the thoughtful planning that went into its creation that it is the only city in India, with a population topping 1 million, that does not have a municipal authority. The residents have repeatedly opted for the Tatas to continue to run and administer the town. Jamsetji also laid the foundation for an ambitious plan to generate hydroelectric power on the edge of the Western Ghats close to Bombay. The project became functional only after Jamsetji's death.

In philanthropy, too, he was a pioneer. Jamsetji believed that education was the key to India's progress. In 1892, he sponsored a scholarship that offered loans to bright Indian students so they could study abroad. Within a short span, one out of every five Indians in the prestigious Indian Civil Service was a J.N. Tata Scholar.[17] Jamsetji's most ambitious philanthropic scheme was conceiving the first Indian university of science, which would provide the best-quality teaching and research facilities for postgraduate students. At the suggestion of his trusted aide Burjorji Padshah, the institute was modelled on the lines of Johns Hopkins University in Baltimore, in the United States. (Padshah, a brilliant scholar who abandoned an academic career to work with

Jamsetji, gave significant inputs for many of Jamsetji's visionary schemes.) Jamsetji offered fourteen buildings and four properties in Bombay and half his fortune as an endowment to the proposed university. He hoped the balance would be made up by donations from enlightened Indian rulers and the British government. However, only the maharaja of Mysore, encouraged by his dewan, Sir Seshadri Iyer, came forward to help. He offered 300 acres of land in Bangalore and an annual subsidy.[18] While Jamsetji's extraordinary generosity was hailed by Indians generally, some from his own community grumbled that Parsi wealth should be utilised for the benefit of Parsis.

The then viceroy, Lord Curzon, was cool towards the proposal, and even hinted that it was a means to an end, that Jamsetji was angling for a baronetcy. Livid, Jamsetji made it clear that he was not interested in any titles or honours from the British. Dorabji and his wife also indignantly denounced the libellous suggestion. It was only after Jamsetji's death in 1904 that Lord Curzon gave the go-ahead for the institute and agreed to match the contribution offered by Jamsetji and his sons, Dorabji and Ratanji. The Indian Institute of Science (IISc) opened for admissions in 1911, when Curzon's successor, Lord Minto, was viceroy. Today, the IISc is routinely ranked among a handful of India's very top universities and its alumni includes many of the country's leading scientists.

After Jamsetji's death in Europe in 1904, Dorabji was appointed chairperson of the Tata group of companies. Dorabji completed his father's unfulfilled projects, including the commissioning of the steel plant. The Tatas had to raise £2 million for the venture. The money market was tight in 1907 and British investors were sceptical. The Swadeshi movement, launched in 1905, was gaining ground. Dadabhai Naoroji had written to Jamsetji in 1903, stressing that India's mineral wealth should not be exploited by British capital and its products taken out of the country. Dorabji issued a patriotic appeal to the people of India to fund the building of a steel plant. Within three weeks, 8000 people had put down the entire capital in return for shares in the steel company. The Tata investment was only 11 per cent of the total stake. When debentures were invited for the working capital, the maharaja of Gwalior bought the entire issue of £400,000 at the suggestion of his financial advisor, Framroze Eduljee Dinshaw, popularly known as FE, a great friend and supporter of the Tatas.

During Dorabji's leadership, three hydroelectric power companies, two cement companies, a large edible oil and soap company, an insurance company and an airline were added to the Tata group. Dorabji's role in building the Tata empire is often glossed over, perhaps because he was overshadowed by two particularly charismatic individuals—his predecessor Jamsetji and his successor JRD.

He studied at Gonville and Caius College, Cambridge University, and shone on the sports fields. He was a visionary who understood the value of a sporting culture to build a nationalist imagination in a country that was still under colonial rule.

Dorabji's younger brother Ratanji was frail and often unwell and very different temperamentally. Although a partner in the family firm, Ratanji did not take an active interest in the business. He was drawn to the arts and to funding worthy causes. While Jamsetji and Dorabji were keen to provide opportunities to the most able and talented in society, Ratanji focused on the welfare of the downtrodden and weak.[19] He contributed generously to Gopal Krishna Gokhale's 'Servants of India Society' as well as Mahatma Gandhi's campaign for racial equality in South Africa.

Ratanji died when he was only forty-eight, spending his last few years in England. After setting aside the family home and a small portion of his stake in Tata Sons for his widow, Navajbai Tata, he bequeathed the bulk of his estate to the Sir Ratan Tata Trust, one of the first major Indian philanthropic foundations in the modern sense of the word. He set up the Sir Ratan Tata Department of

Social Sciences at the London School of Economics and the Sir Ratan Tata Fund at the University of London for studying the conditions of the poor. A great art collector, particularly of Chinese porcelain, Ratanji donated his priceless art collection to the Prince of Wales Museum (renamed 'Chhatrapati Shivaji Maharaj Vastu Sangrahalaya') in Bombay.

Dorabji's major expansion of Tata Steel came at a price. In 1924, the market was unfavourable and the price of iron ore crashed. The Tatas were in such dire straits that a timid director even suggested that the government be asked to take over the company. The story goes that JRD's father, R.D. Tata, pounded the table and declared angrily that such a day would never come. There was even a telegram from Jamshedpur, pleading that there was not enough money to pay wages.

Tata applied to the Imperial Bank for a loan. Dorabji pledged his entire fortune, as well as Esplanade House and his wife's jewellery. (The jewels, incidentally, included the famous Jubilee Diamond, one of the world's largest diamonds, reportedly bigger even than the Kohinoor.) All of this though the Tatas had never owned more than 11 per cent of Tata Steel. To provide the remaining surety for the loan, the financial wizard FE came to the rescue again. FE was the second son of a prominent Karachi philanthropist and businessman, Edulji Dinshaw, who had extensive real-estate holdings in the city. A lawyer by training, FE had moved to Bombay, where he multiplied his father's real-estate portfolio. He was a director and financial adviser to numerous companies and individuals, including maharajas. The Tatas, the fifth maharaja of Gwalior and the Aga Khan were his biggest clients. FE laid the foundation of the Indian cement business, pioneering a merger of ten companies to form the Associate Cement Companies (ACC) Limited. He also helped develop Bombay Talkies, the most modern film studio in the 1930s.

FE agreed to loan Tata Sons a further Rs 1 crore in 1926 to rescue the troubled Tata Hydro. Tata Sons never managed to repay FE in full. Ratan says that FE wrote off all the Tatas' debts. But FE seems to have got back some of his loan indirectly. On 2 July 1927, his firm F.E. Dinshaw Ltd was bestowed a one-eighth share in the commission paid to the Tata managing agency by its steel and power companies.[20] After FE's death, his bohemian and profligate heir, Edul Dinshaw, who spent most of his time in Europe and America and had little connection with Bombay society and its conventions, was keen to leave the country. He sold his father's estate, including F.E. Dinshaw Ltd, to Shapoorji Pallonji. This included not just his Tata shares but also a hefty holding in ACC.

Neither Ratanji nor Dorabji had children. After Ratanji's death in 1918, Dorabji, his wife Meherbai and cousin Nowroji Saklatwala urged his widow Navajbai Seth Tata, still in England, to adopt a son to carry on the Tata name. Perhaps Dorabji did not feel the need to adopt a child because he and Meherbai treated their young nephew, Homi Bhabha, like a son. Even at an early age, it was clear that Homi—son of Meherbai's brother, Jehangir Bhabha, legal advisor to the Tatas and director of many Tata companies—was exceptionally bright. Dorabji and Jehangir hoped that the infant prodigy would become an engineer and eventually join the Tata Iron and Steel company. They dreamt that he might head the group someday. But the boy grew up instead to be the father of India's nuclear programme.

Three months before Dorabji's death in 1932, he formed a trust bequeathing his entire fortune, including the famous Jubilee Diamond, towards opening India's first cancer hospital, the Tata Memorial, in memory of his wife. (The very gifted Lady Meherbai, an accomplished pianist, talented tennis player and a crusader for women's causes, including raising the age of marriage for girls, had died of leukaemia a year earlier.) The Sir Dorabji Tata Trust would later set up the Tata Institute of Social Sciences (TISS), the Tata Institute of Fundamental Research (TIFR) and the National Centre for the Performing Arts. Dorabji nominated as his successor Nowroji Saklatwala, the senior-most director of the firm. (Saklatwala was a nephew of Jamsetji's and cousin to Shapurji Saklatvala. Jamsetji's two sisters, Virbaiji and Jerbai, had married men with the same surname but a slightly different spelling.) It was Saklatwala's misfortune that he took charge during the global depression of the 1930s. He relied heavily on the advice of FE, who was happy to offer his expertise, at a price.

Meanwhile, the boy adopted by Navajbai, Naval Tata, was growing up. There are varying stories on how Naval came to be part of the family. According to one version, Navajbai chose Naval at random from four orphan boys at the J.N. Petit Parsi Orphanage in Parel, Bombay, attracted by his beautiful eyes. The official Tata story is that Naval's father, Hormusji, a spinning master in Tata's Advance Mills, Ahmedabad, died when the boy was four. Hormusji also happened to have the surname Tata. His widow, who had four sons to support, struggled to earn a livelihood through embroidery work and moved from Navsari to Surat. Two of her sons were admitted to the Petit Orphanage in Mumbai as paying boarders for technical training. Naval was taken in gratis. According to Tata sources, Naval's mother, Ratanbai Rao, was Ratanji's favourite cousin, which was why Dorabji selected him.[21] It is said that Dorabji wanted Navajbai to adopt a son so that there would be someone to carry out his brother's last rites. In any case, Naval remained in the orphanage for four more years. Despite the clout of the Tatas, the orphanage authorities stuck to their rules and did not permit Naval to leave until he was thirteen. Overnight, the young boy was transported from a very humble environment into a life of luxury, the adopted scion of one of the richest families in India.

Naval never forgot his humble roots or tried to hide them. He retained his biological father's name, Hormusji, as his middle name. The Petit Orphanage for 300 poor boys was supported on a slim budget and was a bit like a penitentiary. The only glimpse the inmates got of the outside world was a visit to the Victoria Gardens every three weeks. Naval was to say later, 'I am grateful to God for giving me an opportunity to experience the pangs of poverty which more than anything else moulded my character.'[22]

Naval, who graduated from Bombay University before going to England to study accounting, might well have ended up as chairperson of the Tata group but for the fact that, in the same year of his birth, 1904, another little Tata was born in an opulent mansion on the Rue de Halevy in Paris. (1904 was also the year Jamsetji Tata passed away.) Jehangir Ratan Tata (who would come to be widely known as 'JRD') was the son of Ratan Dadabhoy Tata, a nephew of Jamsetji's. (R.D. Tata was the son of Nusserwanji Tata's brother-in-law.) In 1887, when Jamsetji converted his firm into a company under the name 'Tata and Sons', he took on his son Dorab and R.D. Tata as partners. Jamsetji was impressed by RD's financial acumen as a trader in the Far East. While he did join the company, RD did not abandon his own business, perhaps because he did not always get on with Dorabji. According to family lore, Jamsetji's elder son could be prickly at times and was said to have resented any relative in whom the patriarch took an undue interest. Dorabji was similarly jealous of his cousin, Shapurji Saklatvala, with whom (alongside the American metallurgical engineer C.M. Weld) he travelled extensively in Bihar and Orissa, prospecting for iron ore. Saklatvala contracted malaria and settled in England to convalesce, for a while running the Tata office in Manchester. An ardent socialist, Saklatvala eventually joined the Communist Party of Great Britain. He had the distinction of being the third Parsi (and third Indian) to be elected to the

House of Commons, one of the very few British MPs ever to win as a member of the Communist Party. It is said that although he had married an Englishwoman, he ensured that his children had their navjotes, attracting the ire of the Communist party, which was opposed to religion in any form. He claimed that he did it to ensure his children benefited from a family trust fund. His remains were interred at the Tata Mausoleum in the Brookwood Cemetery in Surrey, England.

R.D. Tata was a widower in his mid-forties and living in Paris to learn French when he met the beautiful, young Suzanne Brière. In those days, marriage outside the religion was strictly taboo for Parsis. When RD wrote to the family of his intentions, Dorabji was furious and wrote him an angry letter stating why the alliance was unsuitable and pointing out that Parsis do not marry outside their community.[23] But the family patriarch gave RD his blessing. Jamsetji, as Bakhtiar Dadabhoy suggested in *Sugar in Milk*, is believed to have even attended the wedding in France in 1902. Dorabji too eventually came around.

Suzanne was renamed 'Sooni' because RD wanted his wife to be inducted into the Zoroastrian faith and be accepted by his family and community, a story we have already touched upon. Two high priests belonging to the respected Jamasp Asa line, agreed to perform Sooni's navjote, which really meant conversion from Christianity to Zoroastrianism. They were liberal in their thinking, and perhaps also in awe of the Tata name. The navjote is normally performed during childhood to confirm a Parsi child's entry into the faith by donning the muslin vest (sudreh), tying the sacred girdle made of lambswool (kasti) and reciting the prayers with the priest. In a letter to her mother describing the momentous event, Sooni noted, 'Until the very last moment we weren't sure that it would be allowed. There had been quite a few objections and some Parsis had not come since they were afraid of trouble.'[24]

Sooni's foreboding proved to be justified. The Parsi community was up in arms over the conversion. Protest meetings were held and committees set up to oppose it. Little Parsi boys recited the Gujarati ditty, '*Tata naam no Parsi, Madam parni ayo, dakhma leva gayo to laat khayi ayo.*' (A Parsi named 'Tata' married a foreign madame, when he wanted to have her taken to a dakhma, he got a kick in his behind.) The then head of the BPP, Sir Jamsetjee Jejeebhoy, accepted the community's concerns and approached the court.

The matter went to the Bombay High Court in 1908, with another Parsi baronet, Sir Dinshaw Petit, supporting R.D. Tata and challenging both the punchayet's ruling and the fact that the Jejeebhoys had somehow acquired the authority to nominate the punchayet head, a post which consequently remained within the family. The judgement—a landmark in Parsi history, that continues to be valid—held, among other issues, that Sooni could not be accepted as a Parsi. Why RD was so determined on converting Sooni remains a mystery. The Tatas, despite their priestly origins, were not particularly religious. And it was unlikely that Sooni would have been interred in the Malabar Hill Tower of Silence even if she had been recognised as a Parsi. Most Tatas, starting with Jamsetji, died abroad and are buried in the Tata Mausoleum in Surrey, England.

JRD, the son of RD and Sooni Tata, had a nomadic, itinerant childhood. He was schooled along with his four siblings, Sylla, Dorab, Rodabeh and Jimmy, in both France and India and for a short time, even in Japan. French was the language spoken at home, and with which they were most comfortable. RD's work required that he remain in Bombay but Sooni, soon after her controversial navjote, found the climate unsuitable and spent most of her time in France with her children.

One of the most memorable moments of JRD's life was when, as a fifteen-year-old, he was given a joyride in a neighbour's plane at the beach resort of Hardelot on the Channel coast, where his parents had a summer home. The neighbour was Louis Bleriot, the first man to fly a plane across the Channel in 1909. JRD was bitten by the flying bug. He became the first Indian to get a pilot's licence and his fascination with planes shaped his life.[25] One of the many legends about his piloting exploits was that he participated in the Aga Khan contest, which offered a prize to the first Indian to fly from India to England and back. He lost out to Aspy Engineer, another Parsi, who ended up as the second chief of the Indian Air Force. It was characteristic of JRD's generosity of spirit that he loaned four spark plugs to his rival when the two crossed paths in Alexandria as they flew in opposite directions.

RD's plan was that JRD should study at Cambridge University. But before he could finish his preparatory course, JRD, a French citizen, was conscripted into the French cavalry. On his return to India in 1925, his father, perhaps having a premonition of his own death, insisted that the young man join the family firm. JRD was very conscious of his lack of a college education and often referred to himself deprecatingly as 'semi-educated', although he was a very well-read man indeed. John Peterson, a retired ICS officer who was director of Tata Steel at Bombay, was his official mentor at the firm.

JRD's first major proposal at work was that the Tatas start a postal air service from London to Karachi in partnership with the South African-born Nevill Vintcent, an experienced pilot. Tata chairperson Dorabji was by this time old and unreceptive to new concepts. It was Peterson who pleaded for JRD's project, pointing out that the cost was not prohibitive. On 15 October 1932, a small crowd gathered at the Karachi airport, including the city's postmaster. They had come to cheer JRD as he started on his inaugural run on a Puss Moth, carrying the mail to Ahmedabad and onwards to Bombay. 'Those were adventurous days,' JRD recalled years later in *Beyond the Last Blue Mountain*, a biography of the tycoon by R.M. Lala, a former director of the Sir Dorabji Tata Trust. 'We had no navigational or landing aids on the ground or in the air and no radio.' Two planes, three pilots and three mechanics was what it took to start Tata Airlines. From a mail service, it was just a small step flying passengers. By 1946, Tata Airlines carried one out of every three passengers in the country. JRD's plan was to make his airline international under the name 'Air India International', as a joint enterprise with the government.[26]

JRD was only twenty-two and was still to find his feet in India when R.D. Tata died of a heart attack in Paris. He discovered that his spendthrift father, as described in his biographies by Dadabhoy and Lala, unlike the thrifty Dorabji, was heavily in debt. Dorabji, by this time old, crabby and suffering from severe diabetes, insisted that JRD pay off his father's debts to him, though the debt to Tata Sons was waived in view of RD's lifelong services to the company. JRD was forced to sell the family house, Soonita, named after his late mother, in Bombay as well as the estate in Hardelot and the Poona house. After he had cleared his father's debts, all that was left were the shares in Tata Sons. According to Russi Lala, 'This was a third of the total.' Although RD's will had left JRD the bulk of the money from dividends, the fair-minded JRD insisted on dividing it equally between himself and his siblings. JRD did, however, take his father's place as a director of Tata Sons and also took Indian citizenship.

His siblings were only marginally involved in the family firm. The eldest, Sylla, was a keen tennis player and JRD's favourite. She married Fali Petit who inherited the Petit baronetcy. Darab, the second son, was friendly and popular but had no head for business, though he was a director at Tatas. 'He suffered from a nervous disorder and JRD was rather unsympathetic,' Mithoo Coorlawla, a friend of the family, told me.[27] Rodabeh, JRD's younger sister, married Colonel Leslie Sawhny, who worked at the Tata group and was JRD's executive assistant. Sawhny, Ratan Tata says, was once perceived as a possible head of the group by JRD. Unfortunately, Sawhny died fairly young of a heart attack on the golf course. Rodabeh became a respected interior decorator. The youngest son, Jimmy, a trainee fighter pilot, died tragically in an air crash when he was only twenty.

JRD met his wife Thelly because of his love of fast cars. A police case had been registered against him for speeding his blue Bugatti along Peddar Road and causing an accident. He had been advised to consult Jack Vicaji, a top criminal lawyer. There he met Vicaji's niece Thelly, who was half-Parsi and half-English. Her Parsi ancestors were pioneers in banking in India and were in charge of the Nizam of Hyderabad's mint. The family later became bankrupt after differences with the Nizam, since the ruler borrowed Rs 41 lakh from them and refused to pay it back. In 1840, a silver coin was minted with the initials 'PV' and was called the 'Pestanshah sikka'—the only time a coin was named after a Parsi and not some member of a royal house.[28]

The beautiful and elegant Thelly's life revolved around her husband, but he had other interests as well. Author Zareer Masani, whose family lived next door to the Tatas and whose father Minoo once worked as JRD's executive assistant, wrote that JRD's marriage was unhappy: he was notoriously unfaithful and his wife obsessively jealous. 'His French accent and Gallic charm made him irresistible to the ladies and a succession of pretty women flitted in and out of his long life. One of them, I later discovered, was my mother.'[29] But JRD was too kind-hearted to ever leave his childless wife, fearing it would destroy the fragile Thelly, who had suffered a stroke in the 1980s.

When Saklatwala died in Europe six years after he took over as chairperson, JRD was only thirty-four. Other than Navajbai, he was the only surviving permanent director on the board. The other directors were impressed with his sincerity, dedication and team spirit, with Ardeshir Dalal, the first Indian to be municipal commissioner, as the only sceptic. A severe man, Dalal feared that India's largest industrial empire would be run by a playboy interested in fast cars and planes. Within a year, he admitted privately that he was completely wrong in his assessment. JRD made two important decisions on taking over: he formed a talented, brainy advisory group and delegated authority. He joked that he did not want to end up like his predecessor, Saklatwala, rushing from one board meeting to the next.[30]

JRD persuaded leading luminaries of the era to join the company, either on the board of Tata Sons or as senior executives. J.D. Choksi, John Mathai, Sir Jehangir Ghandy, Kish Naoroji, Sumant Moolgaokar, P.A. Narialwala, Nani Palkhivala, Shahrukh Sabhavala, Bobby Kooka and Sir Homi Mody were some of his notable appointees. The top men in the group had varied backgrounds and temperaments. Dr John Mathai, who was a minister in the interim government under Jawaharlal Nehru, was a very respected economist and was one of the main authors of the Bombay Plan. He had famously disagreed with Nehru about establishing the Planning Commission. Sir Homi Mody, a self-made man, was chairperson of numerous prestigious bodies, served on the Viceroy's Executive Council and was later appointed governor of Uttar Pradesh. Sumant Moolgaokar, a visionary and the father of India's heavy engineering industry and architect of TELCO (later Tata Motors), was a key executive at Tata and a power in his own right. A loner and something of a recluse, Moolgaokar was completely immersed in his job. 'TELCO was his heart and soul and he ruled the company with an iron hand,' Ratan Tata says, 'building it into the foremost engineering company in India in those days.'[31] Despite his non-Parsi surname, Moolgaokar was very much part of the Tatas' inner circle—a man JRD admired greatly and 'one whom no one, not even JRD, questioned,' according to Ratan Tata. The

Tata Sumo car is named after him, being an amalgamation of the first two letters of his name and surname, and not a reference to Japanese wrestling as most assume. The colourful Russi Mody, Sir Homi Mody's son, was chairperson of Tata Steel and in his time regarded as the emperor of the steel town, Jamshedpur. Brilliant at labour relations, he developed close links with several Indian politicians, which stood the company in good stead. Minoo Masani, JRD's former chief executive assistant, was for a time an MP from the Swatantra Party and the leader of the Opposition in Parliament. Bobby Kooka was the witty, offbeat advertising head of Air India whose memorable campaigns sold the airline brand very successfully, even if his irreverent humour tended to infuriate some strait-laced Indian parliamentarians.

One reason why JRD was so admired and respected was because he treated all people equally, with courtesy, kindness and consideration. He hated receiving special treatment, was humility personified, modest about his abilities and loyal and supportive towards all who worked in the group. He might have flared up on occasion but was quick to offer profuse apologies. Sudha Murthy, author, chairperson of the philanthropic Infosys Foundation and wife of Infosys founder N.R. Narayana Murthy, recalls that after her graduation from IISc Bangalore, she saw an advertisement for engineers in TELCO which specified that only male engineers could apply. She wrote a postcard to JRD protesting this requirement, pointing to its retrogressive nature, especially unexpected from a firm founded by Jamsetji Tata. At JRD's immediate intervention, she received a telegram calling her for the interview. She became the first woman engineer to work on the Tata shop floor. Eight years later, when she was leaving the Tatas, Sudha bumped into JRD on the steps of Bombay House. He was concerned that her husband had not arrived to pick her up as it was late and she was alone, and so kept her company and enquired about her future plans. She disclosed that she was leaving the group to help her husband start a new software company and expressed her fears about its future. He assured her the company would do well, and said that if she made money, she must be sure to give some back to society.[32] Murthy still keeps a picture of JRD in her office as a reminder of a man who had time and concern for every employee in his company. In fact, many retired employees still display a photograph of JRD in their homes as a mark of admiration and respect.

Although the expression in India once was 'as rich as a Tata or a Birla', JRD actually had very little ready cash. He lived in a rented bungalow, admittedly in the poshest part of town, owned by his brother-in-law Fali Petit. Kashmiri businessman Vijay Dhar, a friend of Nusli Wadia and also close to the Gandhi family, recalls that he once suggested to Nusli that, since Thelly was bedridden in her last years and spent a lot of her time watching television, JRD should buy her a video player to watch movies from her bed. Nusli vetoed the suggestion, explaining that JRD could not afford a video player, only recently introduced in India at the time. Nor would he be willing to accept it as a gift or charge it to the companies he presided over. JRD, Dhar said, 'was such a simple man that he even washed his own shirts'.[33] (When Dhar mentioned this to Indira Gandhi, she expressed skepticism over this last fact.) In one of his last interviews, JRD recounted to journalist Maneck Davar how, after he and his wife sold their flat in Sterling Apartments on Bombay's Peddar Road, he received more money than he had ever seen in his life. He felt that it was unconscionable to hoard the money and immediately formed a charitable trust in the name of his wife and himself.[34]

JRD had great dreams for India after Independence and was close to the Nehru–Gandhi family socially, though he disagreed violently with their socialist economic model for India. In August 1953, the Congress-dominated Parliament nationalised all nine privately owned airlines and merged them into state-owned corporations: Air India International and Indian Airlines. JRD was deeply hurt that the one company that he had personally given birth to and that he still considered his baby, was snatched away from him. The only compensation was that he was appointed chairperson of Air India and a director of Indian Airlines.

In 1961, the elderly politician C. Rajagopalachari wrote to JRD, asking him to contribute to the newly formed right-wing Swatantra Party. Rajaji said that, though he was aware that the Tatas funded the Congress, he felt it was the group's patriotic duty to also assist the opposition since 'no democracy governs well in the absence of a strong opposition'. JRD accepted the argument. But such was his honesty that he did not fund the party surreptitiously, as did other industrialists; he wrote frankly to Prime Minister Nehru and explained his reasons. JRD pointed out that, in the absence of a constructive opposition, the only option for patriots opposed to the Congress were to 'either to go into the political wilderness where their services will be lost to the country or turn to the Communist Party or some equally undesirable extremist party'.[35] Historian Ramachandra Guha, recounting the exchange of letters between JRD and the prime minister, observed in his *Hindustan Times* piece, 'There is no Indian industrialist alive today who has the political sagacity or moral courage of JRD Tata. No industrialist now would have the guts to tell the prime minister so frankly that he, his party, and his government were not flawless or perfect.'

The Congress campaign against big business inevitably led to a slowdown in the growth of the Tata group during the 1960s. By the 1970s, the Birla companies overtook the Tatas, both in sales and profits. This was the era of the Licence Permit Raj, and JRD made it clear that the Tatas were unwilling to pay politicians under the table, even if it meant that they would not be able to expand the capacity of their industries. JRD once commented to his biographer Russi Lala, 'I don't think I have contributed anything in economic matters except in ethics and values. I believe an ethical life is part of an economic life.'[36] Leading financial journalist T.N. Ninan endorses this, saying that 'the Tata group may have occasionally made compromises because the existing laws made it difficult to conduct business otherwise, but generally the Tatas and other Parsi businessmen preferred to do things the ethical way.'[37]

It is widely believed that JRD privately disapproved of Tata director and constitutional lawyer Nani Palkhivala handing back Indira Gandhi's legal brief after she declared an Emergency, curtailing fundamental rights and civil liberties. In Mrs Gandhi's mind, looking for conspiracies everywhere, Palkhivala's stand put a black mark against the entire Tata group. After the Emergency was declared in 1975, the *New York Times* quoted JRD supporting the draconian measures on the basis that 'things had gone too far', and that perhaps India was not suited to democracy.[38] Ratan Tata recalls that 'JRD was also annoyed with Palkhivala for taking the brief in the first place because there were protests outside Bombay House.' JRD refused, however, to sack Palkhivala from the board, as suggested by some Tata directors. However, when Palkhivala accepted the government's offer to be ambassador to the US in 1978, he did lose out. He left India assuming that his position as a director on various Tata company boards would be kept vacant for him. But this did not happen. While Indira Gandhi was considered hostile towards the Tatas, it was her successor, Morarji Desai, who dealt the unkindest blow. JRD was dropped from the boards of both Air India and Indian Airlines without any prior intimation. His embarrassed successor, Air Marshal P.C. Lal, had to break the news to him.

Ninan's assessment of JRD's half-century-plus tenure as chairperson was that he had done very well in difficult times for business.[39] Tata was once again the leading industrial group in the country when JRD handed over charge to his successor, Ratan, in

1991. It was during his tenure, the longest corporate reign in India, that many of the major Tata companies were launched—Tata Chemicals, Tata Motors (originally TELCO), Titan, Tata Finlay (later renamed 'Tata Tea'), Taj Hotels, Lakmé, Tata Exports and TCS. His strength lay in picking the right people and giving them the freedom to run the company under his benign watch.

In 1969, the government introduced the MRTP Act, which ended the practice of companies being run by a managing agency. Tata Sons looked as if it would lose its relevance, because its shareholding in the various group companies had dropped to minority levels. By then, the group really consisted of professionally managed independent companies, with JRD as the part-time chairperson. Despite the token shareholding, JRD held the group together with the sheer power of his personality. In his lifetime, JRD won honours at home and abroad, including India's highest civilian honour, the Bharat Ratna, and the French Legion of Honour. When he passed away in a Geneva hospital in 1993, he was eighty-nine. The Indian parliament was adjourned as a sign of respect, an honour normally reserved only for parliamentarians. He was buried in the Père Lachaise cemetery in Paris, where his father had bought a plot for the family vault. Two Zoroastrian priests from London chanted religious passages. Later, in Bombay, rituals for his soul were carried out at the Malabar Hill dakhma. The Parsis were keen to claim him as their own, although some orthodox members expressed disapproval. This was largely because JRD did not believe in formal religion. Because his mother had been snubbed by the Parsis, he considered himself a humanist rather than a Zoroastrian.

* * *

When JRD reached the age of seventy-five, there was great speculation about who would succeed him. There was a growing concern among Tata insiders that some heads of Tata companies had a larger stake in those particular establishments than the Tatas did and ran them as personal fiefdoms. In particular, the bosses of the three big companies—Darbari Seth of Tata Chemicals, Russi Mody of TISCO and Ajit Kerkar of Taj Hotels—brooked no interference from Bombay House. According to Lala, in his biography of JRD, the Tata chairperson considered several names in the group, such as Nani Palkhivala, Russi Mody, Sharokh Sabavala and H.N. Sethna, as possible successors. Ratan says that he himself had assumed that the two top contenders for the post would be Palkhivala and Mody.[40]

In fact, Russi Mody, seen to be something of an 'egotist' in popular perception and as per interviews with various other sources, also assumed he was the natural inheritor of JRD's mantle. He was, after all, a quintessential Tata man who had started in the group at the bottom of the ladder. The dilettante son of Sir Homi Mody, a director of the Tata group, Russi was schooled at elite British institutions—Harrow (of which Jawaharlal Nehru was also an alumnus) and Christ Church College, Cambridge University. He was fun-loving, played the piano (he once accompanied Einstein on the piano), had a discerning eye for art and was an avid collector. Most of all, he loved food (his favourite breakfast was a twelve-egg omelette) and his expanding girth was testimony to this devotion. Like many educated Parsis who had no definite career goal, he was sent to work at Tatas. On his first day in Jamshedpur as a management trainee, the story goes, Russi went out for a jog in his shorts. He saw that there was a strike on and that workers were agitating outside the office building. Casually chatting with the strikers, he noted down their grievances while Tata managers watched from the safety of the fourth floor, wondering what the hell the newcomer was up to.[41] The management realised that labour relations was Russi's forte and placed him in HRD. He built up a natural bond with the workers, holding darbars outside his house like a politician. The employees knew they could count on him. And so even-handed were his dealings with the unions that they were almost aligned with the management. Mody became particularly powerful in the group after the Emergency. During the Janata Party regime of the late 1970s, the socialist minister George Fernandes wanted to nationalise Tata Steel. Mody knew most of the politicians in eastern India and he worked on each one of them. The man who epitomised capitalism was even very friendly with the communist chief minister of West Bengal, Jyoti Basu. Mody engineered a petition by the Tata workers' union demanding that the steel company continue to be run by the Tatas. He forced the Janata government to backtrack on its proposal for nationalisation. For JRD, this was a major achievement and it gave Mody special status within the company. It was Mody who gave away the Duke of Edinburgh Award every year in Jamshedpur and it was Mody, not JRD, who presided over lunch at the Taj Hotel for newly selected trainees for the Tata Administrative Services. (The Tata group was the first Indian company to set up a school for the selection and training of its executives.) 'His compassion and ability to get things done was unbelievable,' says Suhel Seth, an unabashed admirer of Mody.[42]

In 1987, it seemed like Mody would indeed succeed JRD. Moolgaokar wanted Mody to be his deputy with an eye to eventually taking over as chairperson of TELCO. He told Mody that he would be stepping down. This would have meant that Mody would be heading the group's two largest companies, accounting for half its turnover. Unfortunately, just before the board meeting, the indiscreet Mody gave an interview to the Calcutta-based *Business Standard* newspaper, suggesting that he was being called in to save TELCO, which was on a downslide. Moolgaokar was furious that Mody had indirectly run him down and rescinded his offer. Even though Mody swore that he had been misquoted, Moolgaokar appointed Ratan vice-chairperson of TELCO. Suddenly, the succession was wide open.

While neither Ratan nor Lala mention Nusli Wadia, many within the group and outside assumed that he would be JRD's eventual choice. The two families were closely connected, and JRD and Nusli shared a father and son relationship. From the time that Nusli was twenty-six, the two met practically every fortnight and spent Sunday mornings together. JRD was impressed by Nusli's capability and hard work, and he particularly appreciated the fact that, unlike other company board directors, Nusli was not overawed by the Tata boss and did not automatically agree with him. At meetings, Nusli often argued with JRD. And quite often Tata executives, including Ratan, would meet Nusli at his own offices, suggesting they viewed him as a possible successor.

On several occasions in the 1980s, JRD had asked Nusli to join the Tata board. But there was major opposition from Naval Tata, who was aligned with Pallonji Mistry. In their efforts to block Nusli's appointment to Tata Sons, Naval and Pallonji even approached Indira Gandhi, who was wary of Nusli because of his old association with Nanaji Deshmukh and the Bharatiya Jana Sangh. JRD was willing to take the two of them on, but Nusli hesitated. He knew he would face hostility on all fronts and he had his own group of companies to run.

Years later, JRD decided to make Nusli a permanent director, a move that reportedly irked even Ratan. According to Jamsetji Tata's will, each branch of the family had the right to appoint one permanent director. In Ratanji's family, Navajbai became permanent director, followed by Naval. Since Naval did not appoint a successor before his death, the right of Sir Ratan Tata's family lapsed. JRD, who inherited his permanent directorship from his father, was the only one still in a position to appoint a permanent director. He invited Nusli in writing sometime after Mrs Gandhi's death. JRD pointed out that nobody could stop him since the board articles allowed it. Once again, Nusli was reluctant. 'I know everyone in this building hates the sight of me. They all resent me,' he reportedly told JRD. When JRD called Ratan into his office, Nusli tore up the invitation letter in his presence, so that there would be no misunderstanding with his friend.[43]

Nusli says that JRD didn't want Ratan to succeed him and was quite hostile to him for years. Ratan and Nusli really came to know each other well after both started working in Bombay, though their mothers Sooni and Dina, were best friends, and Dina was very close to Sooni's daughters from her second marriage. Ratan asked for Nusli's help when he was given charge of the Empress and Tata mills, and an alliance of sorts developed between the two young men. For years, Nusli was Ratan's principal promoter.

Meanwhile, JRD vacillated on appointing his successor. Or perhaps he had not come to terms with his own mortality. JRD only stepped down as chairperson in 1991 at the ripe old age of eighty-six. At this point, he turned to Ratan, the only eligible Tata left. JRD believed that one of the few things that could hold the group together was the Tata name. Apart from Nusli, Sharokh Sabavala, who was JRD's executive assistant, also advocated Ratan's cause.

Ratan regrets that he only got close to JRD in the older man's last six years at Tatas. The first sign that JRD had begun to revise his opinion of Ratan was when he appointed him head of Tata Industries, a holding company promoter of high tech firms. But it was after Moolgaokar chose him over Russi to be his deputy that Ratan truly emerged as the frontrunner to be JRD's successor. Ratan believes that his appointment to TELCO was meant to keep Russi out, and not part of a larger succession scheme. 'JRD did champion Russi's appointment to TELCO but, characteristically, did not interfere with Moolgaokar's decisions, even though he was quite upset that Moolgaokar had changed his mind,' says

Ratan.[44] He also refutes the assumption that, after Moolgaokar singled him out, it was automatically assumed that he would be JRD's successor. 'If I look back at becoming chairman of the group, Jeh called me one morning and told me he was making me his successor and that was literally the morning it happened. He had hinted that one day I would be head of the Tatas but it was read by me as head of the Tatas after somebody else.'[45]

* * *

The succession took place on 25 March 1991, when the board voted Ratan as chairperson. His name was proposed by JRD and seconded by Pallonji Mistry. An ageing JRD remained to help Ratan find his feet. But the new chairperson, now fifty-one, already knew the first step he had to take to establish himself as the boss. He needed to annihilate the three satraps in the Tata empire who ruled without any interference from head office. His father had warned him, 'There is a Mughal emperor in each of the Tata companies.' JRD was not ruthless enough to uproot the very men he had nurtured and built up. At hand to aid and advise Ratan in these crucial hatchet jobs was Nusli, familiar with politics and intrigue from an early age. The two men, ruthless and single-minded, made a formidable team.

From a shy, under-confident youth whose credentials as a business executive were not inspiring, Ratan blossomed into a larger-than-life chairperson of the Tata group. He gave his company new visibility and prominence, both in India and abroad, through a series of bold and out-of-the box gambles. In 2000, he impressed the business world when Tata Tea purchased the British Tetley group, a company twice as big as the acquirer. Today, Tata Global Beverages is the second-largest tea manufacturer in the world. In 2007, Tata Steel announced its intention to take over Europe's second-largest steel manufacturer, the Anglo-Dutch major Corus. What followed was a desperate bidding battle with Brazilian Steel maker CSN for acquiring the loss-making company. Tata Steel went 34 per cent above its original offer for the Corus shares, forking out a whopping US$12.1 billion. Cynics questioned the wisdom of the deal, but it was sweet vindication for the Tatas. A century earlier, the British had scoffed at the very thought of Indians being capable of setting up a steel plant. Now, that same Indian company was not just the owner of the largest steel manufacturing unit in Britain but also the largest industrial employer in that country.

In 2009, Ratan was hailed by the Indian media as the man who would revolutionise the auto industry when he unveiled the Nano, the 'People's Car', available for the spectacularly low price of Rs 100,000 at the New Delhi Auto Expo. It was calculated that millions of Indians would be able to afford the price and give up using two-wheelers for the relative safety of a car. Ratan's dream project would expand the Indian car market by 65 per cent, according to some of the rosier guesstimates.

Before Nano, in 1998, Tata Motors had produced the Indica, billed as 'the first indigenously designed Indian car'. But the Indica was unsuccessful in its initial years and the Tata group contemplated selling off the business to Ford Motor Company. However, when the Tata team, led by Ratan, travelled to Detroit in 1999, they felt patronised by the Americans. The Ford chairman, Bill Ford, asked rather condescendingly why the Tatas had entered the passenger car sector without knowing enough about the business. Ford taunted the Tata representatives, suggesting that they would be doing the Indian company a great favour if they agreed to purchase the Indica. The Tata team was annoyed, and left without completing negotiations. According to one of the team members, Ratan was very tense on the journey back home and felt insulted. The tables were turned a decade later, in 2008, when Ford, in deep financial trouble, was keen to offload its heritage British luxury marques, Jaguar and Land Rover. This time, it was Bill Ford who found himself pleading with Tata Motors, acknowledging that the Indian company would be doing Ford a great favour by buying its luxury car division, which Tata did, to the tune of US$2.3 billion.[46] Ratan's business exploits have earned him adulatory titles such as 'India's best brand ambassador' and 'most admired Indian businessman'. He has been called a model of corporate responsibility, heading trusts that funded many charities in India and also made sizeable donations of US$50 million each to his alma maters, Cornell University and Harvard Business School. Ratan multiplied the group's net worth from a few billion dollars to over US$100 billion. At the first Iranshah Utsav in Udvada, Gujarat, in December 2015, where Parsis from India and across the globe congregated, Ratan Tata was honoured as the leading icon of the community. The entire congregation was on its feet to applaud him.

For all the glossy satin sheen of Ratan's reputation, some business analysts are less than enamoured. Several of Ratan's costly foreign acquisitions have come unstuck, they argue. Tata Steel Europe, for instance, was a white elephant that dragged the group into colossal debt. Ratan's global gambits, wrote T.N. Ninan, were 'a mixture of hubris and bad timing'.[47] The Indian companies fared little better. 'Telecom was the single biggest opportunity in Indian business in the last two decades and Ratan messed it up,' says a financial analyst who did not want to be named so as not to upset the sensitive Tata leader. Business journalist Sucheta Dalal, though, is frank: 'There was blunder after blunder. True, he made Tata global and was willing to do tie-ups. But a lot of the tie-ups flopped. Steel was a big disaster, and the company was overstretched in purchasing Jaguar.'[48] Ratan, many argue, had a brilliant macro view, but when it came to managing the finer aspects of the businesses, he was less successful.

If the Tata group remained pre-eminent, it was largely because of one company alone: Tata Consultancy Services or TCS. It single-handedly bailed out Tata Sons and buffered its losses. In 2015, it contributed over 60 per cent of the group's net profit and two-thirds of the market value of listed shares.[49] In 2016, it had the largest market capitalisation of any Indian firm, ahead even of Ambani's Reliance. TCS was, however, the one Tata company to which the Parsis contributed little more than moral support. It was conceived in 1968 as an in-house data processing unit, initially called 'Tata Services'. Few at Tata, let alone the rest of the country, knew anything about information technology in those days. The men in charge, P.M. Aggarwala and Faqir Chand Kohli, were initially part of Tata Power. 'Kohli was a visionary, way ahead of his time who understood the potential of human capability as capital,' says S. Ramadorai, former vice-chairperson of TCS.[50] Kohli, Ramadorai and other members of the small team pioneered the whole offshore model. Their clients were not Tata companies, as initially conceived, nor many from the domestic market; instead, their services were engaged largely by foreign companies.

Ramadorai estimates that Tata Sons must have invested only around Rs 35 lakh in the fledgling company. After that, TCS survived by generating its own revenue or borrowing from banks.[51] By the turn of the millennium, the IT boom was a major talking point in business circles and the share price of companies like Infosys shot up dramatically when listed on NASDAQ. Nobody focused on TCS, since the company was owned entirely by Tata Sons and did not have to disclose its figures. Few were aware that Tata Sons was sitting on a huge untapped goldmine. Finally, in 2004, Tata Sons, as the sole promoter of the phenomenally successful TCS, offered a sale of some 15 per cent of the company in an IPO, reaping an unbelievable financial bonanza. The issue was oversubscribed 7.7 times, commanding a 41 per cent premium on the issue price. The cash flows that Tata Sons received helped Ratan pursue his agenda of enhancing ownership in group companies and funding their requirement aggressively through preferential issues.[52] (Incidentally, unlike at other IT start-ups, the men who put TCS on its feet never made huge fortunes from their efforts. However, the Tata group did put out commemorative advertisements in all major Indian newspapers when Kohli passed away in November 2020.) One of those who did profit enormously from the TCS IPO sale was Pallonji Mistry, who was canny enough to make a big investment when the shares came on the market.

Business savvy aside, Ratan's image of the old-world aristocrat who, like his predecessors, would not stoop to shady business practices or try to influence politicians to the group's advantage, was dented in October 1997. The *Indian Express* published startling telephone conversations concerning the Tata group. Transcripts of tapped phone conversations among Tata directors indicated that Tata Tea was secretly funding members of the banned terrorist outfit, the United Liberation Front of Assam (ULFA). By all accounts, this was a common practice among tea-garden owners in Assam to ensure the safety of their employees and the smooth running of their estates. The weak state government could not ensure law and order. But the Tatas' attempts to cover up the truth of their misdeeds could not be so easily condoned. Once again, in 2010, Ratan had to face unsavoury headlines with the leak of candid and revealing telephone conversations with Niira Radia, a pushy, enterprising lobbyist with phenomenal contacts among Indian politicians and journalists. From the transcripts published in the media, it was apparent that Radia had a direct pipeline to the then telecom minister, A. Raja of the Dravida Munnetra Kazhagam, who was the decision-maker in allotting 2G spectrum licences to telecom operators. The Tata group, which ran a telecom company, had hired Radia's PR company,

Vaishnavi Communications, and individual companies were urged by Ratan to switch from their longstanding PR agencies to Vaishnavi. Interestingly, Radia at this point also handled the accounts of Reliance. The transcripts suggest that while Ratan did not want to soil his own hands by political manoeuvring in Delhi, he relied on Radia to do the job for him.[53] Questions began to be asked if the Tatas were not after all cut from the same cloth as other Indian business houses. The Tatas' defenders pointed out that the group was frequently penalised because of arbitrary government regulations and backdoor deals with politicians, which is why someone like Radia was needed to speak on behalf of the group. (A bid by the Tatas to start an airline company during the Vajpayee regime in the late 1990s was sabotaged by a rival already in the business.) However, such is the respect for the Tata name that, though the Radia tapes destroyed many reputations and led to some arrests and criminal cases, Ratan's standing remained largely unaffected. In fact, in 2011 Ratan filed a petition in court that his conversations on the Radia tapes should not be made public as it infringed his right to privacy. In 2017 the Supreme Court held that privacy is a constitutional right, but by then the contents of the tapes were already in the public domain. In September 2022 the CBI counsel informed the court that no case had been made out of criminality in the Radia tapes even after fourteen probes into conversations of the Niira Radia tapes. The rejoinder came in response to a long-standing case filed by Ratan questioning how his conversations had been leaked in the first place as per reports in NDTV and *Outlook*.

The selection of Niira Radia, as well as other former Ratan favourites such as the shyster Dilip Pendse, who was charged with major criminal activity during his ill-fated spell in charge of Tata Finance, and businessman C. Sivasankaran, his adviser in the telecom sector who refused to repay company loans, suggested that Ratan's judgment could sometimes be flawed.

Mukund Rajan argued in his memoir that some of Ratan's closest advisers were as different from the patrician Tata as chalk from cheese. Ratan probably felt that 'by taking the risk of associating with adventurous individuals, he could spur the group to bolder accomplishments.'

Despite the faint and occasional whiff of scandal around Ratan, it took Cyrus Mistry's bombshell of a letter to the Tata Sons board members and his petition before the NCLT, accusing Ratan of violating rules concerning insider information, handing out favourable deals to friends and citing other instances of a lack of transparency and ethical corporate governance, to wobble Ratan from his pedestal. Wobbly or not, Ratan remains standing on that pedestal though as arguably the most trusted businessman in India. Ratan has perhaps also had the last laugh over sceptics questioning his business acumen. His choice of Chandra to replace Mistry has proved fortuitous for the group. The marathon man demonstrated that he was a long-distance player and deservedly earned a second term as chairperson in 2022 for his ability to turn-around many of the group's loss-making companies, including Tata Motors, despite the pandemic. Chandra sold the mobile-phone business in an attempt to cut losses. Tata Steel made a spectacular recovery in the domestic market with an upturn in the commodities market worldwide and the acquisition of Bhushan Steel. (Though the European steel business which has drained the company for years has still not found a buyer.) Chandra is now making a concerted effort to embrace e-commerce with the purchase of the e-retailer Big Basket, starting a pharma platform and a digital service platform connecting Tata brands.

Of course, the group's most talked about acquisition under Chandra's stewardship was in October 2021 when the Tatas put in the winning bid for Air India. For Ratan this was sweet vindication; he had coveted the government run Air India every since the private sector was permitted re-entry into the airline business. There was jubilation and sentimentality at the prospect of a *ghar wapasi* (return home) for the once much beloved airline. Honour may have been avenged, but there remains scepticism whether it is in fact a pyrhhic victory. Can the Tatas really turn around the hugely loss-making, overstaffed airlines, which politicians have systematically run to the ground over decades? But even the naysayers concede that if there is any Indian business group up to the challenge, it is the Tatas.

3

The Blue-Blooded Outsider

Nusli Wadia is a descendant of Lovji Nusserwanjee Wadia, the founder of Bombay's shipping industry. Lovji came from a long line of shipbuilders settled in the port of Surat, where the Portuguese, Dutch, French and British maintained trading centres from the fifteenth century. In 1736, the British East India Company contracted Lovji, who had earned a reputation for the high standard of his workmanship, to construct a dock in Bombay. Lovji and his brother Sorabji built the first dry dock in India in 1750.

Seven generations of Wadias continued in the family profession. The British government, in part payment and recognition of their services, deeded large tracts of coastal lands on Salsette Island, immediately north of Bombay, to the Wadia family. The Wadias were among the first great landowners of Bombay. They built the family estate, Lovji Castle, in Parel. Lalbaug, set up by Pestonjee Bomanjee Wadia (1758–1816), which covered 100,000 square yards, was also in the same area.[1] His brother, Horamsjee Bomanjee (1766–1826), was a trader and broker for many British agencies and was granted eight villages on

Salsette Island by the government in exchange for land he owned in the centre of the city.

The Wadias are said to have built more than 300 ships, merchant vessels as well as ships for the British navy. They turned out sloops and schooners, man-o'-war cutters and clippers, frigates and steamships. The longevity of their ships was testimony to the skill of Wadia workmanship and the high quality of the teak they used. One of the Wadia ships, *HMS Trincomalee*, was launched in 1817. Renamed '*HMS Foudroyant*', at the end of the Napoleonic wars, the frigate served in the Crimean War and the Second World War. It is now exhibited at the National Museum of the Royal Navy in Hartlepool and is described as the oldest British fighting ship still afloat. The *HMS Cornwallis*, launched in 1813, took part in the Opium Wars with China and the signing of the Treaty of Nanking, which ceded Hong Kong to the British, took place aboard the ship in 1842.[2]

Another historic ship built by the Wadias is the *HMS Minden*. American lawyer and amateur poet Francis Scott Key was detained on board the British ship in Chesapeake Bay when he witnessed the British attack on Fort McHenry in Baltimore Harbour during the War of 1812. When he saw the American flag still flying high amidst the pounding of the rockets in the early light of the dawn, he was inspired to script *The Star-Spangled Banner*, the US national anthem.[3] The flourishing Indian shipbuilding industry came to a virtual end by 1857 because of colonial compulsions and the introduction of steamships.[4] Being shipowners, several Wadias branched out into allied businesses such as import and export, trade and acting as agents for foreign ships. One branch remained in Surat, and moved from ships to constructing bridges, dams and buildings. Another developed trade in shipping with Europe and America.

Records of these first encounters between American traders and their Parsi business associates have been preserved in the

Peabody Essex Museum in Salem, Massachusetts. In 1799 George Nichols, a merchant from Salem who travelled to India, wrote in his autobiography of his dealings with Parsi merchants, including Nasservanji Maneckji, a descendant of Lovji Wadia. 'The Parsis,' Nichols wrote, 'are some of the most intelligent people I have ever known, rich and very honourable in their dealings.'[5] In 1839, some grandsons of Lovji set up the firm Dossabhoy Wadia, which specialised in trade and sales of imported goods to the US. The then American president, Ulysses S. Grant, visited the company offices in February 1879 while on a tour of India. Dossabhoy was appointed vice-consul for the US in Bombay in 1852.[6]

The Wadias were a wealthy and distinguished clan, many members of which had achieved path-breaking success in their respective fields. Ardaseer Cursetji Wadia constructed the first private Indian-built steamship, the *Indus*. In 1834, he was the first to introduce gaslight in his home in Mazagoan, nearly two decades before the rest of the city.[7] He was among the first Parsis to travel to Britain in 1839 at the behest of the East India Company to study marine steam engineering. He later adapted a steam engine that could be fitted to the *Indus*, the ship he had built back home. For his achievements, he was appointed the first Indian Fellow of the Royal Society of London.[8] After retiring as chief engineer of Bombay in 1857, he settled in Great Britain with his English mistress and raised a second family. His Parsi and English families appear to have been on cordial terms.

Darashaw Nosherwan Wadia, born in 1883, was a pioneering Indian geologist, known for his work on the stratigraphy of the Himalayas. He helped establish geological studies and investigations in India at the Institute of Himalayan Geology, Dehradun, which he founded. A government institute, it was renamed the 'Wadia Institute of Himalayan Geology' in 1976. His textbook on the geology of India, first published in 1919, remains a standard reference book even today.

A Wadia also founded the first official trade union in the country. Bahman Pestonji Wadia, born in 1881, was an eminent Indian theosophist and labour union leader. In 1917, in the course of his political work for Annie Besant, Bahman Pestonji was shocked by the plight of the textile workers in the local Madras mills. He studied their conditions and made suggestions for improvements. On 27 April 1918, the Madras Textile Workers' Union was established with Bahman Pestonji as president, representing the workers. He was also closely connected with the literary and freedom movements of his time. In his later years, Bahman Pestonji opened theosophy centres in the US and Europe, in addition to the ones he set up in India.[9] Two Wadia brothers, Jamshed and Homi, made a name for themselves in the early years of Indian cinema. Jamshed, known generally as JBH, had many firsts to his credit. He produced India's first documentary newsreel, the first Indian movie to be filmed in English and the country's first TV series.

The Wadia family is also renowned for its philanthropy. Two remarkable women, Motlibai and Jerbai Wadia, deserve a special mention for their charities. Motlibai was descended from one of the richest Parsi families, which moved away from the shipping business to become brokers and agents to several European firms and had particularly close relations with the French. Motlibai, who was married to Maneckjee, her first cousin (a common practice among Parsis), was widowed at the age of twenty-six. Despite her huge fortune, Motlibai lived a cloistered, thrifty life and was deeply religious. As a widow, she dressed conventionally, covering her hair with a white cloth (mathubanu) and wearing a black sari, but at the same time, she ran a flourishing business empire. She increased her family's wealth, lent large sums of money to French vessels visiting India and sent both her sons abroad to explore avenues for expanding the business. Apart from opening an obstetric hospital in Bombay, she donated generously to numerous charities and helped countless needy Parsi families in difficult times. She built fire temples in Bombay and Navsari. At Udvada—the village where the Iranshah fire, the holiest of holy fires for the Parsis, since it is the oldest, is now housed—she rebuilt the Iranshah fire-temple building in 1893 on the pattern of an ancient Iranian design. She also constructed the 3-mile-long road from the Udvada station to the fire temple. After her death, Parsi priests decided that her name would be recited along with Iranian heroes and other famous Zoroastrians in the chanting of their prayers—the first time a woman was so honoured.

Her son, Nowrosjee Maneckjee Wadia, born in 1837, on his death, donated his entire fortune, of over Rs 1 crore, a magnificent sum in those days, to the N.M. Wadia Trust, which offered aid to victims of natural calamities such as epidemics, famine, earthquakes and fire. Though the fund is managed by Parsis, the contributions are for all victims, regardless of creed or nationality. Another important Wadia charitable trust is the A.H. Wadia Trust, which is listed in the Mumbai Slum Rehabilitation Authority (SRA) survey as one of the nine-largest landowners in Mumbai. It donates money for medical treatment, research and education.

* * *

Despite all these illustrious Wadias in the Lovji family tree, the focus is usually on Nusli Wadia's family, perhaps because this branch became the wealthiest, being among the first to open cotton mills in Bombay. The community also affectionately remembers Nusli's female ancestress, Jerbai Wadia, who pioneered the concept of building low-cost rental accommodation for poor Parsis in Bombay. This branch of the family also has perhaps the most colourful history, with orthodox Parsis questioning whether Nusli can, in fact, be counted as Zoroastrian, even if he is a Parsi.

Nowrosjee Nusserwanji Wadia, Nusli's great-grandfather, born in 1849, was schooled in England and had a natural flair for engineering. When he returned to India in 1866, he impressed Sir Dinshaw Petit, one of the first to build a cotton mill in Bombay and also, incidentally, a descendent of Lovji Wadia. Frustrated at the failure of some equipment in one of his mills, Petit asked Nowrosjee if he could fix the problem. The flaw was rectified, and Nowrosjee also set up a 4,000-horsepower steam engine in one of Sir Dinshaw's mills.[10] Later, he designed machines for making hosiery and sewing threads. From being a manager in Petit's mills, Nowrosjee decided to branch out on his own, opening a specialised factory for dyeing cloth, and in 1879 the Bombay Dyeing & Manufacturing Co. was born. Nowrosjee went on to design and build several other mills, including Century Mills, National, Neriad, Dhun, E.D. Sassoon, Presidency and Calicut. As a member and chair of various government educational bodies, he took a particular interest in girls' education, advocating physical training for both boys and girls as well as the introduction of the kindergarten system. During famines, he bought cheap food grain for poor Parsis. Nowrosjee's sons, Cusrow and Ness, expanded the family business so that it became one of the largest textile empires in India.

The Wadias lived in the palatial Bella Vista mansion on Peddar Road. At the entrance to the house is a stained-glass window with the ornate Wadia family crest of ships. The grounds of the property covered several acres, extending all the way down a slope from Peddar Road to the Parsi General Hospital. Sir Ness was universally respected for the integrity of his business dealings. However, he shocked his religious, traditional mother, Jerbai, by marrying an Englishwoman and converting to her faith. He became a member of the Church of England. Jerbai was unhappy that both her sons, Ness and Cusrow, had married outside the religion, and had become too Westernised in their lifestyle and alienated from their roots. She herself was born in 1852 in an orthodox Parsi family and studied in a Gujarati-medium school. Her maternal uncle, Rustomji Jamshedjee Jeejeebhai, offered her the services of an English governess so that she would be prepared for the sophisticated life she was expected to lead, well versed in the literature and etiquette of that society. But rather than transform into a socialite in Bombay, Jerbai came to be more interested in the welfare of co-religionists who were less fortunate than her own family. She empathised with the plight of Parsis from the villages and small towns of Gujarat who were keen to migrate to Bombay to earn a better livelihood. When her husband Nowrosjee died in 1907, he left her a substantial sum in his will. Jerbai conceived of a scheme to benefit poor newly arrived Parsi migrants who could not easily afford the city's rental accommodations. Her first housing scheme was in Lalbaug. She personally supervised the planning of the apartments, ensuring that the architecture respected religious conventions. She fixed the monthly rent between nine and eleven rupees. Another housing colony, Nowrosjee Baug, in memory of her husband, was opened in 1917 and six years later, in 1923, it was followed by Rustom Baug, named after her youngest son, who had died prematurely. After her death, her two sons built Jer Baug in her memory.[11]

Jerbai took the unusual decision in her will to decree that the family's baugs would be administered by the BPP and not by her sons. Some Parsis saw this as a snub to her heirs for forsaking the religion of their forefathers. (Cusrow, although he married an Englishwoman, remained a Zoroastrian.) Even if Jerbai's sons privately felt hurt, they continued their mother's tradition of charitable work for the community. The two brothers divided up the family business, Ness taking control of Bombay Dyeing and Cusrow of Century Mills. Since he had no heirs, Cusrow offered his mill to Ness for a token sum of one rupee, but the latter declined. Cusrow then sold his mill to the Birlas and left the money to charity. Cusrow Baug and Ness Baug were built after their deaths in their memory. Cusrow Baug, located in the heart of Colaba in South Mumbai, is a gated community of 84,000 square yards and houses 600 families. It has gyms, football fields, a park and a fire temple. (Incidentally, the estate of Sir Cusrow's widow. Lady Julia Wadia was the largest benefactor to the Medical Research Council, UK, in the late 1950s. It enabled the establishment of the Laboratory of Molecular Biology at Cambridge University.)[12]

Jerbai's innovative cluster-housing concept became the inspiration for future Parsi housing projects. Many other wealthy Parsis followed her example, and cheap housing for Parsis became a favoured form of charity, not just in Bombay but in all Parsi settlements. (Parsis believe strongly that it is their duty to help their co-religionists, and that at least 10 per cent of their wealth should be left to charity. The very affluent leave a much higher percentage.) In Mumbai today, there are thirty baugs, eighteen of which are run by the punchayet. In fact, an estimated half of the city's Parsi population resides in baugs. These large, usually gated, housing complexes have played an important role in preserving the unity of the community and its way of life. Outsiders are amazed to find sprawling, leafy colonies with spacious old-fashioned apartments rented out for a pittance. Rent in prime areas of Mumbai is a tiny fraction of the actual market value of the flats. The downside of the baug system is that people are unwilling to vacate subsidised housing even after they have long ceased to be lower middle class. Some believe that the baug system has robbed the younger generation of initiative, as they know they can fall back on community assistance. And they are unwilling, unlike other Indians, to compromise on living standards and settle for cramped quarters after marriage. A trustee on several housing charities feels the 'Baugerians', as he refers to them, are a trifle too demanding. For instance, some baug residents familiar with the Bombay Tenancy Act, which is weighted heavily in favour of

long-time tenants, take it for granted that they should be paid a
hefty sum (pagree) if they are to vacate their quarters. They see
themselves as bona fide tenants, not as recipients of charity. On
the other hand, Baug residents believe that Parsis living in fancy
flats and mansions in Malabar Hill, Colaba and other upmarket
neighbourhoods in Mumbai are alienated from their roots and
religion and cannot fully appreciate the problems of their less
well-to-do brethren.

Ness died in India in 1952, but his coffin was flown back
to England so he could be buried next to his wife, Lady Evelyn
Wadia, of Irish extraction, at the Brookwood cemetery. He was
succeeded by his son Neville, who was christened with an English
first name and had little ostensible connection to his father's Parsi
heritage in his youth, having been born in England and educated
at Malvern College and Trinity College, Cambridge. But on his
return to India, Neville began work in the bottom rungs of the
family business. It gave him a feel for the basics and, later, as
chairperson of Bombay Dyeing, after his father's death, he paid
special attention to ensuring quality and established the brand
as manufacturers of India's finest sheets and towels. Neville also
invested in Bombay real estate. His obituary in the *Independent*
newspaper, Mumbai, described him as 'gentlemanly, soft spoken
and full of Victorian charm'.[13]

Neville married a girl from the Petit family, Dina. The Petits
were, like the Wadias, one of the leading mill-owning families
of Bombay. Possibly even a step higher in the social hierarchy,
since they had a baronetcy to their name, rather than a mere
knighthood. Petit Hall on Nepean Sea Road was even grander
than Bella Vista: an imposing palace with Grecian marble pillars
and fountains and a series of reception rooms filled with Ming
vases, crystal chandeliers, Louis XV furniture and priceless
carpets. Imported French flowers grew all over the garden,
which was surrounded by a vast park with the sea lapping at the

periphery of the compound.[14] The Petit family's original surname was Bomanjee. They moved to Bombay from Surat. One of the Bomanjees worked as a shipping clerk and interpreter for the East India Company and other European firms. The family's unusual surname came from Bomanjee's French customers, who referred to him as the 'petit Parsi' because of his short stature. The name 'Petit' stuck. Manockji Petit, born in 1803, was a prosperous broker who in 1855, along with some partners, set up the second cotton mill in Bombay, the Oriental Spinning and Weaving Company. Manockji married Hamabhai, the eldest daughter of Jeejeebhoy Dadabhoy, who is credited with laying the foundations for Bombay's industrial age.

A pioneer of steam navigation, Dadabhoy started the Bombay Steam Navigation Company in collaboration with Jamsetjee Jejeebhoy and other sethias. With the coming of steam navigation, commercial and passenger traffic on the west coast of India shot up dramatically.[15] Dadabhoy also helped establish three banks—the Bombay Chamber of Commerce, the Parsi Insurance Society and the Great Indian Peninsular Railways. He even imported a saw machine, operated on steam power, that sped up the construction of buildings. (Incidentally, the first working steam-powered cotton mill in India was also started by a Parsi, Nanabhai Devar, in 1854 in Tardeo, Bombay.)

Manockji's son, Dinshaw, improved upon his father's success. He opened a second mill in his father's name in 1860, and eventually controlled six mills and a dyeing house in Mahim, with major interests in the yarn and cloth trade.[16] An important civic personality of Bombay in the late nineteenth century, he served as sheriff of the city and was a member of the Legislative Council (where he displayed a decidedly pro-colonial bent, even though he was a non-official nominee).

The Petit charities included a hospital, the Parsi General Hospital; a library, the J.N. Petit Library; a college for women;

schools for girls, J.B. Petit School; orphanages, Avabai Petit orphanage and J.N. Petit orphanage; and the Victoria Jubilee Technical Institute. In 1890, Sir Dinshaw was conferred a baronetcy.

Neville and Dina's match ought to have been an ideal alliance. Between them, they could trace their ancestry to many great Parsi doyens, including Sir Jamsetjee Jejeebhoy, Ardaseer Cursetji Wadia and Jeejebhoy Dadabhoy. But there was one terrible blot in the bloodline of Neville's young bride. Her mother, the beautiful, gifted and completely unconventional Ruttie Petit, had defied her family by running away with a Muslim as soon as she turned eighteen. At her secret wedding, Ruttie took the name 'Maryam' and converted to Islam. Parsi society was scandalised. A meeting of Parsi priests decried in no uncertain terms Parsi families whose girls had married non-Parsis. It was suggested that rich Parsi girls, unlike those from other communities, had too liberated a lifestyle, including dancing lessons, English governesses, riding trips and access to the Willingdon Club. The community felt it was time these girls were brought under control and barred from mixing with non-Parsi boys until they were married. The priests warned parents of girls who married non-Parsis that they too could be excommunicated if they had any further truck with their outcast daughters. Excommunication meant that no Parsi priest would be permitted to perform any religious ceremony for the shamed family, including death rites. Some 8,500 members of the community also called for a meeting with the fifth Sir Jamsetjee Jejeebhoy, president of the BPP and a first cousin of Lady Petit. The president called for a general body session of the punchayet, which decided unanimously that in such mixed marriages the girl would be excommunicated and her unborn children stripped of all rights they might have had as Parsis, and that under no circumstances would she be allowed to re-enter the Parsi community and even attend Parsi social occasions. Though

Ruttie's name was never specifically mentioned, it was clear who was being targeted. The Petits, despite their social standing, realised that they had no option but to disown their daughter.[17]

What the Parsis then regarded as the worst possible misalliance is today a badge of honour for the Wadia family. The man Ruttie married was Mohammed Ali Jinnah, the founder of Pakistan. Dina was the product of this doomed marriage of complete opposites. Jinnah, who was almost as old as Ruttie's father, was dour, proud, withdrawn, cautious and from a conservative Khoja Muslim trading family. Ruttie was pampered, impulsive, emotional, extravagant and reckless. She died of an overdose of sleeping pills on her twenty-ninth birthday. A shattered Jinnah, who became increasingly orthodox after his wife's death, was preoccupied with his life's mission to carve out a separate Muslim-majority country from India. He allowed Dina's grandmother Lady Dinbai Petit to have a major say in the upbringing of his daughter, and even permitted the child to take her grandmother's name. (Ruttie had neglected to name her infant daughter.) Dina was brought up as a Muslim but in a largely Parsi milieu. By then, her mother's transgressions had receded into the background, though they were not forgotten. Jinnah was shocked when he heard of Dina's intention to marry Neville, whom she met when she was seventeen. According to Mahommedali Currim Chagla, who was once Jinnah's junior and later became chief justice of the Bombay High Court, Jinnah scolded Dina in his imperious manner, pointing out that there were millions of Muslim boys in India and she could have anyone she chose. Dina, who was more than a match for her father, replied, 'Father, there were millions of Muslim girls in India. Why did you not marry one of them?'[18] Dina passed away in 2017, at the age of ninety-eight. She always maintained that, contrary to the popular impression, there was never a complete breakdown of relations with her father and that he sent her a bouquet of roses on her wedding day. Some years ago, she also wrote a letter to the *Times of India*, questioning the version of people 'claiming falsely to be close to her father'. (This appeared to be a dig at the distinguished jurist Chagla who, incidentally, was the grandfather of Cyrus Mistry's wife, Rohiqa Chagla.) Nusli maintains that Jinnah and Dina always remained in touch and wrote very nice letters to each other, many of which are in his possession. 'My mother,' he told me, 'adored her father.'[19]

Whatever Jinnah's private feelings, her marriage was a political embarrassment. Before leaving for the brand-new country of Pakistan, he met his daughter for the last time, along with her son Nusli and her daughter Diana. The young Nusli was fascinated by his grandfather's fez and asked to keep it. Dina made two trips to Pakistan—once for her father's funeral and, in 2003, to visit her father's grave, accompanied by her son and two grandsons. It came as a shock to many Pakistanis to learn that the descendants of the Qaid-e-Azam were, in fact, Parsis settled in India, since Jinnah's family was a secret that the Pakistani authorities guarded for years.

By the time of Dina and Neville's marriage, the community's outrage over Ruttie's conversion had subsided. In any case, since Neville was Christian and the two were married in church, the Parsis were out of the picture. But nearly half a century later, Nusli's family was once again embroiled in a religious controversy. At the age of eighty-one, Neville expressed a desire to convert to the religion of his forefathers. He wanted to return to his roots and believed that the Zoroastrian creed was the right religious path for him. Since the Parsis in India do not recognise conversion, the request seemed, at the outset, outrageous. But could the priests really refuse a man whose family had done so much, not just for the community but even for the priesthood? Every time Neville returned from one of his foreign trips to visit a Wadia Baug, he was greeted like royalty by the grateful residents.

Five Parsi high priests agreed to sign a letter stating that, in their view, it would be fitting that Neville be initiated into the Zoroastrian faith by performing a navjote. This, unsurprisingly, led to a hue and cry among the orthodox. Navjotes are normally performed when a child is seven or nine years of age and is more a confirmation than initiation ceremony. Ironically, two of the priests who sanctioned the navjote were considered ultra-conservatives. One of them, Dastur Feroze Kotwal, had been particularly harsh towards women marrying out of the religion. Kotwal, however, justified Neville's conversion as an exception. 'He had Parsi blood. The family has done a lot for the community.' Neville's navjote was seen as a genuine spiritual awakening. But when Nusli followed suit a few years later, some sceptics had less charitable interpretations, suggesting that it bestowed on him the right to manage Zoroastrian trusts. However, Nusli says he always wanted to be Parsi, and that he was Christian simply because of his birth. Everything from the food he ate at home to the customs he followed are Parsi. Asked why he had waited so long to convert, Nusli said it was because he had to wait for his father to first become a Parsi. And asked whether his two sons, Ness and Jeh, also planned to convert, Nusli said it was their decision, and he did not wish to interfere.[20] In 2022 photographs surfaced on the internet of Jeh's navjote with his father looking on, clad in the traditional muslin dagli and Parsi pheta, which suggests that at least one son would be entitled to oversee the family's well endowed religious trusts.

Although in her will, Jerbai had specifically excluded her sons and their descendants from any role in the administration of the Wadia baugs, in later years, due to the mediation of trustees well disposed towards Jerbai's descendants, an amicable arrangement was reached. The Wadias formed a committee that jointly, along with the BPP, looks after the upkeep of the baugs. Some Parsis were displeased by this development as it automatically empowered Nusli. But he is emphatic about his genuine concern for the poor in the community, the future of the Parsi priesthood and preservation of the community's scholastic and religious heritage. He even agreed to fund the renovation of the famous Meherji Rana library of Navsari which was in a shambles, offering to foot part of the bill to institute a trust that would provide monetary grants to boys who studied for the priesthood as well as their parents. Nusli also sponsored the scholarly writings of the conservative priest Dastur Feroze Kotwal. 'Which religion allows poor priests to live like derelicts? Catholic priests live in palaces,' Nusli says, though his proposed projects have yet to take shape because of the community's failure to reach a consensus.

By 1971 Neville and Dina were divorced, and she lived largely in New York. Neville decided he wanted to settle in the Swiss lake town of Lugano and sell off the family mansion in Bombay as well as his businesses. He lived most of the year in Switzerland with an aristocratic European as his partner. Neville entered into an agreement to sell his shares in Bombay Dyeing to the Calcutta-based tycoon R.P. Goenka. The deal was concluded in complete secrecy. Neville did not even take his son into confidence, fearing that Nusli would try to dissuade him. Nusli was to learn through the newspapers that the family company was to be sold to Goenka. It was just as shattering for him to discover one day that the family home, Bella Vista, had been sold to Parmanand Patel, a wealthy Gujarati businessman who imported textile machinery.

Then twenty-six, Nusli did not silently fall in with his father's exit plan from India. The columnist Vir Sanghvi wrote that 'Nusli was famously hot headed.' His parents, Sanghvi added, 'had sent him to public school in England (Rugby). He did not get into Cambridge University much to his father's disappointment and joined the University of Florida. Nusli after his return to India was put to work on the shop floor. To everyone's surprise, he proved to be an astute and imaginative businessman and his major contribution to Bombay Dyeing was the introduction of the retail shops (in those days, most mills sold to wholesalers) and the development of the brand name.'[21]

Nusli had no intention of letting his family heritage slip away. (The Wadia group is 250 years old, though Bombay Dyeing itself was started in 1879.) He rallied other family members to his side, including his mother, and won the support of executives and workers on the Bombay Dyeing rolls. In the fight to save his inheritance, Nusli was backed all the way by JRD. With the Tata elder's sage advice, he built up a strong case that his father had no right to sell the company unilaterally. When Nusli flew to London to meet Neville, he found a red rose with a note tucked into the side pocket of his first-class seat. It was a letter from JRD, then chairperson of Air India, wishing him good luck and reminding him that he had his full support.[22]

When he reached London, Nusli confronted his father. There was a stormy exchange. Neville tried to explain to Nusli that it was impossible to conduct business honestly in India any longer. 'Don't be so immature,' he told his son. 'Let's just take the money. We can live like lords in Switzerland.' This infuriated Nusli. 'You can live in Switzerland,' he told his father. 'I don't want to be a second-class citizen in some European country. I am going to live in India. And I am going to run Bombay Dyeing.'[23] Nusli says he never regretted his decision.

Neville gave in. The Goenkas called off their purchase. Incidentally, the Neville–Goenka deal had the blessing of Shapoorji Pallonji, who held a 40 per cent stake in Nowrosjee Wadia and Company, which in turn held 7 per cent of Bombay Dyeing. Understandably, Nusli and the Mistrys did not get off to a good start. Nusli found new investors in the years to come, most notably the Scindias, the erstwhile royal family of Gwalior, who bought Shapoorji's 40 per cent stake in Nowrosjee Wadia and Company. Bombay Dyeing prospered with Nusli in the saddle, and Neville, though still officially chairperson, spent most of his time in Europe.

Nusli was devoted to his mother, and admits he probably inherited more of her temperament and that of his grandfather, Jinnah, than his father's softer, more genteel personality. Nusli is described as short-tempered and couldn't-care-less, known to be emotional and warm with only a few close friends. He is an extremely private individual, who evokes either strong likes or dislikes. The late Muncherji Cama, a former trustee of the Bombay Parsi Punchayet, told me, 'He has a reputation for doing stern, nasty things, but when I worked with him, I found he had a heart of molten gold and was very caring towards poor Parsis.'[24] A businessman who has long had dealings with the family feels that 'Nusli is clever in a street-smart sense. You can't pull the wool over his eyes. But he has this flaw where basically when he feels insecure, he believes it is best to be aggressive. He attempts to dominate by attacking. Look at the long list of cases he has filed against everyone. He wants to settle scores.'

Nusli's defining characteristic is that he never shies away from a fight, even when they are not his own battles—if he believes the cause is just. In battle fatigues he forgets all other concerns. As he tells Sanghvi, 'I have never looked for a fight. It is true that I have often had to fight but every one of these fights has been forced on me. It has not been of my own choosing.'[25]

Many women were attracted to the handsome, aristocratic, wealthy industrialist. But he disappointed all the ambitious Parsi matrons who had an eye on the very eligible Wadia heir for their daughters. Instead, he married a non-Parsi, Maureen, an attractive stewardess working with Air India, and the daughter of an air force officer from Bareilly in Uttar Pradesh. Despite facing some condescension from the Parsi aristocracy, the chic and svelte Maureen blossomed into a successful businesswoman in her own right. She started a fashion magazine, *Gladrags*, and launched a popular beauty pageant. Her discerning eye discovered stars among the many young aspirants to the world of glamour, including Aishwarya Rai, who was crowned Miss World before ascending to the Bollywood stratosphere. Today, however, the couple live separate lives.

Parsi businessmen, by and large, stick to their comfort zone of Mumbai, keeping a disdainful distance from the very different world of Delhi's power politics. Nusli, however, has an amazing ability to forge close friendships across the political spectrum as well as the cultural and social divide. He had powerful and elderly mentors apart from JRD, the most curious of whom was Nanaji Deshmukh. Although Nusli was the grandson of a man that the Hindu right wing bitterly resented, he was also very close to the man who was one of the founders of the Jana Sangh party, and its key organiser and fundraiser. Nanaji, a Rashtriya Swayamsevak Sangh pracharak, was introduced to Nusli by Pratap Singh Vissanji, the owner of Wallace Flour Mills, probably in an attempt to raise funds for the fledgling opposition party. The unlikely pair hit it off. Nusli did not merely contribute to the Jana Sangh, the precursor of the Bharatiya Janata Party, but through Nanaji, he met other top leaders in the party, including Atal Bihari Vajpayee and L.K. Advani. He even helped, in the 1960s, to draw up the party manifesto. Neville objected to the friendship, and JRD was furious about it. But Nusli was so committed to the relationship that, during the Emergency, he hid Nanaji in his own home on occasion. This was an extremely courageous act for an Indian businessman; not only could it have got his companies into serious trouble with the government, it could also have landed him in jail. The Jana Sangh leaders were touched that Nusli was interested in cultivating them at a time when they were considered untouchable in the upper echelons of non-Hindu business circles and among the country's intelligentsia. Nusli's fascination with Nanaji was at least in part because he believed that the ruling Congress was destroying the country by promoting corruption, and that Nanaji would be the right person to lead the country.

Nanaji introduced Nusli to Ramnath Goenka, the Marwari owner of the crusading *Indian Express* newspaper chain, which often took an anti-Congress line. Goenka, like Nanaji and JRD, had a special affection for Nusli, and often invited him to dine at his *Express* penthouse suite at Nariman Point.

On his retirement, Neville moved almost full time to Lugano, and Nusli formally took over as the chairperson of Bombay Dyeing. His priority was to modernise the old cotton mills by producing polyester yarn as well. In 1978 he applied for a licence to manufacture DMT, the raw material needed for it. Nusli was perturbed to discover that his applications were being deliberately stalled by the bureaucracy in Delhi. Meanwhile, a newcomer in the textile business, the freewheeling Gujarati businessman Dhirubhai Ambani, who had started life as a small-time trader, managed to get instant clearances from the Centre for whatever licence policy favoured his business. Wadia suspected sabotage by Ambani, particularly after the appearance of several biased newspaper reports, running down DMT as a product and praising PMT; Ambani manufactured the alternative chemical for producing yarn, PMT, and a Wadia mill manufacturing DMT would have posed a threat.

In 1985, at one of their dinners, Maureen brought to Goenka's notice that false reports, seemingly inspired by Nusli's rival, were appearing in the media, including in the *Indian Express* newspaper chain and the Press Trust of India (PTI) news agency, of which Goenka was then chairperson. When the press baron complained to Ambani, the latter is reported to have remarked arrogantly that everyone had a price, including the *Express* staff. This infuriated Goenka, especially because his *Financial Express* newspaper carried, on the very next day, a PTI item debunking the DMT plant that Bombay Dyeing had applied for. He joined forces with Nusli to fight what he regarded as Ambani's unethical methods.[26]

India's most celebrated corporate battle broke out between the up-and-coming Ambani, who had connections in all the right government offices in Delhi on the one side, and Goenka and Nusli on the other. Some assumed that Nusli's obsession with Ambani's ability to manipulate the entire government was born out of paranoia. But Nusli pointed out that Ambani's rivals in the textile business in the 1980s—Orkay, Baroda Rayon and Nirlon—were all in deep trouble. The *Indian Express* carried a series of well-researched exposés against Ambani's company, Reliance, alleging various financial improprieties, including smuggling into the country a PTA plant without paying customs duty, getting unjustifiable concessions from the government and evading duties. The government investigating agencies started action against Reliance on the orders of then finance minister, V.P. Singh, who was sympathetic to Nusli, as was then prime minister Rajiv Gandhi. Ambani felt he was under siege.

Then, mysteriously, Rajiv became suspicious of Nusli. He was led to believe that there was an elaborate plot by Goenka and Nusli to bring down his government. He was shown forged documents to suggest that a private US-based detective agency, Fairfax, was looking into the bank accounts of Rajiv's Italian in-laws and his good friend, actor Amitabh Bachchan. V.P. Singh was thrown out of the Congress soon afterwards, and raids by government enforcement agencies conducted on the *Indian Express* offices. Nusli himself was charged with travelling on a British passport when he declared himself an Indian citizen. (India does not allow dual citizenship.) Nusli was arrested, his house raided and he was threatened with deportation.[27]

His fellow Parsis had warned Nusli that he would not be able to cope with this kind of an ugly war—the knives were out for him, and the kind of tactics that a new generation of businessmen engaged in was very different from the old order. But Nusli refused to cave in. Meanwhile, Rajiv discovered that the *Indian Express* was a dangerous enemy to make. The newspaper chain mounted a campaign against the prime minister himself over bribes paid to someone in the government for clearing a defence deal with the Swedish arms manufacturer Bofors. Ambani tried to help the government by diverting public attention from the Bofors scandal by spending Rs 100 crore to launch a cricket match series.[28]

In 1987, when Nusli landed in Mumbai, he was informed that he would be externed from the country as his Indian visa had lapsed. He moved court. In a fresh twist to the ongoing drama, an executive of Reliance was charged with plotting to murder Nusli. (The case still continues.) Interestingly, the plot came to light when a hired hitman confessed to the conspiracy to the police. The would-be assassin apparently got cold feet when he discovered that the intended target was actually the grandson of Jinnah. Wadia was saved from further government harassment because soon afterwards, Rajiv Gandhi lost the general elections in 1989, in large part because his reputation was besmirched by the Bofors scandal. V.P. Singh was elected prime minister of the Janata Dal-led National Front coalition that came to power. Shortly before Rajiv's tragic assassination in 1991, he and Nusli reportedly cleared up their misunderstandings, both agreeing they had been misled by a third party.[29]

The bitterness between Nusli and Ambani though, simmered for decades. After Singh's government fell in less than two years, the Ambanis were back in favour in New Delhi under successive governments. Reliance Industries moved from strength to strength. The textile industry, which began the family's fortunes, was now a very minor subsidiary of an expanding business empire that included oil exploration, petroleum refineries and telecommunications. Bombay Dyeing was left far behind. (Dhirubhai's elder son, Mukesh Ambani, is by far one of the richest men in India with a net worth of US$77.3 billion, making him the seventh-richest man in the world, according to the October 2020 estimation of the Bloomberg Billionaire's Index.)

While Ratan eventually changed his opinion of the Ambanis and made peace, attending weddings and other Ambani family functions, Nusli refutes the Ambani camp's claim that, in 1997, Ram Jethmalani succeeded in brokering a truce between Ratan, Nusli and the ageing Dhirubhai, who was recovering from a stroke. 'Why would I make peace with people who tried to murder me?' he still rhetorically asks.[30]

Nusli did not profit financially from his much-publicised battle with Ambani. But in another drawn-out corporate tussle with biscuit king Rajan Pillai, he managed to finally wrest control of India's largest bakery and biscuit manufacturer, Britannia Industries Ltd, through a series of complicated mergers and acquisitions. Wadia believed that Pillai, a cashew trader settled in Singapore and once his good friend, had double-crossed him. After a bitter legal and media war that started in the late 1980s, Wadia finally got control of Britannia in the early 1990s. Pillai, meanwhile, was arrested in Singapore for fraud and fled to India. His former mentor F. Ross Johnson, who headed the American conglomerate Standard Brands, accused Pillai of defrauding him of US$30 million to purchase Britannia. In India, Pillai died in prison within days of his arrest of complications from liver cirrhosis. Jail authorities had ignored his wife's plea that Pillai needed special medical attention.

These battles, Nusli's detractors claim, indicate his ambitions. Ascending to the chair of the Tata group would have given him the stature to which he aspired and, his critics say, he was peeved at not being appointed. But there is enough evidence to substantiate the version that rather than seek the role himself, Nusli went out of his way to promote Ratan's suitability as a candidate, and when the latter was anointed chairperson, Nusli emerged as Ratan's invaluable ally in assisting the new chairperson to consolidate the various Tata companies into one distinct group and strengthen his own position.

A relative of someone who was a casualty of these plans recalls bitterly, 'They worked together as a team, and it seemed as if Nusli was leading Ratan.' Their first target was Russi Mody, then chairperson of TISCO. The lordly, impulsive Mody played into his opponents' hands when he unilaterally appointed his 'adopted son' and long-time live-in partner, Aditya Kashyap, only forty-seven, as joint managing director, putting him at par with an old and trusted TISCO hand, Jamshed Irani. Without seeking the board's approval, in his grand style, Mody then left for his annual holiday on the French Riviera.[31] His actions infuriated the ageing JRD, who was also allegedly upset about the openness of Russi's alleged relationship with Kashyap. (Although Russi remained married to his first cousin Siloo, of whom he was fond, he reportedly never hid his sexuality.) The board challenged Russi on his return. Nusli, who was a director, spearheaded the move to clip Russi's wings at a time when JRD was still in charge. Russi was divested of his executive powers and an executive committee was formed. Irani was retained as the sole MD. Modi appeared to accept the compromise with good grace, insisting, in typical Russi style, that nothing should be announced at the board meeting before chilled bottles of champagne were brought in from the Taj hotel.

When he took over as chairperson of the group, Ratan completed Russi's decimation with a masterstroke. He introduced a rule that all Tata managing directors should retire at sixty-five and chairpersons at seventy-five. The new directive meant that many of the old guard would perforce have to soon step down. Russi, nearing the age limit, felt that the new cutoffs were aimed specifically at him, and declared that TISCO, of which he was still chairperson, would not accept the order. His defiance was based on the fact that the Tatas controlled only 6 per cent of the company's equity holdings against the 48 per cent held by financial institutions (FIs) that were controlled by the government. Russi tried to drum up support from three chief ministers he was close to, including Laloo Prasad Yadav, Bihar being the state in which TISCO was then located, and Jyoti Basu, chief minister of West Bengal. The TISCO trade unions too rallied around Russi. To counter him, Nusli flew down to mobilise his own considerable political clout, including lobbying with both Sharad Pawar and the then prime minister, P.V. Narasimha Rao. In the end, Ratan won the battle and Russi Mody was out of Tata and his former kingdom of Jamshedpur.

Seeing Russi's fate, the savvy Darbari Seth, head of Tata Chemicals, understood that it would be wisest to make a deal with Ratan. He stepped down without a fight and Ratan appointed Seth's son, Manu, in his place. In 1994, the Ratan–Nusli team manoeuvred the exit of Ajit Kerkar, head of Indian Hotels. According to journalist Vir Sanghvi, the Tatas were not convinced there was a future in hotels, so Kerkar, once a catering manager with Taj Hotel, created a chain of hotels almost by stealth without any money from Bombay House, relying on outside funding.[32] Kerkar's ouster was less troublesome than Russi's. For one, the numbers were stacked against him, with the Tatas holding a 37 per cent stake in the company and hoping to swing the government financial institutions' 16 per cent holding. Kerkar was sixty-five years old, the new retirement age for CEOs. But Ratan's most potent weapon was to tarnish Kerkar's reputation. Tata insiders spread stories that Kerkar had amassed immense wealth at the expense of Indian Hotels. Once again, Nusli played a role in detecting alleged financial improprieties. Kerkar quietly stepped down and, though his reputation was sullied, the charges against him were never proven. Some of the transgressions were, in fact, reportedly with the full consent of the board. This was widely reported in *India Today*.

(There are similarities between the manner of his removal and that of Cyrus Mistry, except that, in the latter case, the slander campaign was of incompetence, not impropriety, and Cyrus refused to back down.)

As late as 1997, Nusli was still bailing out the Tatas with his flair for crisis management, as can be seen from the transcripts of his telephone conversations published in an investigation by the *Indian Express*.[33] The Tatas were desperate to prevent the arrest of the Tata Tea managing director, Krishna Kumar, who had allegedly given false information to the then Assam chief minister, Prafulla Kumar Mahanta. He had claimed ignorance of the whereabouts of a Tata executive who was wanted by the state police for harbouring a terrorist.[34] In fact, the wanted man was staying at a company guest house in Mumbai. To prevent Kumar's arrest, Nusli was making frantic phone calls to his political contacts in the government, which was then headed by Prime Minister I.K. Gujral. From the contents of the tapes, it appears as if Nusli was also coordinating the Tatas' legal defence in the Supreme Court. (Many top lawyers have been impressed by his legal acumen and say he has clearly inherited Jinnah's skill in framing arguments.) Nusli is heard on the tapes complaining to his friend, industrialist Keshub Mahindra, that the Tatas are 'left-footed', and indicated that he was far more familiar with the workings of the law than the top men in the Tata group. The mystery of who tapped Nusli's phones has never been revealed, although the Home Ministry probed the case in light of the fact that neither the central agencies nor the Maharashtra government had given such an order. Ratan probably suspected Nusli's corporate rivals since only the Bombay Dyeing chief's phone was tapped.

The biggest favour that Nusli did for Ratan Tata, as believed by industry titans, has never been officially acknowledged or recorded. During Atal Bihari Vajpayee's tenure as prime minister, from 1998 to 2004, Nusli's old contacts with the Sangh leaders gave him total access to the corridors of power. He could walk into the prime minister's residence whenever he chose, and he addressed the prime minister as 'Babji' (father), a term used only by Vajpayee's immediately family. He was also very close to L.K. Advani, the deputy prime minister, with whom he was on first-name terms.

Section 153A of the Companies Act of 1956 had for long been a thorn in the side of the Tatas. It empowered the government to appoint a public trustee to act on behalf of private trusts. Until this section was amended, the Tata Trusts, and Ratan as the head, had technically no say over the running of Tata Sons. (The Tata Trusts, along with the Birla Trusts, are the only two trusts permitted to hold shares in corporate entities, since they had followed this practice long before rules were framed after India became independent.)

Wadia pleaded the Tata case along with JRD when Manmohan Singh was the finance minister in Narasimha Rao's government. However, Rao's government changed the law only for mutual funds, not charitable trusts. With Vajpayee as prime minister, Nusli's task became much simpler. Ram Jethmalani, as minister of both law and company affairs, assured Nusli, a personal friend, that he would ensure the law was changed. But since introducing a bill in Parliament would take time, he passed an order that Ratan Tata would be a government nominee and remain a public trustee with voting rights. In 2002, the Companies Act was amended on several counts, but few seemed to have noticed that the change in Section 153A was Tata-specific. It allowed Tata trusts to vote directly on the Tata Sons Board and not through a government-nominated trustee. Nusli's help was invaluable to the addition of this crucial amendment. Fourteen years later, it was because of this amendment that Ratan held complete sway at Tata Sons and

was in a position to fire Cyrus. A grateful Ratan had offered Nusli
a position on both the main Tata trusts at that time. But Nusli
declined, unwilling to accept a quid pro quo, or for it to appear
as if he chose to help Ratan in order to secure such positions.
In retrospect, he says, he regrets turning down the offer. Instead,
Noshir Soonawala was made a trustee and Ratan never again made
a serious attempt to get Nusli to join the trusts.[35]

Indeed, the relationship between the former friends and allies
was becoming increasingly cool. As a director, Nusli opposed
several of Ratan's major decisions. He vehemently disagreed
with the acquisition of Tata's steel operations in Europe. He was
the only director who opposed the Jaguar–Land Rover deal. He
also protested vocally at the huge donations made by the Tata
companies, as well as the trusts, to Ratan's alma maters, the
already wealthy American universities of Harvard and Cornell.
Nusli argued that it made far more sense to donate to deserving
charities within India, or even possibly set up a Tata University.[36]
Besides, as the media frequently points out, the Tata group's entry
into the airlines business was also a major bone of contention.
Nusli had once hoped for a tie-up with Singapore Airlines.

Although Nusli often came to the aid of the much larger
group, his own businesses, apart from Britannia, did not reach
their full potential. An executive working at a rival corporation
suggests that 'Nusli is not a businessman who fights wars for
profit. He is a businessman who fights for ego and emotion.
He wants to fix his opponents, put them behind bars. One
major reason why his empire never grew the way it should have,
despite the backing of the media and his close contacts with BJP
governments, is that he is a warrior not a businessman.' Nusli
also managed to alienate several of his former politician-friends
because he failed to keep in touch with them when they were out
of power and was quick to suspect their motives if they did not
support his viewpoint.

The *Business Standard*, in a rare interview with Nusli on 5 November 2012, suggested that the Wadia group seemed to have missed the bus. In comparison, the Tatas, in the late 1990s and first decade of the twenty-first century, had managed spectacular growth. Nusli conceded there was some truth to that: 'I didn't manipulate the system. I live by a set of values . . . I want to sleep peacefully at night.'[37] But some believe that Nusli's major flaw as a businessman is that his actions are often ego-driven rather than on purely financial considerations.

The younger generation of Wadias, the brothers Ness and Jeh, have yet to prove their mettle. Nusli has not laid out a succession plan and claims that he has rotated his sons in different posts. But it created some comment in business circles when Ness, the elder, stepped down as managing director of the flagship Bombay Dyeing to take over as MD of Bombay Burmah, a company that handles only plantations and chemicals, and also to look after the firm's charitable works. Jeh, the younger, was for several years the MD of Bombay Dyeing and also Go Air, but stepped down in 2021 and relinquished his executive posts. The Wadias seem to have taken a decision that the group companies will henceforth be run by non-family professionals.[38]

Fortune India magazine speculated that there was a family rift when Jeh in 2021 relocated to London, around the same time that Go Air was renamed Go First. However, a company spokesman refuted the report and explained that the change of name was simply part of a re-branding exercise so that the airline could be re-vamped into an ultra low-cost carrier as the company prepares to go public with an initial IPO to raise funds for its expansion plans. True to character, Nusli, the seventy-seven-year-old head of the Wadia group and perennial corporate samurai, returned to once again don his battle fatigues to fight for his airline's survival in the turbulent aviation sector. The company may be now fully run by professionals but Nusli, as non-executive chairman, keeps an eagle eye on operations and the airlines handles nearly 10 per cent of the domestic passenger traffic. In 2021 Nusli was confident enough of his airline's future to funnel some Rs 2000 crore of his own money into the company, over and above the Rs 3000 crore he has put in as security for Go Air since 2010 to raise funds when required.

Ness is known to the India media less for his achievements in business and more for his lifestyle. His five-year romance with the popular actor Preity Zinta, from 2005 to 2009, was the staple of gossip magazines. During this period, Preity, Ness and another young business scion, Mohit Burman, bought the franchise for Kings XI Punjab, the Indian Premier League (IPL) cricket team. Though they continue to co-own the cricket team, the romance is long over. It ended on such an acrimonious note that, at one stage, Preity even filed a police case against Ness after an ugly spat at an IPL match because her guests in the Kings XI box refused to vacate a seat for his mother.[39]

Bombay Dyeing's most valuable asset today is its real estate. In 2013, the state government gave permission for the land use of the company's abandoned mills to be converted to residential, office and commercial purposes, provided two-thirds of the land reverted to the Brihanmumbai Municipal Corporation for the setting up of green spaces and the Maharashtra Housing Administration and Development Authority for low-cost housing. Bombay Dyeing opened a separate division, Bombay Realty, to handle this business. In fact, some years back Ness estimated that 70 per cent of the textile division's profits would, in the near future, come from the development of land.

Apart from the Bombay Dyeing mill property, Nusli today also controls another vast expanse of Mumbai real estate, though some of this land is under dispute. It is owned by the Eduljee Framroze Dinshaw Trust, of which Nusli is the administrator. Estimates of the size of the landholdings in Malad, a western Mumbai suburb, vary but it is believed to be at least several hundred acres. The origins of the trust go back to F.E. Dinshaw, the man who bailed out the Tatas more than once.

Much of FE's vast wealth seems to have been frittered away after his death. His domestic life was unusual. FE's marriage appears to have been rather formal and Edwardian. His favourite child, Makki, died in a tragic accident when his three children were playing with bows and arrows. FE blamed the two younger children, Edul and Bachoo, and subsequently withheld all paternal affection from them.[40]

FE had a long-standing affair with a fair, light-eyed courtesan of Indo-European stock. While extramarital affairs were not entirely uncommon among wealthy Parsis, FE's was unusual all the same: among other things, he was also on intimate terms with his mistress's niece. This strikingly good-looking bohemian family—some claim they were descendants of devadasis—lived in Goa. FE had several illegitimate offspring. He provided for their education and settled a one-time sum on his unacknowledged sons and daughter. He met each of them only once when they grew up, and never demonstrated any filial affection. Three of his illegitimate sons rose to the very top in their respective professions without any help from their father, whose name they scrupulously avoided mentioning. One was to admit in a famous defamation case against *Blitz* magazine that he was a bastard. The resemblance with FE was too marked for the inquisitive Parsi community not to speculate about the origins of one son in particular who was associated with the Tatas. I have been told by a knowledgeable source, who wishes to remain anonymous, that FE's illegitimate offspring sat at a certain company's boardroom meetings under the portrait of his father, whom he closely resembled.[41]

In contrast, his legitimate Parsi children turned out to be a deep disappointment to FE. They moved to London in the late 1920s, where they lived an extravagant and bohemian life. Edulji had a court of arty hangers-on. He was on the fringes of fashionable, gay intellectual circles. At one stage, he was reputed to have been a member of the chorus of the Vic Wells Ballet (the predecessor of today's Royal Ballet).

On FE's death, he left both his children a charitable trust, and also a great fortune in a separate trust for them, designed so that they could never touch the capital. One of Edulji's gay friends, the brilliant young Chancery lawyer, John Sparrow, helped Edulji and his sister break their father's trust fund. Thus, the leading Bombay lawyer was bested by his son's equally clever, but much more raffish, friend. Sparrow later became the notoriously reactionary Warden of All Souls College in Oxford.[42]

When the Second World War broke out, the brother and sister moved to New York. Bachoobai married a down-at-heel Russian nobleman, Woronzow Daschkow. They mostly lived separate lives, according to friends. A New Yorker remembers that it was a regular ritual on New Year's Day for Edulji to throw his cast-off couture ball gowns down to the streets from his room in the Algonquin Hotel on Times Square to be fought over by throngs of cross-dressers waiting below. Edulji was a connoisseur of pre-revolutionary French furniture. His Rococo antiques, including a cylindrical desk used by Marie Antoinette at Fontainebleau, were sold after his death at a major auction by Christie's in 2008. Edulji died in the US in 1970, leaving his personal fortune to Bachoobai, with the stipulation that, upon her death, the corpus should pass to two US charities—the Salvation Army, New York and the American Society for the Prevention of Cruelty to Animals.

Bachoobai successfully challenged her brother's will. The division bench of the Bombay High Court ruled in her favour that the bequests to foreign charities were invalid. She, however, reached a settlement with the US charities for a lump sum to be paid to them, and additionally decided to give her share of the money inherited from her father and brother to charity. Bachoobai then requested Nusli to form a trust in her brother's name to handle FE's vast real-estate holdings in Mumbai. He was appointed the trust's administrator. The reason Bachoobai chose him was that she was very close to Dina, who also lived in New York, and was virtually a surrogate mother to Dina's son. Recalling the friendship between Dina and Bachoobai, Nusli says, 'They were sisters in every respect of the word. When I was a young boy, Bachoobai was closer than any blood relative.' Nusli says he has no idea just how much land the Edulji Framji Dinshaw Trust owns, but a lot of the land is under dispute or encumbered. (FE was reputed to be one of Bombay's largest landowners at the time of his death.) In 1995, Nusli entered into an agreement with the Ferani Hotel, owned by leading Mumbai real-estate developer Gopal Raheja, that the Rahejas would develop the Edulji Dinshaw Trust land and pay a fixed percentage of the sales realisation to Nusli. But the two parties fell out and the matter ended up in litigation.

The Wadia family also feel that South Court on Malabar Hill in South Mumbai—now generally referred to as Jinnah House—legitimately belongs to them, but it has been under dispute for even longer. Valued at over US$400 million, the stately bungalow, badly in need of repairs, is surrounded by 2.5 acres of garden, with overgrown shrubbery and towering palms. Jinnah personally supervised the building's planning and construction, and lived there until he left for Pakistan. Jinnah House is historically significant: it is the place where Jinnah, Jawaharlal Nehru and Mahatma Gandhi met to discuss the formation of Pakistan. Technically, the building should have been declared an evacuee property and all rights of ownership should have been extinguished in 1947 but Nehru delayed doing so, knowing how attached Jinnah was to the building. The Qaid-e-Azam appears to have imagined he could return someday to live there. The property was leased by the deputy British High Commissioner for several years. After Jinnah's death, the Pakistan government wanted the property handed over to Pakistan. The Indian government pointed out that, in his will, Jinnah left the property to his sister Fatima, who had also passed away. For decades, the government dithered about what to do with Jinnah House. In 2001, when Atal Bihari Vajpayee was prime minister, Nusli's mother Dina wrote a letter asserting her claim as the rightful heir. Jaswant Singh, as external affairs minister, had agreed to return the property to Dina Wadia on a long-term permanent lease on the assurance that the family would not exploit the property for financial gain. The file was cleared by the Ministry of Home Affairs, the Ministry of Urban Development and the Department for Evacuee Property before it was finally approved by Prime Minister Vajpayee. However, shortly afterwards, Yashwant Sinha took over as external affairs minister and appeared to obstruct the move.[43] Nusli had no option but to go to court, where the issue became complicated after a nephew of Fatima Jinnah laid claim to a share of the property on the grounds that he was his aunt's legal heir. Dina Wadia's counsel contended that, since Jinnah was a Khoja Muslim, a community that follows Hindu law and not Shariat, Dina, his daughter and an Indian citizen, was the rightful heir to the property.[44]

* * *

Those who know them well saw the relationship between Ratan and Nusli begin to deteriorate in the last decade. One reason for friction was the growing clout of Krishna Kumar, known simply as 'KK', a Tata executive who had Ratan's ear. (Incidentally, KK was the Tata Tea MD who had the arrest warrant against him in Assam.) Perhaps Ratan too was beginning to resent Nusli's assumption that he knew best and should be allowed to call the shots. The conversation in the 'Tata Tea Tapes' certainly suggests that Nusli was playing the commanding role. Another Ratan protégé whose selection as a consultant shocked Nusli was Niira Radia. A Tata insider recalls, 'Everyone at Tata was abuzz, wondering what was the special clout of her company, Vaishnavi Communications. Several suites at the Tata-owned President Hotel, Mumbai were reserved for Radia's office and she spoke directly only to the chairperson.' Apart from presumably helping the Tata group in obtaining a 2G licence for its telecom company, Radia was also part of Ratan's negotiations with the Gujarat state government to shift his Nano factory out of West Bengal. The Gujarat government offered extremely favourable terms to the Tatas on the land offered for the plant. Narendra Modi, then chief minister of Gujarat, was in a vulnerable position with the media and international minority rights groups questioning his administration's role in the 2002 violence against Muslims in the state. At that point, a vote of confidence from a respected name like the Tatas was very welcome.

However, until Nusli came out in the open and backed Cyrus, there seemed nothing to suggest to outsiders that the long-time alliance between Ratan and Nusli was fraying. A few years ago, when Tata Sons drew up a detailed agreement to redefine the contours of the relationship between the Tata Trusts and the Tata Sons, it was Nusli who sat and worked on it along with trust officials.

By the time of the showdown with Cyrus, Ratan no longer needed any intermediaries to speak on his behalf to the powers that be in Delhi. He is today a personal friend of Prime Minister Modi. He was, for instance, the only businessman invited to the exclusive ceremony where Modi laid the foundation ceremony for the new Parliament House in December 2020. After the feud between Cyrus and Ratan, both men met the prime minister to explain their side of the story. But Ratan went a step further. On 28 December 2016, his birthday, he met RSS chief Mohan

Bhagwat. JRD's advice to keep a distance from politicians has long been forgotten.

When Cyrus was appointed chairperson of Tata Sons in 2012, Nusli did not know Cyrus personally and felt Noel Tata was the better choice. His history with the Mistrys was not amicable. Shapoorji Pallonji, as a big investor in Nowrosjee Wadia and Company, had backed the sale of Bombay Dyeing to R.P. Goenka. Besides, Shapoorji and Naval Tata had opposed Nusli's appointment to the Tata Sons board. However, three months after Cyrus was made Tata chairperson, Nusli called on him. Speaking frankly, he said that, although he had opposed Cyrus's appointment, he had no prejudice against him. Nusli would support Cyrus if he did well in the three Tata companies of which he was a director, but oppose him if there was need to. Nusli came to respect Cyrus's hard work, and his low-key, earnest, straightforward efforts to bail out the flagship companies of the group that were burdened by the costly, ambitious ventures of his predecessor. He was sympathetic that the new chairperson did not appear to have a free hand and that some of the executives he had inherited were taking orders from elsewhere. The two trust members, Ratan Tata and Noshir Soonawala, appeared to be exercising veto powers.

When records revealed a dud loan from a Tata finance company to a friend of Ratan, C. Sivasankaran or 'Siva', who refused to pay back the amount, Cyrus had to make a difficult call. Should he opt for legal action against Siva or should it be buried under the carpet? The mild-mannered Cyrus is not a man who enjoys a confrontation. Nusli, on the other hand, appears to like nothing more than to take up the cudgels if he believes a cause is just. Ratan's supporters, at any rate, suspected that Nusli had a hand in the events that led to the showdown on 24 October 2016. Dorab Tata Trust member V.R. Mehta told a journalist, 'They (Nusli and Cyrus) are working in tandem and the entire support is being orchestrated by Wadia.'[45] Some speculate that Ratan might not have viewed Cyrus as a major enough threat, one he had to perforce dismiss overnight, had he not believed that Nusli was prodding him on. But Nusli was not even in India when the Tata–Mistry showdown took place.

4

Missing the Midas Touch

The Mistry family's business venture started on a much humbler scale than the Tata and Wadia empires. Carpentry was Cyrus Mistry's great-grandfather Pallonji Shapoorji Mistry Sr's vocation and so he felt the name 'Mistry' (which means 'craftsman' in Gujarati) was a more appropriate surname than 'Contractor', the more anglicised name that he used occasionally. Generally, however, he was addressed as 'Shapoorji Pallonji'. In 1865, he established Messrs Littlewood, Pallonji and Company. Littlewood is believed to have been an English clergyman who helped write letters and fill out tenders since Pallonji Sr knew very little English, while the latter and his team of labourers handled the construction work. The firm was subcontracted to build a section of the water reservoir below Hanging Gardens on Malabar Hill and help bring piped water into Bombay city in 1879. It was the fledgling firm's largest contract yet, but Pallonji Sr still had a modest income and the entire family lived cheek by jowl in a single flat in Khetwadi on Grant Road, a largely Hindu-dominated area in central Bombay. It was outside the walled Fort area, which was mostly reserved for the British and large commercial establishments. It was also far from the upper-class neighbourhoods facing the sea, such as Malabar Hill, Churchgate and Colaba, where well-to-do Parsis had built their homes. But Pallonji Sr was fighting hard to support his eight children and the four who belonged to his widowed sister.

The family originally came from Vesu, a palm-fringed village beyond the suburbs of Surat, where most Parsis were engaged in making liquor from toddy trees. It is not recorded exactly when the family moved to Bombay. Pallonji Sr's father, Shapoorji Jivanji, even used the surname 'Vesugar' on occasion to indicate his native village.

Shapoorji Pallonji Jr was Pallonji Sr's sixth child. He was only thirteen years old when he was moved enough by his father's business struggles to decide he would help out. His father had just won a contract to build a pavement out of the loose sand at Girgaum, Chowpatty.[1] In 1900, Shapoorji dropped out of school after completing the fifth grade to help his father with the project. His frugal habits were acquired early in life, walking to Chowpatty every morning and saving the small coin his father gave him for transport. After six months, Shapoorji earned a profit of Rs 2000 and calculated that he was probably making more than his educated friends who earned Rs 500 a month at most.

The family's early contracts were mostly military and PWD projects. In 1919, Pallonji Sr bequeathed his business to his son and asked him to rely on Bhagoji Keer, his assistant, for advice. Keer, whom Pallonji Sr had picked up as a twelve-year-old on the streets selling oranges, joined as a labourer but soon mastered the finer techniques of the trade. He was so grateful to Pallonji Sr for giving him a break and transforming him from a labourer to a contractor that, in 1922, he installed a marble bust of Pallonji Sr at the Bhageshwar temple in the Ratnagiri Fort and, ten years later, commissioned a bust of Pallonji's wife at a charitable trust he had started. (A modest commemoration compared to the twenty-five full-length statues of illustrious members of the Tata family, including twelve statues of Jamsetji Tata alone.[2])

By working with experienced British army engineers and government civil engineers, Shapoorji gained invaluable technical experience and knowledge.[3] The military establishment, impressed by his thoroughness, steadily awarded him bigger contracts, including a military hospital and ammunition factories in Bhopal and Kanpur, a hospital in Sagar, a prisoner-of-war camp for Italian prisoners, training camps for American soldiers and the military engineering mess in Colaba. Another area the company specialised in was renovating, expanding and modernising buildings for Bombay's expanding mill industry.

By 1943, Shapoorji Jr formed his own company, Shapoorji Pallonji Construction Private Limited (SPCL) and moved into the big league. He focused on building smart residential flats and houses. His first multi-storey apartment complex in Colaba had grandiose Mediterranean names: 'Acropolis', 'Patropolis' and 'Heliopolis'. It was the first apartment complex in the city to have a private swimming pool. It was considered prestigious to live in an apartment block or building constructed by SPCL, recognised for its high standards. Shapoorji's wealthy clients included Sir Nowroji Saklatvala, Sir Byramjee Jeejeebhoy and Sir Sorabji Pochkhanawala. In the 1920s, F.E. Dinshaw asked the British architect George Willet, who had designed Tata House and the Gateway of India, to provide the concept for his house in Poona. When Dinshaw showed his building plans to Pochkhanawala, he recommended Shapoorji as his contractor. Shapoorji and Dinshaw, two men with widely disparate backgrounds, struck up an unlikely friendship. The closeness between them is ascribed partly to the fact that Shapoorji helped the financier tide over a temporary monetary crisis when some investments he had made on behalf of the maharaja of Gwalior turned bad.[4] Dinshaw opened the doors of the Tata group to Shapoorji's company, which now counted on the former as a major client. F.E. Dinshaw's house in Pune, with its fifteen-acre compound, was built by Shapoorji, and is today the Tata Management Training Centre. JRD, who sometimes stayed at the bungalow, believed it to be haunted and later declined to sleep there.

In his career stretching over seven decades, Shapoorji's firm played a major role in shaping Bombay's skyline. Many of Bombay's landmark buildings were executed by SPCL. These include the RBI building, the Bombay Central Station, the Cricket Club of India, the Taj Hotel extension, the Oberoi Hotel, the Shankmukhananda Hall, TIFR, the Homi Bhabha Auditorium and the Breach Candy Hospital. The firm also built many of the headquarters of major banks and insurance offices in old Bombay.

Despite his success, for most of his life, the master-builder operated out of a dark, Dickensian office on the first floor of the erstwhile Meadow Street, in the heart of the Fort commercial district. His desk was of black oakwood, with two drawers and an inkwell. He sat in his swivel chair, and his brother at an adjoining desk.[5] Shapoorji was a shrewd judge of men, and tended to keep his engineers on their toes by paying surprise visits to the site. Since he was not proficient in English, his secretary Mr Dumasia translated his instructions for the benefit of his staff. While most of his senior engineers were Parsis, his accountants were Gujarati and maintained their ledgers in the language. Every engineer reported to him daily and, without the help of any notes, he knew from memory which material supplies and labour requirements had to be dispatched to different sites. An employee recalls his long, frayed coat that had numerous pockets in which he kept wads of cash, his chequebook and spectacles. Shapoorji was not a lavish paymaster but inspired loyalty in his team all the same. He looked after staff members and their families when they found themselves in difficulties, and was always there for marriages or funerals—more a father-figure than boss.[6]

A devout Parsi, he would start each day with a visit to the fire temple at five in the morning and spend almost two hours in prayer. His neighbour at Windmere Apartments, Cuffe Parade, Hormazdiyaar Vakil, recalls how the old man would religiously observe the Muktad prayers for dead ancestors for eighteen days. A priest's wife would be called to ensure that all the traditional rituals were carried out in the approved manner. Shapoorji believed in the old-fashioned Parsi convention that his head should always be covered, so if he was not wearing a pagree, he donned a simple prayer cap.[7]

He worked morning till night, except for a short nap at noon. He would begin each morning by taking a round of his construction sites and visiting clients before arriving at his office at midday. Among his few relaxations was a tot of Scotch and a round or two of bridge on the weekends. Shapoorji was not fond of high society and avoided cocktail parties and dinners. He hated travelling. 'I once took a plane to Bangalore,' he told a friend, 'but never again. It was crazy up in the air with nothing to cling to. I prefer to stay in Bombay on firm land.'[8]

The construction czar also formed an investment company titled 'Sterling Investment Corporation' (SIC). Its subsequent and continued success showed that he truly had the Midas touch. Once, after an illness, he returned to his office to find a Sikh gentleman, who worked in a neighbouring office, waiting for him. Shapoorji inquired what he wanted. The man replied, 'I just wanted some of your good fortune to rub off on me.'[9]

Take, for example, Shapoorji's investment in the Bollywood film *Mughal-e-Azam*. Movie production is considered a high-risk business, and many have lost fortunes in film ventures just to rub shoulders with the glamorous stars. Shapoorji's connection with Bollywood came about by chance. The script for the now iconic movie—based on a mythical romance between Prince Salim and a dancing girl, Anarkali, against the wishes of his father, the Mughal emperor Akbar—was presented to him as payment for a debt. The writer, who subsequently left for Pakistan, owed Shapoorji money for the construction of a studio and gave him the script in lieu of cash. When another film producer approached Shapoorji for the script, he sensed that it might be valuable and decided to finance the film himself. Director K. Asif hired three famous stars—Dilip Kumar, Madhubala and Prithviraj Kapoor—to play the lead roles. Asif was, however, a perfectionist, and Shapoorji, uncharacteristically, kept shelling out more money to fund this perfectionism. He hired one of the top music directors of the time, Naushad Ali, and constructed a series of spectacular sets, including one of Sheesh Mahal (the palace of mirrors). To add to the cost, just as the film was nearing completion, the technology for colour cinema came to India and the director insisted that a part of the film be reshot in colour. By this time, the cost of the movie, Rs 15 million, had mounted to ten times the normal budget of a Hindi film and had taken eight years to make. Shapoorji's son, Pallonji Mistry, was convinced his father was wasting good money in a bid to recover a dead loss. Some suspected it was the beauty of Madhubala that had dazzled Shapoorji, others felt it was his fascination with Prithviraj Kapoor's Urdu dialogue, which Shapoorji recited enthusiastically while climbing the stairs, that made the normally shrewd and cautious businessman throw money at a white elephant. Of course, all the doomsday predictions came to naught. *Mughal-e-Azam*, the first Indian film to be shot partly in colour, turned out to be one of Bollywood's biggest gross earners of all time. Because of his friendship with actor Dilip Kumar, Shapoorji later invested in the former's film *Ganga Jamuna*. The actor was in financial difficulties and had trouble raising the money for the film, a simple Bhojpuri village story which he wrote, produced and starred in and turned, against the odds, into a hit. Shapoorji earned huge profits.[10]

'Shapoorji ran his company in the sethia style,' reminisces a source familiar with the family. 'No open governance, no proper scaffolding, no one cared. He was a completely hard-nosed businessman who always looked to how he could maximise his money. But in those days, when he came up during the Great War, it was a different era. He was a tough customer when it came to doing business.' When his client was unable to pay, he was happy to take an IOU, which he encashed later (usually at a profit). He was known to drive a hard bargain, and when someone failed to pay up in full for services rendered, he would settle for property instead.

Shapoorji kept a low profile and was frugal. Once, a deputation of high-society Parsi women from the Time & Talents Club, a charitable organisation, called on him, requesting a donation. Shapoorji prevaricated, a lady present at the meeting told me. He protested that his wealth was vastly exaggerated and that, at times, his monetary situation was so bad that he barely had enough money to buy himself a cup of tea. The president of the club, Gool Shavaksha, was so incensed by his reluctance to commit—she was accustomed to all the major Parsi companies and Parsi businessmen graciously and unquestioningly sanctioning advertisements and contributions for the T & T's concert programme brochures and the worthy charities for which they raised money—that she drew herself to her full height and imperiously informed her companions that it was best they left. But before departing, she opened her purse and took out a rupee to offer as a donation for his cup of tea.[11] Shavaksha felt free to be so cutting because she was the daughter of the legendary Sir Dinshaw Mulla, a member of the Viceroy's Privy Council and a renowned judge.

It was not that Shapoorji was ungenerous. He was helpful to those he knew personally, especially his employees when they were in distress. When he was older, he passed out Rs 100 notes to the labourers on his son's building site. He donated to fire temples, cow shelters and animal hospitals. In 2018, his grandsons, Shapoor and Cyrus Mistry, set up the Institute for Zoroastrian Studies at the School of Oriental and African Studies, London, in his memory.

As Shapoorji's fortune grew, so did the family's social status. By 1912, the entire joint family had moved from their modest residence in Khetwadi to the large, old-fashioned four-storey Dantra House on the erstwhile Barrow Street, with each floor occupied by a different family unit. Later, Shapoorji Jr moved into one of the poshest apartment buildings in the city, Windmere, in Colaba, constructed by his own firm and set within a garden complete with marble statues and fountains. After the patriarch's death, the family built a mansion, Sterling Bay, in Walkeshwar, with a spectacular view of the Arabian Sea from Marine Drive to Nariman Point.

Since Shapoorji named his son 'Pallon', there was some confusion about whether one was referring to the former's father or his son. The joke goes that when people called the family phone, the man servant would inquire whether they meant the upstairs Pallonji or the downstairs Pallonji. Shapoorji's standing in the community moved up several notches when his son Pallonji married Perin (nicknamed 'Patsy') Dubash in 1958. The Dubashes are a prominent, well-connected business clan who made their money in the maritime and barging business. Soli Sorabjee, the former attorney general, whose mother was a Dubash, recalls the balls his grandfather would throw in the family mansion, Mount Nepean—a distinctive structure shaped like a wedding cake, located on the hillock above Nepean Sea Road. British captains and other seamen, on whom the family's trade depended, were invited to these parties. When he was tired and wanted his tipsy guests to depart, the old man would order the band to play the tune *Goodnight Ladies* and would escort his reluctant guests to the elevator.[12] The mansion has now been divided between two family members, both named 'Adi Dubash', who were once at loggerheads over control of the family company but are now reconciled. The only shared space in the mansion remains the large ballroom, reserved for special family occasions, such as navjotes and weddings.

Patsy had a privileged upbringing: holidays abroad, horse-riding and a Swiss finishing school. Her two daughters, Laila and Aloo, would also go on to make very suitable matches. Laila married a wealthy international investment consultant (a Readymoney) and a relative of the aristocratic Cowasjee Jehangir family, while Aloo married Noel Tata, half-brother to Ratan. However, the Mistrys were conservative and patriarchal and it was understood that (unlike, say, with the Godrejs) only the men in the family would inherit the bulk of the wealth.

In the early 1970s, when India was still a closed economy, Pallonji looked overseas to expand. In 1971, he won the contract to build the ceremonial palace in Muscat for the sultan of Oman and produced a flamboyant example of contemporary Islamic design. As a result of the stunning palace and the impressive Al Khor mosque in Qatar, the firm gained recognition in the Middle East. Large projects followed in Abu Dhabi, Qatar and Dubai.

Pallonji was even more private than his father. And, like him, a hard-nosed businessman and shrewd investor. At a young age, he advised Shapoorji to go beyond construction, as he, Pallonji, was not quite comfortable in the rough-and-tumble of building sites. It was at his suggestion that the family business diversified and invested in companies. For instance, through one of his tenants, the respected businessman Jamshed Gazdar, Shapoorji was introduced to Neville Wadia, who was looking for capital to branch out into other businesses. Shapoorji bought a 40 per cent share in Nowrosjee Wadia and Sons, the managing agents for Bombay Dyeing. At a young age, Pallonji became a director in the company. In the 1960s, Shapoorji acquired the Brady Group, an old English managing agency, which ran several businesses including the Belapur sugar mills, the Caxton printing press and Brady flats. The family eventually divested their stakes in both Nowrosejee Wadia and Brady as well as firms such as Special Steels and United Motors. Apart from F.E. Dinshaw's share in the Tata managing agency's commission, Shapoorji also acquired his Associated Cement Companies (ACC) shares. Dinshaw had merged his cement company with ten other companies to form the ACC, of which Pallonji was chairperson for many years. When the Tatas offloaded Forbes & Company, the Mistrys bought it. Besides company shares, the family's portfolio includes a sizeable real-estate holding.

But, the most prized asset in the Mistry share portfolio was its 18.37 per cent stake in Tata Sons. For years, the Tatas were not transparent about the circumstances in which the shares were purchased. Trusted insiders suggested that the share transfers were made by Dinshaw back in the 1930s. While the Mistrys refuted the claim, it was repeated regularly in the pink papers as gospel truth. The Mistrys' explanation that the shares had in fact been purchased much later from Tata family members was ignored. An affidavit submitted by the Tata Trusts before the NCLT now confirms the Mistrys' version. The shares were bought on three separate occasions. JRD's widowed sister Rodabeh Sawhny sold her stake of 5.9 per cent shares in January 1965[13] with her brother's blessings as she was in need of funds. In July 1969, the Sir Ratan Tata Trust, of which Naval Tata was then chairperson, raised funds by selling a 4.81 per cent stake in Tata Sons to Pallonji's investment company, Shapoorji Pallonji Investment Advisors Pvt. Ltd.[14] Why the Ratan Tata Trust sold some of its shares in 1969 has not been explained. One theory is that Shapoorji had accumulated a large number of IOUs from Tata companies.[15] Whether the outstanding debts were connected with construction works or to settle long-pending unpaid commissions owed to F.E. Dinshaw Limited is a matter of conjecture.

However, as noted earlier, the last Mistry purchase in 1974 was without JRD's consent, and the Tata chief had a shouting match with his younger brother, Dara, who never had much of a head for business. He was said to have been envious of his elder brother and sold his 6.68 per cent stake in the family business in a fit of pique. The reason this sale created such a scare in the group was the introduction of the MRTP Act in 1969 and JRD complained privately that the Mistrys took advantage of people who were weak and credulous.[16]

It was only as late as 1980 that JRD grudgingly agreed to make Pallonji a director on the Tata Sons board. (Shapoorji had passed away by then.) The unassuming Pallonji was a chip off the old block, and perhaps it was he, not his legendary father, who was the real brain behind the purchase of Tata shares. As a director, Pallonji made it clear he would abide by the decisions of the Tata management, offering little resistance to JRD. 'Pallonji never interfered, never challenged, never sought any power,' a Tata insider recalls.[17] The Phantom of Bombay House was rewarded for his unstinting support, winning all the major Tata construction contracts, such as the Tata Thermal Power Station at Trombay. He also was offered first rights on any company the Tatas were keen to sell, such as Forbes & Company.

By the late 1960s, it was generally acknowledged in the community that Shapoorji was among the richest of them all. But few in the rest of India were aware of the extent of his wealth. Most assumed that the richest Parsis were the Tatas and the Godrejs. It was only much later, when TCS went public, that financial journalists calculated the value of the Tata Sons shares and discovered that Shapoorji, because of his Tata holdings, was among the wealthiest Indians.

When Ratan took over in 1991, he and Pallonji were united in a common goal to strengthen Tata Sons' control over the group's individual companies and unseat the satraps who were entrenched in various parts of the Tata empire. Within days of assuming office, Ratan penned a handwritten note to Pallonji stating that 'Our common agreement and mutual faith will foster a true and lasting relationship. Our standing together will be a matter of strength.' For the Mistrys, the most ironic line of this letter of support is 'Let me reiterate that I will never do anything to hurt you or your family.'[18]

But though Pallonji backed Ratan's manoeuvres to wrest control of the group's companies, observers close to both noticed that Ratan rarely spoke to Pallonji and that there was little chemistry between the two men. Pallonji stepped down from the Tata Sons board in 2005, when he turned seventy-five. Two year earlier, he had taken Irish citizenship (since his wife Patsy was born in Ireland and is an Irish national). He was replaced on the board by his younger son, Cyrus, who also holds an Irish passport. Pallonji Mistry passed away in June 2022 at the age of ninety-three. Tragically, his last years were bogged by ill health which rendered him incommunicado. And he was probably unaware of the confrontation between Ratan Tata and his son.

According to the grapevine, Ratan insisted that Cyrus be the Mistry family's representative as director, rather than his older brother Shapoor, who is believed to be Pallonji's favourite. The two brothers are unalike. Shapoor is sharp, ambitious, flamboyant, fun-loving and, unlike his brother and his parents, outgoing and a great communicator. He likes fast cars, and breeds horses at his 200-acre Manjari stud farm, acquired from the Gwalior royal family. The difference between the two brothers was once highlighted by their mother, Patsy, as revealed in *Changing Skylines*, Aman Nath's coffee-table tribute to the Shapoorji Pallonji Group to mark the company's sesquicentennial anniversary. Both

Shapoor and Cyrus received a car from their parents when they turned eighteen. Shapoor asked for a red Ferrari even though he did not have enough pocket money for petrol. Cyrus asked for a black Cosworth, a limited edition, high-performance Ford Sierra. Cyrus, as his choice of car indicated, is the more serious brother, a shy and earnest family man. He married the girl-next-door Rohiqa Chagla, who lived in Pallonji Mansion on Cuffe Parade, adjacent to Windemere. Rohiqa, a half-Parsi, is the daughter of leading lawyer Iqbal Chagla and the granddaughter of eminent jurist, diplomat and cabinet minister, M.C. Chagla, who served for a while as Jinnah's junior and sketched an unflattering portrayal of him in his autobiography, *Roses in December*.

A qualified civil engineer with a degree from Imperial College, London and an MBA from the London Business School, Cyrus was fond of working with his hands and has an eye for detail. When he completed his studies and returned to India in 1991, he helped grow his father's company from one worth millions of dollars to one worth billions. A.K. Bhattacharya, the former editor of *Business Standard*, notes that the remarkable success of Cyrus's performance can be gauged from the fact that the annual cumulative growth of their business was over 30 per cent at a time when the Indian economy grew by 14 per cent annually.[19] The Mistrys went about restructuring the group by putting Shapoor in charge of the real-estate business, while Cyrus handled construction, though each brother kept abreast of what the other was doing.[20] They lunched together and both were aware of the other's projects. Even after the Tata confrontation, which has undoubtedly hurt the SP Group's business, Shapoor has made it clear publicly that he and Cyrus remain united.

Over the years, the group has diversified into avenues other than its core business of construction and real estate. In 2000, SP bought Afcons and ventured into the infrastructure space. By 2016, the revenue of the privately held SP group was US$4.2

billion, operating in over forty-five countries worldwide. The group also invested heavily in renewable energy projects.

While his father and grandfather, beneath their soft-spoken and unassuming exterior were both hard-nosed businessmen with a ruthless streak, the plump, bespectacled, earnest Cyrus grew up in a different era and environment. He had a reputation for sincerity and straightforwardness. A nice guy who was diligent, dedicated and keen to be a team player. He deliberately kept a low profile as Tata chairperson, giving no interviews or press conferences because he believed the CEOs of the respective companies should be projected instead. Even cynical journalists who have interacted with him declare that he 'seems incapable of guile and is very genuine. What he says is generally backed by documents.'[21]

It remains an enigma as to why Ratan named Cyrus as his successor, given that the Tatas had long been suspicious of the intentions of the Mistry family. A prominent Parsi businessman who observed the succession recalled that 'The Tatas considered themselves saintly and noble and the Mistrys mere real estate people. Many of us suspected privately that this arrangement would come to grief at some point.' Besides, the businessman added, 'Cyrus was only forty-four and not quite experienced enough for the job.'

Cyrus was not the first choice for the position. The board set up an international search committee, which included Ratan, Cyrus and Lord Kumar Bhattacharyya, to select a top global business head to steer the Tata ship. Lord Bhattacharyya was the man to whom Ratan turned to for recommendations. A senior professor at the University of Warwick, Bhattacharyya was chairperson of the Warwick Manufacturing Group and his job included brokering partnerships for UK manufacturing units. He was rewarded for his work by being made a baron by the Labour party. Bhattacharyya, who passed away in 2019, was reportedly also influential in the Tatas' decision to buy Jaguar–Land Rover and in the ill-fated purchase of Corus. He was close to several prominent Indian tycoons whose children studied at Warwick, including Nusli Wadia and Venu Srinivasan. It was Wadia, in fact, who introduced Bhattacharyya to Ratan, though the academic subsequently became closer to Ratan.

In the end, either the search committee found no one suitable or else the suitable candidates, including Indra Nooyi, CEO of Pepsi, declined the offer. The financial newspapers speculated that the eventual choice would be Noel Tata, Ratan's half-brother, who had the double advantage of the Tata name and Pallon as his father-in-law. Noel had acquitted himself very competently in the retail business, heading Tata Trent. Unlike many in the group, this was a company that made steady profits. But, for whatever reason, Ratan never entrusted Noel with additional responsibilities or appointed him as a trustee on the family trusts, though his own brother Jimmy had long been accorded that privilege. The Parsi gossip mills churned with speculation that Ratan resented his father's second family because he was not made to feel welcome in the family mansion when he returned from the US. And Noel, at the time, was the indulged baby boy, twenty years younger than his half-brother. Ratan was generally not present at Noel's mother Simone's Christmas and New Year bashes, even though he lived next door.

After the search committee could find no suitable candidate, Ratan and Lord Bhattacharyya invited Cyrus, a member of the search committee, to take over. Some speculate that Pallonji might have put a bit of pressure to appoint someone from his family, either his sons or son-in-law. There was an apprehension in the Tata group that if Pallonji did not get his way, he might have sold his shares in the market. While Tata Sons was perhaps no longer vulnerable, TCS was. Once TCS became a public-listed company, the value of its shares started climbing. If a new, aggressive minority shareholder came into the picture, he might attempt to raise his stake in TCS from 18 to 26 per cent, at which point a shareholder could do a significant amount of damage. Cyrus initially declined the offer. His brother Shapoor, however, egged him on to accept, chiding him that as usual he was overanalysing things. When an opportunity came his way, he should be ready to jump in. Cyrus conceded that he does have a tendency 'to think things through in depth which gives everyone a hard time effectively'.[22] A friend describes Cyrus as 'serious, focused, meticulous and extremely well-read. He applied himself assiduously, but perhaps he didn't have the entrepreneurial spirit.'

Ratan retired in December 2012, leaving his successor to settle into the chairperson's job. But before he retired, Ratan ensured that the trusts had tightened their grip over Tata Sons. The Articles of Association relating to the appointment and removal of future chairpersons were revised with Nusli's guidance, so that all appointments and removals of directors had to be cleared by the trusts. The two main trusts, the Sir Ratan Tata Trust and the Sir Dorab Tata Trust, had the right to nominate one-third of the directors to Tata Sons. Cyrus would become the first Tata Sons chairperson in the group's history who, during his tenure, was never made chairperson of the Sir Dorab Tata Trust, which together with the Sir Ratan Tata Trust holds 66 per cent of the shares of Tata Sons, giving the trusts near-absolute control of the group's holding company.[23] Ratan retained his position as chairperson of the trusts, and thus sowed the seeds for potential discord. Mistry did not really have the powers a normal chairperson of the board would have had. Nusli recalls that when Ratan asked him for his views on choosing Cyrus as chairperson, his cynical response was that Ratan had not really retired: 'All you have done is move the power centre from the board to the trusts.'[24]

For the first year, Ratan remained in situ to mentor Cyrus, just as JRD had been there for Ratan. Although Ratan claimed he had no intention of constantly looking over Cyrus's shoulder after that year of apprenticeship, this was not how things panned out. The honeymoon was short-lived. Nine months after Cyrus took over, in a curt handwritten note, Ratan demanded that Cyrus ensured there was no conflict of interest with the Shapoorji Pallonji Group, and that Cyrus should put a ban on all business deals between the two houses. Even ongoing contracts with the SP Group were to be completed within a fixed timeline. Cyrus eventually acquiesced, though he believed it was not a part of the original understanding. The remaining contracts between the SP Group and the Tata companies ran into huge amounts.

Cyrus consciously tried to keep a low profile. 'For three and a half years,' Cyrus told me, 'I never gave a press interview. I never tried to project myself as the face of Tatas. I didn't come to overshadow anyone. I came to make sure the group was put on an even keel.'[25] He worked overtime, poring over company reports and data. He was slow to take action but gradually, as a meticulous and conscientious chairperson, he raised uncomfortable questions about individual companies. This was not to the liking of the old guard, all of whom were close to Ratan. Equally, it irked Ratan's confidants that Tata Sons board members and trust members were no longer automatically appointed as directors on individual Tata companies. This was seen as evidence of Cyrus trying to cut them out. In any event, Ratan's closest advisors, who were also trustees at that point, R.K. Krishna Kumar and Noshir Soonawala, were past the retirement age of seventy-five that Ratan had himself had put in place. Another minefield on which Cyrus stepped was trying to set in order the expensive acquisitions in steel and telecom that his predecessor had made. He was veering round to the view that it was in the company's best interest to exit from the European steel sector and to sell off the telecom company. Cyrus also wanted to wind up the Nano—Ratan's dream project. These decisions were seen as casting aspersions on Ratan's business judgement and legacy.

Cyrus was keen on institutionalising the Tata group so that it was not run by any single individual. He suggested that a corporate governance framework be drafted to clearly spell out the role of Tata Sons, the role of the trusts and the role of the operating companies. His fear was that 'after some years the trusts could be lost to the wrong people.' He asked Nitin Nohria, dean of Harvard Business School, an academic whom Ratan relied on, to take responsibility for working out the framework. Nohria has been a member of the Tata Sons board since 2013. Though he sent several drafts to Nohria, Cyrus received no response. Attempts to meet Ratan and discuss the issue also failed. Finally, Cyrus decided to make a preliminary draft that could be put before the board at its meeting on 24 October 2016. That draft was never to be discussed.[26]

A few minutes before the meeting, Ratan and Nohria walked into Cyrus's office. Nohria came straight to the point. He told Cyrus, out of the blue, that he knew that relations between Ratan and Cyrus were not great and that the trust had taken a decision that morning to replace him. It was suggested that he resign gracefully or prepare to be removed. A shaken Cyrus, who was given no reason for his sacking, is reported to have responded, 'You do what you have to do, I will do what I have to.' Ratan's only comment was, 'Sorry that things have reached this stage.'[27] Cyrus's protests that the sacking was clearly illegal—it was not even on the meeting agenda, but included in the clause of 'any other business'—were ignored.

Cyrus claims he was clueless about his planned ouster, though Lord Bhattacharyya had conveyed to him Ratan's unhappiness more than once. He felt his relationship with Ratan might not have been the best, but it was not as if they were not talking. Until their last meeting, Cyrus assumed that the disagreements were 'crisis challenges which could be overcome. I tend to look at the glass as half full, not half empty.' He always showed the utmost respect and deference towards the patriarch. He would personally escort Ratan to his car every time he came to visit Bombay House. Cyrus was under pressure from Ratan on the one hand, and from irate shareholders at every annual general meeting. He felt that Trust nominated-directors were taking their instructions from Ratan Tata. Soonawala's demands for information on the group, Mistry would later complain to the tribunal, were in violation of the newly framed government rules concerning regulations of insider trading.

If Cyrus's protestations of having no knowledge of his imminent dismissal are to be taken at face value, he was extraordinarily naïve and insulated from the ground reality. There were enough straws in the wind to suggest that his relations with Ratan were fast deteriorating to a point of no return. The move to oust him was systematically planned for over two months. The trusts obtained legal opinion from two eminent jurists about whether the sacking would stand up in a court of law. Most of India's leading senior counsels were engaged on retainers to ensure that they could not appear for the opposite side. Several public relations firms were hired by the trusts and tasked with handling the possible fallout of the sacking.[28] One of those involved in the PR exercise recalls that the operation was done so systematically that various possible scenarios were worked out in advance. Ratan had built his own team, which was quite apart from the Tata machinery. Three members from the trusts were actively involved in planning the ouster. A participant in the strategy sessions in September confessed that things seemed 'more Byzantine than the Borgias'.

Cyrus claims he was far too involved with trying to resolve the many grave issues facing the Tata group to be aware what others were plotting behind his back. But at the very least, he should have been alerted by the sudden induction of three new members to the Tata Sons board in August, two months before he was fired. One of the new directors was Ajay Piramal, chairperson of the giant Piramal group, a diversified conglomerate which includes pharmaceuticals, financial services and real estate. Piramal, incidentally, is a very close friend of Mukesh Ambani, son of Nusli's old bête noire. Within two years, he would be father-in-law to Ambani's daughter, Isha. Another recent non-executive director was Amit Chandra, managing director of the investment firm Bain Capital. Both Chandra and Piramal have links with Nohria. Chandra is Nohria's brother-in-law, and the then dean of the Harvard Business School was an advisor to the Piramal group. Both Nohria and Chandra were on Piramal's boards. The third inductee was industrialist Venu Srinivasan, chairperson of the Sundaram Clayton group, one of India's largest two-wheel manufacturers, producing TVS motors. Srinivasan's wife, Mallika, is a director of Tata Steel and Tata Global Beverages. Shortly after Srinivasan's induction on the Tata Sons board, he was also appointed a trustee of the Dorab Tata Trust. Lord Bhattacharyya had introduced Srinivasan to Ratan Tata.

When Cyrus entered the boardroom, the cards were clearly stacked against him. The move to remove him was put to vote. The directors, all Ratan appointees—Ishaat Hussain, an old Tata hand and group finance director; Ronen Sen, former Indian ambassador to the USA; Vijay Singh, former defence secretary; Nohria; Chandra; Piramal and Srinivasan—voted against Cyrus. The only director who broke ranks and abstained was Farida Khambhata, a global strategist and the only Parsi on the board, apart from Ratan and Cyrus. Ironically, the board had, earlier, given Cyrus a glowing annual evaluation as chairperson of the group, not once indicating its unhappiness with his performance.

Nohria's role in Cyrus's removal was later questioned as a conflict of interest. John C. Coffee, director of the Center on Corporate Governance at Columbia Law School, commented that it was 'exactly the kind of incestuous corporate dealing that an academic of Mr Nohria's stature would be expected to guard against'.[29] Significantly, in October 2010, the Tata Trusts made a US$50 million grant to the Harvard Business School, the largest single donation in the school's history. Nohria had joined as dean in July 2010.

What Cyrus suspected could have been the possible motives are listed in the Mistrys' petition before the NCLT. Cyrus felt that, in spite of being in charge, he really had not been in control. He pointed out he wanted to register a legal case against C. Sivasankaran (Siva), a friend of Ratan's who had defaulted on a loan from a Tata company. He mentioned that he had cancelled Mehli Mistry's lucrative barging contracts with Tata Power to lift Indonesian coal, which he felt was overpriced. The petition questioned the overriding powers of the Tata Trusts in the management of the group. In the end, however, the Supreme Court in March 2021 dismissed all Cyrus's charges of mismanagement, even upholding Cyrus's abrupt removal as being in conformity with the law. The court held that a private company is not subject to the norms of good governance for public and listed companies.[30]

The crux is that while Cyrus believed he was fixing things, Ratan thought the man was trying to undo his legacy.

Cyrus, an introvert who had shied away from publicity all his life, was thrown unceremoniously into the limelight in an ugly, no-holds-barred fight. He was badly shaken by the whole affair, and unable to conceal the shock and hurt he felt. Within a day of his ouster, he wrote an explosive letter to the board, which was leaked to the media. He accused Ratan of creating an alternate power centre in the group, questioned some of his past business decisions and even pointed out what he considered corporate malpractices. Ratan's men hit back, suggesting that Cyrus was making excuses for his poor performance as chairperson, which was the reason the trusts were compelled to get rid of him. (In fact, Tata shares fared better during Cyrus's tenure than average on the Bombay Stock Exchange.) They also wondered how such a detailed response could have been prepared in twenty-four hours, which implied that the reply had been worked upon for a while as Cyrus knew full well what was brewing.

If he was hurt by the accusation that he could not fill the shoes of his eminent predecessor, Cyrus can now feel vindicated. His successor, N. Chandrasekaran, would go on to implement most of the measures Cyrus had already conceived in his recovery plan. The loss-making Tata telecom business was unburdened. Nano production was closed down. The board also made provisions in its budget for the bad loan made to Siva.

Mukund Rajan, who had worked with Ratan and was appointed as the group's first brand custodian by Cyrus, pays glowing tribute to the latter: 'Cyrus Mistry worked incredibly hard to make a success of his role; he seemed to be always on the job.' Rajan adds, in his memoir of his time at Tatas, that 'Cyrus is one of the smartest people I have ever met. He lived up to my definition of a great leader by voluntarily surrounding himself with people with great talent, skills and strong opinions, unlike many other leaders I have seen.'[31]

Many wondered why Cyrus continued to remain entangled in a long, messy legal battle, when he had his own businesses to look after. His father-in-law, the leading lawyer Iqbal Chagla, would surely have warned him against what is perhaps a dead-end litigation. But could Cyrus really afford to walk away from a legal battle when he had to protect his family's 18.37 per cent shares in Tata Sons? The trusts seem determined to make the Mistry family's shareholding irrelevant. Tata Sons has been converted into a private company, and the present rules, formulated after Mistry's removal, do not permit the Mistry family to sell its shares without the consent of the board.

Respected economic commentator Swaminathan Aiyar wondered whether the entire debate on majority versus minority shareholders' rights misses the elephant in the room: 'Why trusts set up for charitable purposes given tax exemption status should be allowed to control one of India's greatest industrial empires.'[32] Even a Tata loyalist like Rajan conceded that the 'charities and Tata Sons, consequently, have to introspect, unambiguously define their preferred mode of governance, address critical issues of succession and leadership and seek stakeholder endorsements of their decisions. In the case of the charities, it may well become necessary for them to refocus their efforts purely on their philanthropic endeavours and distance themselves from the business of Tata Sons and the Tata companies.'[33]

Critics of the sacrosanct Tata Trusts point out that their value today is highly disproportionate to the amount they spend on charitable activity. In 2016, the Tata Trusts were valued at around Rs 350,000 crore, making it the third-largest trust in the world after the Bill and Melinda Gates Foundation and the Welcome Trust. But according to official figures, it spent only Rs 750 crore on charities in 2016. In contrast, the Bill and Melinda Gates Foundation donates some US$3 billion annually. So are the trusts really functioning for the purpose for which they were intended? Part of the trusts' original charter, on the basis of the will of Sir Dorabji Tata, was to support the institutions set up by the Tatas, such as the TIFR, TISS and Tata Memorial Hospital. Today, the trusts have little need to help out these institutions as their funding comes from the government. Nirmalya Kumar, one of the members of the disbanded Tata Group Executive Council set up by Cyrus, and now a business school professor, feels, 'If the share value of some US$50 billion is invested in 8 per cent government bonds, the returns would be around US$4 billion a year. Not the US$100 million that Tatas presently spends.'[34] Financial analysts agree that the trusts should be spending far more for charitable purposes, instead of creating fixed assets for earning more profits. In 2013, the Comptroller and Auditor General (CAG) had also questioned the ratio of the trusts' earnings and charitable works. The Ratan–Cyrus clash once again put the spotlight on the trusts.

An overriding concern is: who gets to control the trusts in the future? When Cyrus was thrown out in 2016, the Mistry camp believed that there was an insidious power struggle afoot between three influential groups. The three industrialists brought in just before Cyrus's ouster were backed either by Bhattacharyya or Nohria. At that time, Venkat, a protégé of Krishna Kumar, as permanent managing trustee of all the main trusts, would have had a pivotal role as decision maker.

But since 2016, much water has flowed under the bridge. Once all-powerful, Venkat stepped down as permanent managing trustee of the main trusts after the Income Tax Department withdrew tax exemption for the Sir Dorab Tata Trust as Venkat's annual salary of Rs 2.66 crore exceeded the permissible tax bracket. Venkat is also being investigated by the Central Bureau of Investigation in a case regarding the joint venture of Air Asia India and Tata Sons. To the business world's surprise, after stepping down from the trusts, Venkat did not rejoin the Tatas. He is, instead, working for Mukesh Ambani's office, looking after health and education initiatives for the Reliance group. The Tata Trusts are at present in search of a CEO, rather than a managing trustee, to fill his former position.

Both Nohria and his brother-in-law Amit Chandra are no longer on the board. Ajay Piramal continues on the board, as does Venu Srinivasan. The latter was subsequently also appointed deputy chairperson of the Sir Dorab Tata Trust, while Vijay Singh took over as deputy chairperson of the Sir Ratan Tata trust. Lord Bhattacharyya, as we have already noted, passed away in 2019.

What is Ratan's future vision for this once quintessentially Parsi business house? To the query whether, under him, the number of Parsis on the trusts has declined dramatically, Ratan wryly points out, 'If we looked at the trusts as a percentage of the country's total population, there would be far more Parsi representation than in the national population.'[35] He says there has not been a conscious decision to reduce the proportion of Parsis on the trusts or the board. 'We are not a Parsi company, we are an Indian company. Large corporations all over the world, even if started by a Catholic or a Jew, do not continue to be dominated by people from the same religion. The people on the trusts are the best people we could find.'

As mentioned earlier, Noel Tata was appointed a trustee of the Sir Rata Tata Trust only at the late age of sixty-three. However, the bonds between the two half-siblings appear to have become stronger post 2016. The *Economic Times* quoted the soft spoken, low key Noel remarking that he looks upon his elder brother as a mentor and they enjoy regular meetings.[36] In 2021 Noel stepped down as managing director of Tata International on turning sixty-five, in accordance with the group's policy. He, however, continued as non-executive chairman and vice chairman on several prestigious Tata companies. In February 2022, Noel was finally inducted as a trustee of the Sir Dorab Tata Trust. The *Business Standard* interpreted this as a signal that Ratan wanted to ensure the Tata family's association with the charitable trusts, which control the Tata group, continued. Significantly, at the same time Tata Sons, at a board meeting, with chairman emeritus Ratan as a 'special invitee', passed a new rule stipulating that the two key positions of chairman of Tata Sons and chairman of the Tata Trusts could not be held by the same individual, which was the practice until 2012 when Ratan retired.

If the Tata group's reputation was mildly singed by the confrontation with Cyrus, the Mistry family was brutally bruised by its decision to take on the Tata behemoth. When Cyrus was still Tata chairperson, the family firms lost substantial revenues that they had traditionally enjoyed through their dealings with the Tatas. The complicated litigation has not just been hugely expensive but has also consumed much of Cyrus's time and attention, which could have been utilised instead in managing his new venture capital business. The 2019–20 economic downturn badly affected the construction and real-estate markets and the SP Group, like others in this business, has taken a huge financial hit, its debts shooting up. Prior to the COVID-19 lockdown, the Mistrys were in the process of selling off some of their assets, including Eureka Forbes, their solar companies and a portion of their TCS shares to raise liquidity and pay off an inter-company loan. The family approached Canadian financial giant Brookfield to raise a reported US$2–2.5 billion by using part of its Tata Sons stake as collateral. But Tata Sons firmly opposed the loan in court, arguing that the company's new Articles of Association did not permit such a transaction. The right of first refusal of share sales rested with Tata Sons, and the Mistrys would have to first get the board's approval. The SP group's argument that the AoA do not prevent the pledging of shares and that the proposed deal with Brookfield did not amount to selling its stake was not accepted in court. With time not in its favour, and in an uncomfortable position, the SP group issued a statement that the action of the Tatas to block crucial fundraising, jeopardising the futures of 60,000 employees and over 100,000 migrant workers, was indicative of its vindictive mindset. With the court staying the Mistrys' deal for securing the loan, the Mistry family felt it was being squeezed by the Tatas at a time when funds were desperately needed.

Finally, in a dramatic turn of events, the Mistrys approached the Supreme Court in September 2020, claiming that they wanted a separation with the Tata group, after seventy years in business together.

On 26 March 2021, a three-member bench of the Supreme Court headed by then Chief Justice S.A. Bobde gave its ruling. The court backed the Tatas on all issues raised by the Mistrys and completely overturned the judgment of the NCLAT. Senior lawyer Rajat Sethi described it as 'a knock out' verdict.[38] The judges accepted all of the Tatas' appeals, including the decision to sack Mistry, and held that the '. . . removal of a person from the post of executive chairman cannot be termed as oppressive or prejudicial'. Ratan, in a social-media post observed, 'After relentless attacks on my integrity and the ethical conduct of the group, the judgement upholding the appeal of Tata Sons is a validation of the values and ethics that have been the guiding principles of the group.' Cyrus commented sportingly, 'We will take the knocks on our chins. My conscience is clear. My aim at Tata was to ensure a robust brand driven system of decision making and governance that is larger than any one individual.'

After his exit from Tata Sons, Cyrus did not take back management control at SP and Co. and instead carved out something for himself. He floated a venture capital fund, Mistry Ventures, to back startups. In 2022, the Shapoorji Pallonji Group cleared a major portion of its huge outstanding debts by selling its entire stake in Eureka Forbes and Sterling and Wilson Renewable Energy companies. The family also put some Rs 5,100 crore of its own money into the holding company. Post the COVID-19 pandemic and subsequent lockdowns, its real-estate division finally started picking up by 2022.

A question mark remains over the worth of the Mistrys' 18.37 per cent stake in Tata Sons. The Supreme Court has yet to adjudicate on the formula by which the Mistry shares should be evaluated or even if it is possible for the construction magnates to sell or stake their shares as collateral without the permission of the board. (While the SP Group pegs the worth of their Tata shares at Rs 1.76 trillion, the Tatas value it at a mere Rs 80,000 crore.) In 2022, for the first time in decades, Shapoorji Pallonji Mistry was no longer listed by *Forbes* magazine as one of the ten richest men in the country. The family's wealth rating had fallen steeply.

For the present, at least, the family seems to have lost some of its Midas touch.

Post-Script

On 4 September 2022, Cyrus Mistry died in a tragic accident when the speeding Mercedes in which he was travelling crashed into a culvert on the Ahmedabad–Mumbai highway at Palghar. Cyrus and his school friend Jehangir Pandole, a former national squash champion, who were sitting in the backseats, were not wearing seat belts and died instantly. The driver of the car, well known gynecologist Anahita Pandole and her husband Darius Pandole who were in the front were seriously injured. Cyrus's death came just over two months after his father Pallonji Mistry passed away. Cyrus had recently masterminded the well thought out business plan to set the family companies on a recovery path after freeing them of their debts.

The Mistry family was flooded with messages of sympathy. Commiseration from the business community, media and people from all walks of life affectionately recalled Cyrus as soft-spoken, highly intelligent and extremely humble. From Prime Minister Narendra Modi to the chairman of the Tata group, Natarajan Chandrasekaran, the who's who of India condoled with the shattered family on their loss. The public silence from Ratan Tata on Cyrus's death was noticeable. It seemed to indicate that Ratan was not yet ready to forgive or forget the embittered relationship.)

5

The History of an Entrepreneurial Community

Long before the arrival of the Tatas and even before the Parsis' pioneering role in the development of the city of Bombay, the Parsis of Gujarat had made a name for themselves as entrepreneurs. As early as the fifteenth century, Parsis were trading from Gujarat with merchants in Persia, Arabia and South East Asia. They would handle supplies to ships for trade in salt, corn, wheat and cotton in exchange for spices from the southeast which were then shipped onwards to West Asia and Europe.[1]

But it was with the arrival of Europeans in India that the Parsis really came into their own. Parsis, perhaps because they eschewed caste and appeared to have few religious and social taboos, were uninhibited about mixing with foreigners. Added to this relative openness was the adventurous spirit of a migrant community that knew they had to seize every opportunity to establish themselves in their new homeland. They learnt the languages of the Europeans and developed a reputation with their colonial masters for hard work, honesty and integrity. By 1580, Portugese, Dutch, French and English companies all had

Parsis as agents.[2] As their wealth grew, these merchants became brokers and moneylenders.

Rustom Manock, a prominent Parsi of Surat, for instance, made a name for himself by liaising between European companies, the nawab of Surat and the Mughal emperor. Manock was a very wealthy trader who owned several ships and traded with West Asia and South East Asia. He did much to foster and promote the welfare of his community.[3] In 1720, the Rustom family moved to Bombay and their descendants were referred to respectfully as the 'Seth khandan', the leading family of the community. He was the first of the Parsi merchant princes who became known as 'Sethias' for their wealth and influence. His son, Naoroji Rustom Manock, was the first Parsi to visit London, arriving in the city in 1723 to negotiate with East India Company directors for the release of his brothers whom the company had imprisoned because of a dispute over a large sum of money owed to the family. The company eventually repaid its debts to the Manocks in several instalments and also released Naoroji's brothers.[4]

The pioneering role of Lovji Wadia, the master shipbuilder who came to Bombay in 1736 with ten carpenters in tow, has already been mentioned. The dockyards of Bombay became so active under the Wadias that Bombay became the foremost shipyard of the British empire. Trade between India and China had already been in place for centuries, but in the eighteenth and nineteenth centuries there was a boom, thanks to the ship trade. The Parsis, who were entrenched in the shipping industry and owned many vessels, had a head start over other communities. In western India, the majority of private shipowners were Parsis and, by the eighteenth century, the Parsis had become the foremost maritime traders in the country.[5] The bulk of the exports were raw cotton, textiles and opium from India and the ships returned laden with Chinese silk, porcelain and tea. The exchange of opium for tea dominated trade relations.

Unlike in Calcutta, the East India Company was not able to monopolise the opium trade in Bombay. Local merchants controlled a sizeable share of the market and the profits. The Parsis, in contrast to other Indian trading communities, did not simply dispatch their goods to the ports, they transported their cargo to Canton themselves and sold it, competing with European and American owners and traders.[6] The Readymoneys, the Banajis, the Camas, the Tatas and the Dadyseths were among the leading Parsi families involved in the China trade. They made fortunes which subsequently funded the creation of other enterprises.[7]

In the nineteenth century, the richest Parsi by far was Sir Jamsetjee Jejeebhoy, whose wealth was as legendary as his generosity. Rising from humble roots in Navsari, he became the most successful of all the Parsi merchant princes in the China trade. He got his start as an apprentice for a maternal uncle, Framji Battliwala, a junk dealer selling old bottles and cans. Despite some early setbacks, Jamsetjee eventually established a shipping and commercial business empire at the start of the nineteenth century and formed a partnership with William Jardine—a friendship which came about quite by accident. Jardine was the ship's doctor on the passenger liner *Brunswick* bound for China, on which Jamsetjee was travelling as a trader. The ship was taken hostage by the French and both men were temporarily stuck in South Africa, where they struck up an acquaintance. Historian Jesse Palsetia describes this chance encounter as 'changing both men's lives and influencing the course of history'.[8]

Jardine gave up his medical practice and started what would be the largest trading house in Canton, and managed to corner a major share of the opium trade.[9] The British found it hugely profitable to trade the comparatively cheap opium to the Chinese in return for their more costly products.

Jamsetjee began his trading firm, Jamsetjee Jejeebhoy and Company, with three non-Parsi Indian partners who helped him procure opium from Malwa and ship it along with cotton from the ports of Bombay and Daman, which was then under Portuguese rule. He selected his partners with care: Motichand Amichund, a Jain, had close ties to the opium producers in the western central plateau of Malwa; Mohammed Ali Rogay was a Konkani ship-owner and captain; and Rogerio de Faria was a Goan Catholic who liaised with the Portuguese authorities who controlled the port of Daman. Jamsetjee owned opium warehouses in Malwa and his letters to agents show that he carefully monitored the prices at which to buy and sell his stock. He was a remarkably perceptive judge of the market.[10] The Chinese were impressed with his integrity in business dealings, as were others with whom he came in contact. Jamsetjee was recognised as the foremost member of his community and the British government honoured him by making him the first Indian baronet with hereditary rights for his descendants. If Jamsetjee's early life had centred on trade and making his fortune, after he turned forty, he focused on philanthropy and civic affairs. He set up more than 125 charitable institutions and donated a reported £2,450,000 over the course of his life.

Philanthropy is another defining expression of the Parsi conscience. Those Parsis who have done well for themselves have tended to set up foundations that funded public welfare initiatives, including schools, colleges, scholarships, educational facilities for women, hospitals, orphanages and infrastructure. The entire causeway linking Mahim to the mainland, for instance, was constructed by Sir Jamsetjee so that people would no longer have to hire a ferry to get from Bandra to Mahim. When the British imposed a grazing fee on cattle owners, Sir Jamsetjee bought grasslands where all the city's residents could graze their cattle for free. The area is still known as Charni (grazing) Road. Among his many charitable ventures were a hospital, a medical college, an obstetrics institute, an art school and Asia's first free home for the elderly. At the time, wealthy Hindus donated their money to temples, or put it towards feeding pilgrims or poor Brahmins, their charity usually having religious connotations or overtones. Unlike other religious denominations in India, the Parsi priesthood was weak and did not have the power or influence to impose its diktats on the laity. Parsi charities, despite little religious pressure, could rely on sufficient community support to ensure that not a single Parsi beggar was found in the 1864 Bombay census.[11] The Parsi wealthy thought they owed it to their community to give back. Even among the Parsi middle classes, most were brought up to believe that a certain portion of their earnings had to be devoted to the upliftment of those less fortunate than themselves. In 2019, Rayoman Ilavia, a Surat-based philanthropist, argued in a *Times of India* blog post that, regardless of the power of Parsi clerics, the driving force behind Parsis' charitable instincts are their religious convictions. 'From a religious point of view,' he wrote, 'Parsis consider poverty, suffering and want as an affliction of evil. To remove poverty, disease and suffering is not only a religious duty, but an act of spiritual merit, depriving "evil" of sustenance. Zarathustra asked his followers to attain happiness by making others happy.'[12] Naushad Forbes, a co-chair of the Pune-headquartered multinational Forbes Marshall and former president of the Confederation of Indian Industry, told me that, even more than religious impulse, philanthropy is deeply embedded in the Parsi psyche because of role models from the past. 'Most Parsis,' he says, 'like to live a good life, but we do not need to live over the top, ostentatious lives. There are exceptions, but most of our wealthiest families are pretty humble.' His own family set up the Forbes Marshall Foundation many decades ago to fund work in health, education and the upliftment of women.

Parsis were also the most global and cosmopolitan of India's business communities. Sir Jamsetjee and other Parsi traders mimicked Western culture, turning their homes into copies of grand European houses, with their chandeliers, paintings, carved furniture, fine porcelain and *objects d'art* from around the world, particularly China. Trade with China had spawned some exquisite Indo-Chinese products. Intricately woven and patterned Tanchoi silk saris are popular across the country, but few are aware that the style was introduced to India by Sir Jamsetjee. Struck by Chinese techniques in jacquard weaving, he arranged in the mid-nineteenth century for three Parsi weavers from the Jokhi family in Surat to visit China and learn this new art of weaving.[13] Into the woven fabric, the Parsi weavers incorporated traditional Persian patterns and motifs such as sets of birds, flora and fauna and circles of pearls. (The name 'Tanchoi' appears to be an amalgamation of the Gujarati word for the number three and the name of the Chinese weaver who taught the three Parsi brothers the style.) Tanchoi saris lost their popularity among Parsi women by the early twentieth century when French chiffons and georgettes imported from Europe were in vogue, and blouses with lace and puff sleeves imitated European fashions. In the 1940s, though, Mahatma Gandhi encouraged the Jokhi family to set up centres throughout the country to teach others the art of the Tanchoi, which led to a revival in the style and accounts for its pan-Indian ubiquity.

Gara was the other sari inspired by interaction with China. Unlike the Tanchoi, though, the Gara has remained a signature of Parsi women. Shernaz Cama points out that Parsis have long been known to be skilled weavers and embroiderers and this reputation long preceded trade with China. In keeping with the cosmopolitan nature of the community, though, Parsi embroidery is an amalgam of Iranian, Indian, Chinese and later European influences, all of which can be seen on heirloom Garas. The original Garas were brought from China by Parsi traders who commissioned Chinese workmen to embroider borders and pallus on thick Chinese silk yardage. Parsi women back in India would draw patterns of their requirements for embroidery. Cama believes Parsis can rightfully take credit for being among the first to introduce temperate silk to India and also for popularising heavily embroidered saris and pallus.

Compared to some of the new Parsi billionaires, many descendants of the old Parsi aristocracy today live relatively modest lives, their family fortunes having been much diminished. The eighth Sir Jamsetjee Jejeebhoy, Rustom Jejeebhoy, for example, describes himself, albeit with some understatement, as 'merely comfortably off'.[14] The baronet worked for fifteen years as an employee for Tata Exports before leaving in 1998 to help his father run their family's charitable trusts. The Jamsetjee Jejeebhoy family was so closely associated with the BPP that, at one point, the tradition was that that the current baronet automatically became the BPP chairperson. A court order in 1906 ended this cosy arrangement, ruling that the BPP chairmanship could not be hereditary. For a century and a half, the Jejeebhoys hosted the BPP's offices in a family building in the Fort area. But for the last two decades, the JJ charitable trusts have been fighting to evict the BPP, claiming that they need the space (some 5,000 to 7,000 square feet) to expand their charitable schools. The BPP, though, refuses to move out, claiming tenancy rights under the Bombay Tenancy Act. Ironic, considering that the punchayet is perhaps the biggest private landlord in Mumbai.[15]

In the mid-nineteenth century, after the first Opium War (1839–42), Parsi merchants began to retreat from the China trade and search for new areas to do business. It was the age of industrialisation and commerce and Parsis were at the vanguard of change in western India. It was through the far-sightedness of Jeejebhoy Dadabhoy, an agent, broker, merchant and banker, that steam navigation for commercial and passenger traffic was introduced on the west coast of India. Jeejebhoy was also the first to import a saw machine from England which worked on steam power, helping greatly to speed up construction while also cutting costs. He helped in the establishment and running of three banks in the city—the Bombay Chamber of Commerce, the Parsi Insurance Society and the Great Indian Peninsular Railway.[16]

By this time, cotton had become the main export from India. The impetus to found the cotton industry came largely from Indians, rather than the British. Indeed, the first Indian cotton mill, the Bombay Spinning and Weaving Company, was opened in 1854 by a Parsi, Cowasji Nanabhai Davor, though it only spun cotton. By 1858, Manockjee Nusservanjee Petit had established the first composite spinning and weaving mill. As we have seen in earlier chapters, three Parsi families—the Petits, the Wadias and the Tatas—dominated the manufacturing of cotton in Bombay, opening the largest number of cotton mills. Until 1925, Parsis controlled about 30 per cent of Bombay's cotton mills.[17]

During the American Civil War, from 1861 to 1865, there was huge demand for cotton from Bombay, since the export of cotton from the plentiful fields of the southern states of the USA had stopped. But after four years, when the civil war ended, the Bombay cotton market and speculators were caught off-guard and there was a financial crash. Many Parsi families, including the Jamsetjee Jejeebhoy family, lost vast fortunes, though some recuperated their losses over time. One of the few Bombay businessmen who sensed that the cotton market was heading for a crash after prices had skyrocketed for years was Cowasji Jehangir Readymoney. As a director of the Bombay Presidency Bank, he wrote a report warning of the looming crisis, but few of his colleagues and market speculators, including his own brother Hirji, heeded his advice. A year later, when the scandal over the cotton crash speculation came up for debate in the British parliament, Cowasjee Jehangir's report was read out. He was praised widely for his financial acumen and asked to help revive the Indian economy.[18] He was a highly respected figure, knighted in 1870 and commonly referred to in the newspapers as the 'Peabody of the East', after the American banker and philanthropist. Among Cowasji Jehangir's contributions to Bombay was the elaborate Gothic convocation hall of the university, while he is remembered in London because of the ornate fountain he erected at Regent's Park with an inscription that it was built as a mark of gratitude from the Parsis for the protection that the British government had extended to them.

Sir Cowasji was a descendant of the Readymoney family, a prominent Parsi family from the days of the China trade. Hirji Readymoney, who came from Navsari, was originally a moneylender. In 1778, the family came to the rescue of the East India Company by contributing cartloads of silver to its war effort, as the company fought the Marathas. The Readymoney family's misfortune was that, for three generations, there was no male heir to take over their affairs in China and men like Sir Jamsetjee took over the China trade. Hirji Readymoney had three daughters. The son of one of Hirji's daughters, Soona Banaji, was married to the daughter of her sister, a Dadyseth. Both Soona's husband and her son Jehangir Banaji proved to be terrible businessmen. So, the shrewd Soona bypassed her son and left the fortune, inherited from her father, to her grandsons, who assumed the Readymoney surname.[19]

When they were fifteen, Soona sent her grandsons to work in godowns and as cashiers for a British trading company, believing that this would be the best commercial education she could give them. It was her second grandson, Cowasji Jehangir Readymoney, who made his mark in the financial world. Cowasji Jehangir had no children, and so adopted one of his brother's grandsons. When he died in the 1870s, he left two-thirds of his fortune to charity and one-third to the grand-nephew. Like his grandmother, Soona, Cowasji Jehangir had chosen his heir wisely. Jehangir Cowasjee Jehangir Readymoney also turned out to be a finance wizard and his wife, Dhanbai, was equally brilliant with figures and money matters.[20] He was knighted in 1895 and appointed a baronet in 1908 for his contribution to commerce in the city of Bombay. His son, the second baronet, was active in civic affairs and restructuring and reviving the Bombay Municipal Corporation after an outbreak of plague in the city. As a member of the Liberal Party of India, he believed that independence from the British should come about only very gradually. His grandson, Adi Jehangir, jokes that 'people used to say, except for Dadabhai Naoroji, all you Parsis are lackeys of the British.' The Cowasji Jehangir Hall, which today houses Mumbai's Museum of Modern Art and the Jehangir Art Gallery, is an example of the largesse of the Cowasji Jehangir baronets. The present baronet, the fourth, Jehangir H. Jehangir is a low-key philanthropist who shuttles between Pune and Mumbai, looking after the 400-bed Jehangir Nursing Home in Pune and, along with his brother Adi, handles the family property portfolio in both cities and its numerous charities. Like his father and grandfather before him, the present baronet does not care to use the illustrious surname 'Readymoney'. In 2019, Jehangir H. Jehangir was appointed a trustee of the Sir Ratan Tata Trust.

The Readymoney-Jehangirs are known not merely for their commercial successes, but the genius, idiosyncrasies and the passions of some in the later generations. The second baronet's daughter, Meherbai, universally known as 'Bapsy', was highly individualistic, eccentric and committed to her convictions. She was one of India's first suffragettes and an animal rights activist. Despite their unconventional childhood, both Bapsy's sons, Sharokh and Jehangir Sabavala, distinguished themselves. The elder, Sharokh, was a respected journalist who later joined the Tata group as a director and worked closely with JRD as his executive assistant. The second son, Jehangir, became one of India's best-known artists. This impeccably dressed scion of the

Cowasji Jehangir and Readymoney family, with his silk cravat and groomed moustache, was a simple, unaffected artist, even if some critics viewed his elite background with suspicion and suggested his romantic depictions of an alternative world were out of touch with the real India. He was at a tangent to the various directions taken by contemporary Indian artists.[21] At the time of his death in 2011, his paintings commanded some of the highest prices in Indian art.

Among the many distinguished Parsi bankers, economists, chartered accountants and financial consultants, the name Sorabji Pochkhanawala stands out. Orphaned early in life, Pochkhanawala, who grew up in straightened circumstances, helped found the first genuinely swadeshi bank, controlled solely by Indians and meant for Indians. With the help of other like-minded individuals, the Central Bank of India was opened on 11 December 1911; Pochkhanawala was the manager and the board consisted of prominent merchants from all Indian communities, with Sir Pherozeshah Mehta, the eminent barrister, chosen to serve as the first chairman. Pochkhanawala grew up in straitened circumstances after his father died. He was only six then and the family had to struggle to survive because it lost its savings in a bank which went bust. Despite these hardships, Pochkhanawala became the first Indian to qualify as a banker through the Institute of Bankers in London, where he experienced the racism of the snobbish British banking system. When he returned to India, he worked for a while at the Chartered Bank and the Bank of India. Conscious that the British totally dominated banking in India, Pochkhanawala was convinced that it was imperative for Indians to exercise control over their own financial affairs. He resigned from his job and with the assistance of a business acquaintance, Kalianji Vardhanaman Jetsey, who provided the seed capital, set up a small office with two chairs and a table. He succeeded in enlisting many prominent merchants from all communities to back his vision of the first swadeshi bank. Banking and accountancy continue to be a favourite profession among Parsis. Zarin Daruwala, for instance, is among the select few Indian women to have broken the glass ceiling, becoming the chief executive of the Standard Chartered Bank.

By the beginning of the twentieth century, many Parsis, not just the cotton mill owners and the Tatas, had entered the manufacturing sector. Some of these early entrepreneurs are now almost forgotten names although, in their heyday, their brands dominated the market. In 1901, Dr Darab Writer hit upon the idea of manufacturing sugar-coated quinine pills. He did so well that he opened a sweet factory. His sons expanded the business to start a canning factory. The Writer family sold its jams, pickles, preserves and savouries under the popular brand name 'Dipy's'.[22]

Parsis were also pioneers in the development of dairy products on an all-India scale. The Anand Dairy Farm near Ahmedabad and the dairy in Bangalore were developed by the Kothavala brothers during the Second World War for the British government. Pestonji Eduljee Polson continued their good work by setting up the Polson Model Dairy at Anand, which supplied butter all over India along with the popular Polson's coffee powder, prepared from a French recipe. By 1945, the Indian government recognised Polson's achievements, making the dairy responsible for the supply of whole milk to the city of Bombay.[23]

Surprisingly, for a community of celebrated entrepreneurs, there have also been several pioneering Parsi unionists, starting with B.P. Wadia who, in 1918, founded the first labour union in India, the Madras Labour Union. As far back as 1875, Sorabji Shapurji Bengali was actively concerned about the plight of labour in Bombay's textile mills. He advocated progressive social and factory legislation and, in 1878, forwarded a draft Factory Bill to the then governor of Bombay.[24] He was opposed by the mill owners, many of whom were Parsis. Bengali travelled to England to campaign for his bill, which was passed in 1881, and assisted Narayan Lokhande, a worker in the railways, in founding the Bombay Millhands Association by the end of the decade.

Following in the footsteps of Wadia and Bengali were the trade unionists S.H. Jhabvala and F.J. Ginwala. They were 'outsiders', in the sense that they were not employed in any of the firms or banks for which they founded unions.[25] Jhabvala, an author of several religious and biographical books, attempted to start a 'Workers and Peasants Party' in 1927 with two British Communists, P. Spratt and F. Bradley. His connections to the Communist Party of India led to his indictment with thirty-one others in the famous Meerut Trial of 1930–33 for allegedly organising an Indian railway strike. He was later among the top functionaries in the All India Trade Union Congress.[26] In the early 1940s, Homi Daji, a leading advocate of the Indore High Court, defended many labour cases. He joined the Communist Party and represented it in Parliament.[27]

In the twenty-first century, despite the doomsday critics who say that Parsis have lost the entrepreneurship spirit of their forefathers, Parsi firms continue to hold their own and branch out into new directions. This includes engineering firms Forbes Marshall and Thermax, the latter controlled by the charismatic billionaire Anu Aga and her family. Ronnie Screwvala built the media and entertainment conglomerate UTV, which he eventually divested to Walt Disney for US$1.4 billion in 2012. Ronnie's surname may be the subject of many jokes but if it is indicative of anything, it is that his head is screwed firmly on his shoulders. He and his wife Zarina run a charitable foundation, 'Swades', focused on rural development while also heading several ventures, including a media content company and a digital platform.

Parsi businessmen have also made a mark outside India. An inspiring example is London-based Karan Bilimoria. The first Parsi to sit in the House of Lords as a baron, he holds the title

Lord Bilimoria of Chelsea. The Indian-born Parsi built his fortune manufacturing Cobra beer, which he successfully marketed as the perfect drink to down while eating 'curry'. Bilimoria, whose father was a respected Lt General, moved to the UK for his higher education. He studied chartered accountancy and later took a law degree from Cambridge University. Cobra beer, originally made in India and sold in the UK, is described as a mixture of ale and lager. The beverage is now manufactured in the UK, and Bilimoria is a respected figure who has held many prestigious positions. In 2014, he was nominated chancellor of the University of Birmingham. He is the founding chairman of the UK India Business Council.

Undoubtedly, Parsis are still disproportionately represented in the list of the country's wealthiest people. Naushad Forbes believes Parsis can still pride themselves on having become rich without compromising their principles. 'One cannot be deferential to the government,' he told me in an interview, 'dependent on it for favours, and then be critical of it. So being ethical makes being outspoken possible. I think any criticism we provide is also somewhat positive and in the national interest. We do not come across as criticising to further our own agenda. Also, our criticism isn't political. We have, I think, been outspoken across governments.' Certainly, Parsi entrepreneurs have thrived both under colonial rule and, now, in India's raucous democracy.

6

Billionaires, Old and New

Vaccine king Cyrus Poonawalla, who made his fortune in the second half of the twentieth century, best exemplifies the continued success of Parsi entrepreneurship. Cyrus is today the richest Parsi in India. His company, the Serum Institute of India (SII), is the largest producer of vaccines in the world in terms of dosages and has been in the global spotlight because of the coronavirus pandemic. Cyrus is the chairman and managing director of the privately owned company and his son Adar is the CEO. *Politico* magazine described Adar as 'Perhaps the most important figure in the global vaccine race who isn't working in a laboratory.'[1] Because of SII's reputation for selling quality vaccines at relatively low prices and its huge production capacity, international vaccine developers lined up for a possible collaboration with the group from early 2020, as the coronavirus spread rapidly around the world.

SII had to choose from nearly a hundred vaccine candidates, settling for five, most notably the vaccine developed by the British-Swedish company AstraZeneca and Oxford University which was rolled out in India in January 2021, as Covishield.

Courtesy: Indian Express

Ratan Tata, patriarch of the Tata group.

Courtesy: Indian Express

The late Cyrus Mistry challenged the Tata behemoth.

Courtesy: Author's Collection

Nusli Wadia, the corporate Sumurai who doesn't shy from a battle.

Courtesy: Archives

Freddie Mercury (born Farrokh Bulsara), the greatest frontman of a rock band.

Field Marshal Sam Manekshaw, who
led the Indian Army to its greatest
war victory.

Homi Bhabha laid the foundation for
science in post-independent India.

The celebrated conductor Zubin Mehta (left).

Madame Cama was one of the first supporters of Veer Savarkar and actively backed him.

Nani Palkhivala, the greatest Indian jurist of his time.

Feroze Gandhi, the parliamentarian who was married to former Indian Prime Minister Indira Gandhi.

Kobad Ghandy, the twenty-first-century Parsi revolutionary.

Cornelia Sorabji, the first Indian woman law graduate and lawyer.

Jerbai Wadia, the pioneer of Parsi housing colonies.

Mithuben Petit, a disciple of Mahatma Gandhi who took part in the Salt march.

Avabai Wadia, one of the first to preach family planning and contraception in India.

Dadabhai Naoroji was an early advocate of Swadeshi philosophy and one of the founders of the Congress party.

Sir Dinshaw Maneckjee Petit, Bart.

Sir Dinshaw Maneckjee Petit was from a family that pioneered the cotton manufacturing industry and believed in philanthropy.

Sir Jamsetjee Jejeebhoy, legendary merchant prince and philanthropist.

Statue of Jamsetji Tata, one of India's most iconic businessmen.

Rustom Manock was the first of the great Parsi merchant princes.

Ardeshir Godrej, the inventor of foolproof locks and soaps made from vegetable oil extracts.

Pirojsha Godrej, founder of House of Godrej.

The first all-Parsi Indian cricket team to England (1886).

Courtesy: Cyrus Poonawalla

The vaccine barons, the Poonwallas.

Courtesy: *Parsiana*

Meherwanji Pavri, the first Indian cricketing icon.

Courtesy: Archives

Actor Sohrab Modi, remembered for playing historical roles.

Courtesy: Meher Mafatia. Laughter in the House

Adi Marzban, the genius entertainer.

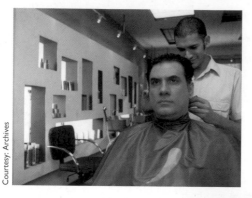

Boman Irani, the popular
Bollywood actor and comedian.

Author's navjote
ceremony (1954).

Early Parsi family drawn by James Forbes,
engraved by T. Waganan (1810).

A Parsi mother and her children
(1884).

Adar struck a deal to produce a billion doses of the Oxford AstraZeneca vaccine for developing countries, including India. The world anxiously watched the Covishield trials, since it hoped the vaccine could prove to be the silver bullet to deal with the pandemic. Adar appears to have selected his choice of Oxford AstraZeneca vaccine wisely. It was not just one of the first vaccines to be granted approval, but unlike vaccines in the West produced by pharmaceutical giants Moderna and Pfizer, Covishield is relatively inexpensive and, importantly for developing countries, it can be stored at a much higher temperature of -2 - to -8°C as against the extreme -70 to -90°C cold chains required by some of the other vaccines.

Adar sees his role in the Corona pandemic as 'a commitment to the country and the disease and not for monetary gain'. He took a major gamble by beginning the manufacturing process for the AstraZeneca vaccine in October 2020, long before he got the go ahead for the licence from the Indian health regulatory authorities responsible for maintaining safety standards. He also drastically expanded his manufacturing facilities so that they could increase productivity. 'I risk losing $200 million if it doesn't work,' Adar said in an interview to the journalist Barkha Dutt in 2020.[2] But he termed it 'a commitment to the country and the disease and not for monetary gain'. He added that, 'Some people called me crazy, but if we didn't commit to the trials, we would have lost six months.' Apart from their own investment, the Poonawallas had to raise an additional $600 million, some of which came from the Bill and Melinda Gates Foundation and some from private equity networks. SII was meant to provide the vaccine to some ninety-two countries, including much of Africa, and several of the world's poorest countries that are part of the Global Alliance for Vaccines and Immunisations (GAVI). Bill Gates has been involved with the group as a mentor for years, and his foundation has been working with SII to bring affordable drugs to poor countries.

The coronavirus crisis no doubt presented a huge opportunity for SII but the scrutiny and pressure on the company has been enormous. Adar concedes that 2020–21 were stressful years where every week a new challenge popped up. The SSI, which produced around 90 per cent of the COVID vaccines in India at the time the vaccination programme in the country started, faced some unforeseen hiccups. The Indian government took charge of vaccine distribution and prioritised the country's needs. The export of vaccines was temporarily banned. The SII, which had already delivered 60 million doses abroad, could not meet the remainder of its time-bound overseas commitments, much to the company's embarrassment. In fact, the media questioned how earlier vaccine stocks were in the first place permitted to leave India when there was a crying shortage back home. The company claimed a financial squeeze since the government purchased the vaccine at a subsidised rate, compared to the price globally and it's business model went awry.

For several months there was an acute vaccine shortage in India, with state governments vying with each other to procure more stocks. After Adar received threats from some politicians demanding more vaccine supplies for their respective regions, the Modi government had to provide Adar with special police protection. The Poonawallas became unwitting scapegoats in the tussle between the central government and opposition ruled states over vaccine procurement. The company was at a loss dealing with bureaucratic red tape and government diktat since in recent years 80 per cent of SII's business was out of India. In what was viewed as a public relations disaster, in May 2021 Adar Poonawalla flew to London to join his family, just a day before the UK put India on its red list and banned Indian travellers as the second corona wave was raging in the country. He gave an interview to the *Times*, London, stating that he had left the country because he felt there was a grave threat to his life in India. 'The level of expectation and aggression is really unprecedented,' the tycoon told the newspaper. Senior bureaucrats from the health ministry did not take kindly to Poonawalla announcing his predicament to the world. Meanwhile, Cyrus's innocent response to a journalist that he came to London every year for his summer vacation and to attend the Derby reinforced the family's jet-setting image. Subsequent to the *Times* interview, Adar in a tweet clarified that he was in London to hold meetings with stakeholders to discuss how to meet the demand for the vaccine and not on a holiday. He returned to India shortly afterwards to review production facilities in Pune.

SII managed to ramp up its production capacity sharply, helped by a belated financial incentive from the government. By the end of 2021, it had the capacity to manufacture 3 billion doses of vaccine against COVID and was in a position to raise it to 4 billion doses by 2022. In fact, by 2022 the Poonawallas were on a roll. While COVID and the general economic downturn in India had a negative impact on some major Parsi fortunes, a graph of the Poonawalla wealth shows a steady steep rise. The Hurun Global rich list pegged Cyrus as the fourth-richest Indian with a net worth of $26 billion, up by 41 per cent from the earlier year. In fact, Poonawalla topped the list of global health care billionaires.

Cyrus Poonawalla, the septuagenarian chairperson of SII, achieved billionaire status fairly recently. He was not born to great wealth. His great-great-grandfather, Dhanjishaw Ankleshwaria, was a leading contractor who built or developed some 135 properties, mostly in Poona and a few in the nearby hill resort of Mahabaleshwar. He was known respectfully as 'Poonawalla seth', which is why some branches of the family took on the surname 'Poonawalla'. Dhanjishaw had eleven sons and three daughters, so each offspring effectively inherited 'only' some eight properties. The fact that Dhanjishaw's descendants were not as wealthy as they might have been because of the large size of his clan seems to have had an impact on Cyrus, who consciously decided to keep his family small. He was once quoted as saying, only half-jokingly, 'I cannot afford more sons.' He concedes he said that because had he had more than one, 'I would see a fight. Which has happened in most families.'[7]

Cyrus's grandfather, Burjor, lost much of his share of the family fortune, except for the stud farms and a real-estate business; Cyrus's grandmother used to bemoan the fact that her good-hearted husband had turned his gold into dust. After graduating with a degree in commerce in 1962, Cyrus saw that there was little future in running the businesses he had inherited from his father, Soli. Stud-farming was not a going proposition after the then Bombay state chief minister, Morarji Desai, an ascetic killjoy, had banned horse racing. Things have come full circle, complains Cyrus, now that the government's high GST rates, as a result of categorising horse racing as gambling rather than as a sport, have once again made it difficult to make a profit from breeding horses.

Instead of racehorses, Cyrus considered producing race cars. Though he put together the prototype of a Jaguar-type luxury sports car, he realised it was not going to be commercially viable in India back then and dropped the idea. It was a vet, Dr Balakrishnan, who gave him the idea that would transform his fortunes. Balakrishnan pointed out that the Poonawallas had been donating their horses, after breeding, to Mumbai's government-run Haffkine Institute where they were used in the production of antiserum for the tetanus vaccine. He suggested that Cyrus put up a processing plant in a corner of the Poonawalla farm and get into the business himself. The family's advantage over the big pharma companies was that they had plenty of land to house the horses. Cyrus and his brother Zavereh soon realised they were on to a good thing. The family doctor, Jal Mehta, who subsequently became vice-chairperson of SII, introduced Cyrus to Dr P.M. Wagle, who had just retired as director of the Haffkine Institute.

Cyrus employed two scientists to build a small laboratory in a corner of the farm, which had a lot of barren land for breeding.

In 1966, on Cyrus's wedding day, the foundation stone for the SII was laid. It was a small-scale industry, with a capital of Rs 5 lakh. The company's rather grand name, Cyrus admits, was a bit of an exaggeration of both the scale and standing of the business at the time. Adar Poonawalla concedes that perhaps the company is misnamed since the word 'Institute' implies it is also a research centre. But the name has proved so lucky that no one is in a hurry to change it. In 1967, SII began making serum for the tetanus antitoxin, of which there was a huge shortage in the country. Cyrus, who has always loved horses, stopped using them to produce the serum, moving on to discarded army mules instead. The company quickly became hugely profitable and branched out into the manufacture of other vaccines. Today, SII specialises in the DPT, MMR and Pentavalent vaccines and has expanded to produce pneumococcal and rotavirus vaccines as well. The SII would have grown even faster had the brothers looked for partners or opted for a public listing. But Cyrus did not want to lose his independence and control; in fact, he always had concerns about retaining control. So much so that even when his brother Zavereh wanted to bring his son into SII, Cyrus demurred: 'I feared that at some stage it could lead to a rift with my only son.' Zavereh decided to exit the company, a decision he probably now regrets. He encashed his holdings and distributed the money among his three children. Zavereh also took possession of the Poonawallas' three flourishing engineering firms for his son to develop. Cyrus, who was the majority shareholder and CEO of SII, says he advised his brother against selling out.[8]

The company's big break came when it got WHO accreditation to produce vaccines. UNICEF is now one of the SII's biggest customers. Another major client is the Pan American Health Organisation, which honoured Cyrus in 2010 for his contribution to eliminating rubella in the region. The Gates Foundation has often pumped cash into the SII and has credited the company with helping to eliminate meningitis in hard-hit parts of Africa.

Before the pandemic, the SII had manufactured nearly 1.5 billion doses of vaccines for use in around 170 countries in the developing world. Cyrus has transformed the global industry by offering large volumes of serums and vaccines at half, and sometimes even one-tenth, the cost of such vaccines elsewhere. Understandably, big pharma in the United States and Europe is anxious that SII be kept out of their markets, which they guard zealously through byzantine patents and intellectual property laws. Despite hurdles placed in its way in Europe, America and China, SII has conquered much of the rest of the world. Cyrus is confident that the firm now has the financial clout and infrastructure to enter the developed world. The pandemic might prove to be the global health crisis that paves the way for SII to do just this.

The big pharmaceutical companies in the West accuse firms like SII of piggybacking onto their costly research to produce inexpensive copycat vaccines. Adar wants to pressure Western companies and governments to start changing the landscape, using the example of COVID-19, and the global need for inexpensive vaccines on a massive scale, to illustrate the flaws in the current system.[9] In some cases in the West, companies have retained sole control over major scientific products for decades. The SII vaccine was bought in bulk by the Indian government and the price was easily affordable, Adar points out.

Opening up the West would be fantastic for SII's business and for its owners' profits. Adar believes that to ensure a fair global health system, there is no other option but to adopt a Global Pandemic Treaty aimed at building a common regulatory framework which would enable knowledge-sharing, provide resources and logistical support and maintain a transparent approval system of vaccine certificates. Cyrus Poonawalla does not believe in hiding his wealth. He is candid about his taste for the good life and has a reputation for flamboyance. 'I am proud of spending the money with which I have enriched myself, without compromising my principles and being ruthless,' Cyrus told me. He has a reputation for style and enjoys being photographed in the company of glittering international celebrities, or in his trademark hat and long cigar, celebrating his thoroughbreds in victory enclosures at racetracks around the world. His son, Adar, and glamorous daughter-in-law Natasha are often the subjects of glossy magazine features salivating over their jet-setting lifestyle. Cyrus says he sometimes cautions them about their extravagances, but resigns himself good-naturedly to the younger generations' consumerism. 'What is life all about,' he says they believe, 'if you can't enjoy your wealth.'[11]

Natasha, born to a Parsi mother and a Punjabi father, is close friends with several Bollywood and Hollywood stars and rivals them in both looks and attire. She figures regularly on the list of the best-dressed women in India. 'I have been a clotheshorse all my life,' she once told a writer for a weekend supplement. 'Dressing is a creative outlet for me.'[12] But the London School of Economics graduate dislikes being portrayed as a beautifully dressed airhead and party girl. She takes her work as chairperson of the Villoo Poonawalla Charitable Foundation very seriously. Inevitably, Natasha has been compared to the late Parmeshwar Godrej of the Godrej group, who was similarly smart and stunning.

The Poonawallas' conspicuous consumption extends into various spheres. They are an auctioneer's delight; once they bid, they seldom quit until they have made the purchase. Apart from an impressive collection of modern Indian art, they have also acquired paintings by the Dutch masters Rembrandt, Rubens and Van Gogh, the great French impressionist Renoir, through to the likes of Picasso and Marc Chagall and the contemporary

English artist Damien Hirst. Their opulent Pune mansion is stuffed with priceless artefacts, not to mention racing trophies won by Poonawalla stallions bred at their three stud farms, two of them co-owned with his brother, Zavereh. (Horses from the Poonawalla stud farms have, over forty years, won several Derbies and 364 classic races).

Though their home base is Pune, Cyrus in 2015 made a successful bid at an auction for the former palace of the maharaja of Wankaner—a 50,000 square foot palace standing on a two-acre palm-fringed seafront compound in South Mumbai's trendy Breach Candy. The palace was renamed 'Lincoln House' when it was bought by the US government and served as the US consulate in Mumbai for over half a century. When the property was finally auctioned, the winning bid was a reported Rs 750 crore, described by the newspapers as the costliest purchase of a property in India. Thanks to the Indian government's various interdepartmental wrangles, though, the Poonawallas are yet to take possession of the palace. Still, there are other baubles with which they can console themselves—a Gulfstream jet, a luxury yacht, three aircraft simulators and over thirty supercars, including Rolls Royces, Ferraris, Bentleys, Lamborghinis and several rare vintage models. Adar even modified a Mercedes-Benz S-Class to look like a Batmobile for his elder son Cyrus's sixth birthday.

Because of Adar's love of the deluxe, international jet-setter lifestyle, many observers underestimated his business acumen and ability when he took over as the SII chief executive officer in 2011. Adar proved the sceptics wrong, guiding SII to an over 30 per cent rise in profits, while Cyrus remains the chairman of the company. His father had inducted Adar into the firm as soon as he graduated with a degree in business management from the University of Westminster in England, at the age of just twenty; as Adar turned forty, the number of countries being supplied by SII had grown to 170. In its early days, SII struggled domestically because of chronically delayed payments from government departments. The firm then changed its business model and focused on overseas clients. Before the pandemic, nearly 80 per cent of the company's revenues were generated outside India. Adar took the company into newer segments and ploughed most of the profits into building quality, technology and capacity.[13] The firm adheres to the highest standards. Everything in the two huge plants in Pune is imported from Europe and the USA and the automation is state of the art. Both father and son have similar temperaments and are not averse to some risk, though they have to be the ones taking the decisions. They do not extend trust and relinquish responsibility easily. Adar accepts that he might be guilty of micromanaging the business, 'but we do not believe in allowing the grass to grow under our feet'.[14] Cyrus says he is not as tough or as much of a disciplinarian as his son, which is why he was comfortable with letting him take charge at an early age.[15]

When Cyrus was growing up in Poona, he was a little envious of the cars and houses of the two richest Parsi families in town—the Jehangirs and the Jeejeebhoys. The Jeejeebhoys were descendants of Byramjee Jeejeebhoy, a wealthy businessman and philanthropist to whom the East India Company had gifted seven villages covering some 12,000 acres from Jogeshwari to Borivili, in what later became part of Bombay. This included the Bandra Land's End cape, which was renamed 'Byramjee Jeejeebhoy Point'. The Cowasji Jehangir family also shuttled between Bombay and Poona. Cyrus cites the Jehangir family as an example of being unnecessarily low-key. They did not even care, he says, to use their famous surname 'Readymoney' or the full baronetcy title of Sir Cowasji Jehangir. 'If you have such an illustrious name, why not use it?' he asks matter-of-factly. Cyrus's firm belief is that when he donates, as he frequently does, to a worthy cause he wants his family name to be attached to those deeds.[16] Hence, Poonawalla is not an easy name to escape in Pune. For instance, the road leading to his stud farm offices and factory is named 'Poonawalla Road' after his ancestor, Dhanjishaw. He pays for private traffic wardens on the long stretch of road so that the family and its visitors enjoy VIP movement privileges. When Cyrus came to Delhi in 2016 for the inauguration of the 'Everlasting Flame' exhibition, organised by the School of Oriental and African Studies, London, which he had partly sponsored, he did so in typical Poonawalla style. He sent his personal chauffer with his Rolls-Royce to Delhi in advance so that he could travel in the style to which he was accustomed.

In 2013, three years after Cyrus's wife, Villoo, died, the family set up the Villoo Poonawalla Charitable Foundation. Cyrus, unlike some other Parsi industrialists, takes a keen interest in community affairs. That year, a sharply divided BPP threatened to back out of hosting the Tenth World Zoroastrian Congress in Mumbai as scheduled because of the inclusion on discussion panels of liberal Parsis who mocked orthodox punchayet members. Cyrus stepped in to broker peace between the liberal and orthodox factions. He personally shuttled back and forth between both camps, cajoling them into a compromise. He also footed the bill for the congress. He was appointed chairperson. At the first Iranshah Utsav in Udvada in December 2015, Ratan Tata was felicitated with a standing ovation. But there was also applause for Cyrus, who had paid for the show. In fact, Cyrus has seldom turned down a request from his fellow Parsis. When a former BPP chairperson, Dinshah Mehta, requested that the SII reserve 60,000 vials of the Covid vaccine for Parsis—since the community is an endangered micro-minority and over forty people from the community had already died from the virus, far above the national average, in part because the community is ageing—Cyrus instantly acceded to the request. Adar seconded the generous gesture in a tweet, pointing out that it would be just a day's production. However, since the

Government of India is fully in charge of the vaccination drive, a special concession to the Parsis was not possible.

Adar's pet charity is a drive to clean Pune. The Clean City project has over 110 sophisticated vehicles, including cranes imported from Belgium and Holland, to lift large mounds of garbage. It is meant to serve as a model to other Indian cities. The Villoo Poonawalla Foundation has also built toilets in Mumbai and Pune and set up water treatment plants. Adar's drive for a clean Pune took its inspiration from Prime Minister Narendra's Modi's 2014 Swachh Bharat campaign and perhaps Modi's visit to the Poonawalla factory in 2016 was a gesture of appreciation for this support. The prime minister visited the SII once again in December 2020 to oversee preparations for the COVID vaccination preparedness. In January 2022 Cyrus was awarded the Padma Bhushan, the country's third highest civilian award.

Without doubt, the Poonawallas' most significant philanthropic contribution is the low price at which they sell their vaccines. Before the pandemic, it is estimated that two-thirds of all the children in the world born from 2015 onwards have been administered at least one dose of a vaccine produced by SII. Cyrus believes that some 30 million children in poor countries have been saved because of his low-cost vaccines. Of course, post-pandemic the number of vaccines and lives saved has increased exponentially. The pricing policy is a conscious decision not to exploit the health of people for outlandish profit margins. Cyrus's philosophy in all business dealings, even real estate, is to strike a bargain that pleases both sides. But the low cost of Poonawalla products proved to be a good marketing strategy as well. 'Everything fell into place,' Cyrus says. 'You are saving children's lives and you are keeping the competition away. There could not be a better way to be proud of making a living.'[17]

* * *

If there were a roll of honour for Parsi billionaires, one name which would have figured prominently for over a century is 'Godrej'. If the Tatas are the first family of the Parsi business world, the Godrejs likely occupy second place. The House of Godrej took root just before the start of the twentieth century. Despite heading a major industrial empire, the first two generations of the Godrej family were far less grand than the Tatas. The Godrejs prided themselves on being a simple, down-to-earth, middle-class, closely knit family. As Pheroza Godrej, the multi-talented wife of Jamshyd Godrej (a third-generation Godrej and the billionaire managing director of Godrej & Boyce), put it to me: 'One defining trait in the family was frugality. They genuinely believed, why do you need more? If you generated more, it was ploughed back into the karkhana. When I got married, I hadn't realised how much this family had to struggle to set up their businesses. It was a real eye-opener.'

As with the Tatas, the Godrej name became so popular and respected that it inspired trust in generations of consumers. 'A Godrej safe in every home' was an iconic slogan from the early twentieth century, while a Godrej steel cupboard was found to be the second-most popular item for the trousseau of an Indian bride.

The founder of the Godrej empire, Ardeshir Godrej, was a very private and individualistic man who met with a great tragedy early in life. Ardeshir could be both extraordinarily parsimonious (people sometimes ask if the word is derived from Parsi—it is not) and extraordinarily generous. He had a strict working arrangement with his brother, Pirojsha, whom he kept on a tight budget. Rather than use cars, which he could well afford, he would take public transport or simply walk. It wasn't about the money. Back then, in 1921, he didn't think twice about donating Rs 3 lakh, a huge sum, to the Tilak Swaraj Fund for the upliftment of the Scheduled Castes and to fight prohibition. Gandhiji expressed his gratitude, noting that 'during collection week in Bombay, not a day has passed without Parsi donations . . . but Mr. Godrej's generosity puts the Parsis easily first in all India.' The donation irked the colonial government; a secret circular was sent to all departments prohibiting them from purchasing any Godrej product.[18]

Ardeshir started his career as a lawyer in Zanzibar in 1884 but, feeling that he was not cut out for the law because of his straightforward character, returned to Bombay, where he pursued his natural bent for innovation and invention. Like Dadabhai Naoroji and Jamsetji Tata, he strongly supported the Swadeshi movement, believing that genuine Indian independence required self-reliance and an end to the demand for foreign-made goods. Taking a loan of Rs 3,000 from a wealthy Bombay landowner, Merwanji Cama, he started his own business. His first venture was repairing surgical instruments. But he came to public attention when he focused on devising a trustworthy Indian-made lock. Though locks were made on a small-scale in the country in both Aligarh and Howrah, the technique was generally crude and time-consuming. Ardeshir experimented with mechanised locks. He invented a sophisticated lever lock without springs, the first of his thirty-six patented inventions.[19] The Godrej name came to be synonymous with Indian locks which form, even today, an important segment of the company's turnover. From locks, it was a natural progression to safes. Ardeshir's advertising and marketing ideas were often out of the box. He took up the challenge thrown by one Dhunjibhoy Batliwala to break open a safe made by a well-known foreign brand. He managed to figure out the workings of the safe in a few minutes and expose its contents. He then issued a much-publicised challenge to anyone to try and break open his own safe. Three professional safecrackers conceded defeat. Among Ardeshir's clients were His Majesty's Mint and the Imperial Bank of India. Ardeshir's final triumph was to force the British firm

Chub and Milner, which had a near-monopoly on safes in India, to transfer its entire sales operations to Australia.[20]

At Bal Gangadhar Tilak's suggestion, Ardeshir took up the manufacture of soap. While the first soap factory in India was established in Meerut in 1897, the complaint about Indian soaps was that they became soggy easily and melted fast. Ardeshir experimented with the proportions of chemicals and came up with a washing soap bar, Chavi Chaap (literally, key brand), which lathered better and retained its shape. In 1918, the same year Chavi Chaap hit the market, another of his soap products was an even bigger technological breakthrough—the first soap made from vegetable oil. Until then, all soap manufacturing required the use of animal oils. The first vegetable-oil-based soap was a popular concept in a country with a large vegetarian population and made sound economic sense. Prominent nationalists Rabindranath Tagore, Annie Besant and Dr M.A. Ansari testified that the quality of Godrej soaps compared favourably with the best imported soaps. The highest tribute came from Gandhiji himself who refused to give his blessings to a rival soap manufacturer, saying he held brother Godrej in too high a regard.[21]

Ardeshir had no offspring. His child bride, Bachubai, died within a year of the marriage. She and her cousin had climbed to the top of the Rajabai Clock Tower of Bombay University for a panoramic view of the city. Once up there, though, they were accosted by a man. To save their honour, the frightened ladies plunged to their death 200 feet below. The Parsi community was so outraged, it took to the streets to demand the arrest of the suspect, who it was alleged was related to an influential businessman and therefore let off by the police. While it became a cause célèbre in his community, a shattered Ardeshir retreated further into his shell and took no part in the unsuccessful bid to bring the suspect to justice. After Bachubai's death, Ardeshir effectively became a recluse.

Ardeshir and his younger brother Pirojsha had a highly fruitful and long business partnership but a prickly personal relationship. Ardeshir would go to the factory in the morning and early afternoon, while Pirojsha arrived at the workplace only when his brother left. The division of labour was clear-cut. Ardeshir was the inventor, the ideas-generator. While his better-known inventions were soaps, locks and safes, his fertile imagination experimented on various fronts. Later in life, he even tried his hand at farming, hoping that he could grow fruit and vegetables for processing and preserving and dreamed of starting a canning factory. His agricultural plans never fructified. But his thinking was far ahead of his time. Another unfulfilled dream he had was the setting up of a Parsi agricultural colony as he believed that fully a quarter of all the Parsis in Bombay were subsidised by dole from Parsi charities. He thought handouts were an unproductive and morally questionable way to assist the poorer members of the community.[22]

If Ardeshir was given space to experiment and think, Pirojsha was the administrator who followed concepts through the manufacturing process. Ardeshir had three brothers and two sisters, but only Pirojsha entered into a partnership with him. The elder brother would sell his patents to Pirojsha at the market price and the latter then manufactured them and built up the company. It was Pirojsha who set in place the policies that guided the future of the company. He emphasised ethics, workers' welfare and quality. Though he was not a bookish man, he understood instinctively the need for a modern, efficiently laid out factory in pleasant surroundings that would make the lives of the workers less arduous.[23] Ardeshir did not believe in inheriting wealth or bequeathing it. He left his soap company to the BPP from whom Pirojsha bought it back at a discount.

Pirojsha's three sons, Sohrab, Burjor and Naval, were very different in temperament. Sohrab, the eldest, felt like a misfit in the family. He was not interested in the factory, which was his father's whole life. The practical, business-minded father and his sensitive son, uninterested in business, were often at loggerheads. As a teenager, the physically frail, daydreaming Sohrab believed he was a disappointment to his father and at one stage even reportedly contemplated suicide.[24] When Soli, as Sohrab was known, went abroad to study further, Pirojsha insisted he study the sciences, when the young man's interests were entirely in the humanities. The second son, Burjor, was an intellectual and studied in Germany. He obtained a degree in mechanical engineering, followed by a doctorate in technical chemistry. He came back to India during the Second World War, before returning to complete his doctorate. Burjor's side of the family was particularly academically inclined. His younger son Nadir described his father in an interview as being 'hard-working, charismatic and threateningly intelligent'.[25] Naval, the youngest and Pirojsha's favourite son, did not go abroad to study. Instead, he joined his father at the factory. Naval became Pirojsha's right-hand man and it soon became obvious that he had an instinctive flair for managing and containing the many problems that cropped up at the factory.[26]

Pirojsha died in 1972, without leaving a will. At the time, Soli was convinced that he would be cut off from the family business.[27] But at the first board meeting, Naval announced that Soli, as the eldest, should be made chairperson of both Godrej Soaps and Godrej & Boyce.[28] So united was the family that nobody argued. Under Soli, Burjor took charge of the soap business and Naval took over Godrej & Boyce, which dealt largely in steel furniture, locks and safes. (The name 'Boyce' was added to the firm, founded in 1897, as a gesture of gratitude to Merwanji Cama, who had loaned Ardeshir Rs 3,000 to get going. Cama said that Ardeshir could repay his loan by making his nephew Boyce a partner. Boyce, a shirker, took no interest whatsoever in the business but the family felt it had a moral rather than a legal obligation to retain his name.)

During his father's lifetime, and guided by Pirojsha, Naval bought, in 1935, the entire 3,500-acre village of Vikhroli at an auction, despite having to incur heavy debts to make the purchase.[29] Five years later, he transferred the land to the Godrej & Boyce Manufacturing Company. Through Naval's ingenuity, skill and hard work, what had once been wasteland was transformed into a socially progressive industrial garden township with many facilities for the workers, including an excellent school started by Burjor's wife, Jai. The sprawling Vikhroli estate is today amongst the family's most valuable assets. It is estimated to be worth around US$12 billion if developed. In Vikhroli, some 1,750 acres—nearly three times the size of Manhattan's Central Park—are occupied by mangrove forests, trees, shrubs and plants growing in saline tidal waters. Mangroves once formed much of the natural habitat of the islands of Bombay, but have almost disappeared, thanks to development, landfills and reclamation. The Godrej family, dedicated to ecology and wildlife, had once vowed to protect one of the city's last few large green stretches. 'The mangrove is sacrosanct,' Pheroza says, 'we can never touch it.'[30] The Godrej family's interest in protecting the environment and fighting pollution preceded by decades the current urgency to slow down our ecological impact. In 2012, *Forbes* listed the Godrejs as among the richest 'green billionaires' in the world.

At the time of Pirojsha's death, his three sons and daughter, Dosa, also decided they would start a foundation in his name. Twenty-five per cent of Godrej's holding company are held in trusts. Apart from environmental causes, the Godrejs focus much of their philanthropy on education.

To get back to the question of succession. On the face of it, Soli seemed a totally unsuitable choice to follow Pirojsha as the family patriarch. Friends described him as 'in the hippie

mould', a man whose heart bled for underdogs and green causes.
He was an avid traveller and would go on long trips to obscure
and faraway locations. Even in his dress, with his frayed, shabby
trousers, colourful tribal shirts, chappals and straw hats, Soli
defied corporate culture.[31] On his sleeves, he would often wear
black bands to indicate sympathy for some or the other lost cause.
He was known to doze at meetings, though Pheroza loyally insists
that he would suddenly spring to life, raise his hand and ask very
pertinent questions.[32]

Despite his idiosyncrasies, Soli became the face of the
company. He was a friend to several Indian prime ministers and
was on intimate terms with many international leaders. His friends
in high places were impressed with the Godrejs' work in family
planning and in preserving the environment and conservation.
Soli won several national and international awards from the
Padma Bhushan to the White Pelican award. During his many
travels, he built up the Godrej image. Soli opened the Indian
office of the World Wildlife Fund and was its chairperson until
his death. While Soli became a distinguished international figure,
his brothers grew the business. Burjor experimented with new
soaps and detergents and engaged in fierce competition with the
multinational Hindustan Lever. And Naval, with his mechanical
bent of mind, ventured, in the early 1950s, into manufacturing
typewriters. So successful did Godrej typewriters become in India,
that Remington retreated. From typewriters, Naval moved on to
refrigerators, machine tools and hi-tech electronics.

In January 1979, a terrible tragedy struck Naval and his
family and sent shockwaves through the city of Bombay. A few
months earlier, the Godrej & Boyce workers' unions had broken
away from the Indian National Trade Union Congress to form
an independent union to negotiate with management for their
demands. It was alleged that, in a case of inter-union rivalry,
militant trade unionist Dutta Samant had masterminded the

attack in which Shankar Savardekar, a union man, burst into Naval's house with a Rampur knife. He stabbed Naval twice and when his pregnant daughter-in-law Pheroza and his elderly mother-in-law Gulbai Dastur tried to come to his rescue, they too were assaulted. Hearing the screams, Jamshyd, his son, rushed to the scene. He found the two women unconscious, the apartment splattered with blood and Naval, despite his deep wounds, desperately trying to call for help. The victims were all rushed to Breach Candy Hospital and, miraculously, survived, though Pheroza lost the baby she was carrying. A huge public meeting was held in Bombay to express outrage at the gangsterism that had infiltrated the trade unions.

After two major operations, Naval appeared to have recovered, though his health was never the same again. He died prematurely of liver failure caused by the infusion of infected blood during his operations. According to Parsi custom, after a person dies, the body is bathed and a sudreh and kusti are tied round the waist. It is then taken immediately to Doongerwadi for the last ceremonies and non-Parsis do not get to see the body. But in Naval's case, in a departure from religious tradition, and out of respect for the workers, the body was first taken to Pirojshanagar, where over 10,000 workers waited to pay their last respects.[33]

The Godrej women, like the men in the family, were greatly influenced by Gandhian philosophy. They worked hard at social welfare and education, dressed simply, kept a low profile and strove to be earnest and conscientious. Jai, Burjor's wife, spent a lifetime running a school for workers' children, which had a reputation for excellence. As if to offer proof of the school's high standards, some of the Godrej children were also enrolled as pupils. Both Jai and her mother were intellectuals and poets. Naval's wife, Soonoo, was deeply committed to worker welfare. She had been inspired by the Mahatma as a child. When she asked him for an autograph, he made her promise that she would wear only khadi. This was highly unusual for a Parsi in those days. Naval's daughter-in-law, Pheroza, Jamshyd's wife, is an art historian, teacher, art collector, custodian of the family archives, environmentalist, scholar and author. Nadir Godrej's wife, Dr Rati Godrej, is a very well-respected physician on the board of several charitable trusts.

The one Godrej wife who did not conform to the family's low-key image was Parmeshwar, a spirited Punjabi beauty and wife of Burjor's eldest son Adi. Once an airline stewardess and briefly a successful designer and interior decorator, Parmeshwar was one of Mumbai's best-known hostesses and invitations to her parties were much sought after. Her guestlist mixed Bollywood stars and top industrialists with international celebrities such as Richard Gere, Imran Khan and Oprah Winfrey. Soli, her husband's uncle, disapproved of Parmeshwar's socialite image, which ran contrary to the family's ethos and did not hide his displeasure. But Soli had underestimated her impact. When Parmeshwar died in 2016, the *Mid Day* columnist Malavika Sangghvi wrote, 'She taught Indian society how to dress, decorate and entertain.' Well-known writer Shobhaa De recalled, 'She was a dazzling beauty with more blinding wattage than a movie star.' The obituary writers noted her work with Richard Gere and Bill and Melinda Gates on AIDS. Parmeshwar's socialising, so frowned upon by Soli, meant that the Godrej soap brand Cinthol found it easy to garner celebrity endorsements, boosting the brand's profile and the company's profits.

As a family, the Godrejs represent a uniquely Indian mosaic. In our interview, Pheroza told me that they don't see themselves as a particularly Parsi family. 'We are an Indian family, proud of our Indianness.'[34] The Godrej family has often been at the forefront of reform in the community but in a quiet, understated way. But they are also so obviously rooted in the Parsi community and religion that few have ever dared to cast a stone at their pan-Indian cosmopolitanism. For instance, Naval's daughter,

Smita, is married to Vijay Crishna, a Christian. Along with four other Parsi women who married outside the faith, she formed a group dubbed the 'Association of Inter-Married Zoroastrians' more than twenty-five years ago to fight for their right to remain Zoroastrian. In the Godrej family, the various children have all had their navjotes, regardless of whether their father was a Parsi. Pheroza recalls that when Smita's elder daughter, Freyan, was to have her navjote along with her own daughter Raika, Naval, then a trustee of the BPP, was very worried the night before the ceremony. He asked Pheroza, his daughter-in-law, if special security arrangements should be made in case some Parsis tried to disrupt the festivities. But Naval's wife Soonoo said firmly that she would handle anyone who dared protest. When the priest hesitated about performing the navjote, Pheroza's little daughter Raika gave him a scolding for being so orthodox and the ceremony took place without further ado. Soonoo herself was unafraid to buck tradition. She had long made it known to her family that she wanted to be cremated after her death, rather than go through with the traditional Parsi funeral rites of a dakhma. Most Parsi priests did not generally agree to say prayers for a body that was to be cremated, but the Godrejs refused to be browbeaten. They found a Parsi working in a Godrej company who was a qualified priest, having trained as a navar.[35]

On Soli's death in 2000, Adi took over as the chairperson of the group, being the eldest among the cousins. The chairperson may have been the face of the group, like Soli was, but not necessarily the sole power. The family businesses had branched out into several fields, including real estate, property development, electronics, IT, agriculture, retail marketing, aerospace, info-tech and robotics. Jamshyd took over from his father Naval as the chairperson of Godrej & Boyce. It remains one of the largest privately held companies in India, even as other Godrej companies have gone public.

The family's fourth generation has now entered the business. The Godrejs have never discriminated against women and this latest generation to lead the group includes three bright, personable businesswomen with degrees from the world's best universities—Adi's daughters, Tanya and Nisaba, and Smita's daughter Nyrika Holkar. When Adi retired as the chairperson of the group at the age of seventy-five in May 2017, he appointed Nisa, his second child, as the executive chairperson of the flagship Godrej Consumer Projects. At thirty-nine, Nisa became one of the youngest women to head a large Indian company. Her younger brother, Pirojsha, was appointed chairperson of Godrej Properties. Adi remains chairman emeritus of Godrej Consumer Projects. His cousin, the more low-key Jamshyd, continues to head Godrej & Boyce. In Naval's branch of the family, only Nyrika continues to work for the company and is an executive director. Her uncle Jamshyd confirmed to the *Times of India* that Nyrika is being groomed to take over from him as chairman cum managing director.

The younger generation has made some changes to the group's ethos. There is reportedly a greater emphasis on profit. The frugality of the earlier generations is no longer evident in the younger Godrejs' life choices. Pirojsha lived together with his brothers and sisters on a house off Forget Street, near Grant Road in South Mumbai. Later, they bought a property on Ridge Road and built a bungalow in which they even rented out some rooms. They converted the property into an apartment building and Soli and his two brothers each occupied a flat. In contrast, a few years ago, Smita Godrej-Crishna, Naval's daughter, created a flutter by purchasing one of Mumbai's most expensive homes at an auction. The old-fashioned bungalow, Mehrangir, on Malabar Hill, with its large garden, was the family home of nuclear physicist Homi Bhabha. Smita bought it for Rs 372 crore, to the dismay of some scientists who petitioned for the house to be made a museum.

By the fourth generation, many Godrej family members have married outside the community but remain proud of their Parsi roots. Some in the family are still religious and frequently go to the fire temple. The family, though, is perhaps less tightly knit. Some media reports suggest that high-profile Adi's branch and the more retiring Jamshyd's have different strategic visions for the Godrej group's future. A bone of contention is reportedly a 1000-acre mangrove plot that belongs to Godrej & Boyce, led by Jamshyd, which the group's publicly listed company, Godrej Properties, headed by Adi's son Pirojsha, would like to see developed. Lawyers and bankers have been retained to act as mediators.[36] But while there may be differences and a group restructuring is on the cards, the Godrejs are too genteel for the family dispute to spill out in the open.

7

The Community's Backbone

The Parsi aristocracy, merchant princes, business families, chikoos, Tanchois et al. is one part of the Parsi tapestry. But probably the greatest gift from the Parsis to their adopted homeland is the community's professional middle class, which is the true backbone of the community. According to Berjis Desai, the popular tongue-in-cheek chronicler of the Parsi community, social standing was determined to a great extent by when one's family migrated to Bombay from Gujarat. The early migrants were richer, spoke better English, went to the best English schools, made their homes in the posher parts of the city and were usually connected to prominent business families. The later migrants went into the professions, becoming doctors, lawyers, engineers and architects or finding employment in the big Parsi business houses.[1]

The real key to general Parsi success was that they took advantage of British schooling at a much earlier stage than other communities, aware that education was the road to advancement. Many of the charities established by wealthy Parsis in the nineteenth and twentieth centuries focused on opening schools, colleges and professional institutions in Bombay and Poona for their community but also the population at large. The extent to which the Parsis of Bombay were ahead of the rest of India in terms of education, in both Gujarati and English, is illustrated by these telling statistics: in 1860 there were 615 Parsi students in high school in Bombay, compared to 441 Christians, 239 Hindus, just 15 Muslims and 22 others; that same year there were 66 Parsis enrolled in Bombay colleges, compared to 82 Hindus, 3 Muslims and 27 others. At that time, the Parsi community comprised less than 10 per cent of the city's population.[2] In the early 1920s, Parsis formed .03 per cent of the country's population, but they earned 7 per cent of the engineering degrees, 5 per cent of the medical degrees, 2 per cent of the science degrees and 1 per cent of all Western degrees granted in India.[3]

Armed with their education, Parsis made a name for themselves in every conceivable field, excelling in the sciences, the arts, academia and even sports. But in no field did educated Parsis make as seismic an impact as in the fields of law and medicine. Some of the greatest legal minds in the country have been Parsi and even today it remains among the most favoured careers for bright Parsi youth. Two Parsis, Sam Bharucha and Sarosh Kapadia, have served as chief justice of the Supreme Court of India, several as top law officers and the landmark legal battles to interpret constitutional issues have often been dominated by Parsi lawyers. For instance, the 'Kesavananda Bharati judgement' (1973), which held that the Indian parliament had no absolute right to repudiate or alter the basic foundation of the Constitution, featured Parsi counsels for both petitioners and the government. Nani Palkhivala, assisted by Soli Sorabjee and Fali Nariman, represented the petitioners, while another Parsi legal luminary, Homi Seervai, was such a respected name that he preceded the then attorney general, Niren De, in opening the government's argument.

On the criminal side, over the last century, in the Bombay High Court, Parsi lawyers have dominated proceedings. One of the most scandalous crimes in India was the 'Nanavati case', named after Kawas Nanavati, a dashing, decorated Parsi naval officer who shot dead his wife's lover, the rich businessman Prem Ahuja. Despite the overwhelming evidence against Nanavati, his crack legal team led by the suave, sophisticated, criminal lawyer Karl Khandalavala—who would be appointed years later as the main government counsel in the Shah Commission, instituted to investigate the Emergency—persuaded the jury to acquit him. The verdict led to the end of jury trials in India, with the judge describing the jury's decision as perverse. Leading Parsi lawyers involved, in one way or another, with the strange twists and turns of the Nanavati case included, Khandalavala apart, the likes of Palkhivala, Homi Seervai, S.R. Vakil and Tehmtan Andhyarujina—an all-star team.[4]

Born in 1920, Nanabhoy Palkhivala, known universally by his pet name 'Nani', is regarded as the greatest jurist of his day. Leading lawyer and member of the Rajya Sabha, Abhishek Manu Singhvi, when paying tribute to Palkhivala at an event to mark the centenary of his birth, described Palkhivala as the 'best finance minister this country never had, the best law minister which this country never had, and undoubtedly the best attorney general this country would ever have had'.[5] Palkhivala persistently defended the individual—be it a prince or pauper—against the State. Beginning with the 'Golaknath case' in 1967, a precursor, both literally and in spirit, to the 'Kesavananda Bharati judgment' which prevented Parliament from altering the fundamental rights provided by the Indian Constitution, Palkhivala fought a series of historic cases in the Supreme Court. He was the lead defence counsel in the so-called 'bank nationalisation' case in 1970, in which the court decided that the government owed monetary compensation to those whose property the government wanted to appropriate for public use. He was also lead counsel on the abolition of privy purses, in which the Indira Gandhi government backtracked on a deal with the rulers of princely states to pay a stipend in lieu of their agreeing to join the union, and a case to prevent the government from interfering in the educational choices, institutions and language of instruction in schools and institutions run by minority communities.

In his argument before the Supreme Court, Palkhivala framed the term 'basic structure of our constitution is inviolable', a phrase now used repeatedly in courts. His plea to ring-fence fundamental rights from Parliament was agreed to in a narrow 7-6 verdict by a thirteen-judge bench in the 'Kesavananda Bharati judgement'. It is considered by many to be the most important verdict in the history of democratic, independent India. Tyranny and autocracy, Palkhivala wanted to convince the court, could not be allowed to masquerade as constitutionalism. Hans Raj Khanna, a judge on the Supreme Court bench that heard the case, observed that 'the heights of eloquence which Palkhivala reached have seldom been equalled and never been surpassed in the history of the Supreme Court'.[6] The former attorney general, Soli Sorabjee, who worked with Palkhivala closely on numerous matters, believed that he was unmatchable when it came to clarity of thought, precision and alacrity in his response to a judge's query.[7]

On the principle that every litigant has the right to the best defence, Palkhivala defended then prime minister Indira Gandhi, accused by her opponent Raj Narain of electoral malpractice. On 12 June 1975, the Allahabad High Court found in favour of Narain; within days, Indira imposed a state of Emergency, effectively turning India into an authoritarian state. Within hours Palkhivala returned Indira's brief, declaring that her actions were inconsistent with the lifelong convictions and values he cherished. During the Emergency, Palkhivala played a heroic role in defending those whose rights were trampled on by the State, particularly those imprisoned without trial under the dreaded Maintenance of Internal Security Act (MISA).[8]

Apart from his legal genius, Palkhivala was also a brilliant economist who championed economic liberalisation and free enterprise at a time when socialism was the mantra in government. He was a trenchant critic of the economic policies of successive Congress governments, arguing that under the License Permit Raj, businessmen were denied an opportunity for fair competition on a level playing field. Government policies, and decisions were bogged down in bureaucratic red tape and favouritism. Palkhivala's interest in economic issues was aroused while arguing about taxation laws in the courtroom.

Keen to educate the public on the benefits of a free market economy, Palkhivala, in March 1958, gave the first of his budget lectures. This incisive, often scathing and, above all, public analysis of the budget became for many an eagerly awaited annual ritual. By the mid-1960s, his audience filled the vast Brabourne Stadium in Bombay, after which he travelled to other parts of the country speaking at jam-packed auditoriums.

Despite joining the Tatas as their legal adviser in 1961, Palkhivala continued to take up cases of national importance and even some private consultations. The Tatas took not just his legal advice but also his advice on matters of taxation and management. Palkhivala was the chairperson of several of the group's companies, including Tata Steel and TELCO. He was also the chairperson of the money-spinning TCS in its early years, and Subramaniam Ramadorai, the former CEO of TCS who was with the company almost from the beginning, credits the rapid growth of the start-up partly to Palkhivala, who 'gave the professional management a free hand and did not interfere'. At the same time, Ramodorai added, 'Palkhivala had the ability to clarify concepts when giving advice.'[9] J.R.D. Tata, however, decided against appointing Palkhivala as his successor because, he believed, Palkhivala had too many outside interests which could clash with the company's neutral position. In 1977, then prime minister Morarji Desai offered Palkhivala the post of ambassador to Washington with the rank of a cabinet minister. Palkhivala agreed only after much persuasion. During his tenure as ambassador, he was a popular guest speaker at numerous American universities and institutions.

Palkhivala came from a humble background. His grandfather died when his father Ardeshir was only eighteen. Although Ardeshir had a BA degree, he joined his uncle's business making palanquins (palkhis), which, of course, accounts for the family surname. When palanquins and coaches were no longer used, Ardeshir tried to earn a living first by starting a taxi service and then a laundry business. Palkhivala recalls his father as a perfectionist, teaching his son to follow his example. He also inculcated in Palkhivala a love for reading. As a boy, Palkhivala would spend all day at a bookshop close to his house on Grant Road where the kindly proprietor would allow him to browse until closing time.[10] Palkhivala's other interests included playing the violin and piano, fretwork paintings and photography. He overcame a stutter as a boy to become a most eloquent orator and could recite from memory his favourite poems and passages from literature.

His unfailing courtesy and humility were much admired by his peers. Self-important senior lawyers can often be seen trailed by respectful juniors and sycophantic hangers-on. Palkhivala would walk into the courtroom holding his own briefs and books. His successors, as moral forces in public life and outstanding jurists, are fellow Parsis, Fali Nariman and Soli Sorabjee. Nariman initially specialised in corporate law and acted as the lead counsel in several high-profile corporate battles (including the civil litigation arising out of the Bhopal gas tragedy). But over time, his contribution to jurisprudence and public affairs earned him greater respect and renown. He was appointed additional solicitor general of India in 1973 but resigned in 1975, the day after Indira Gandhi announced Emergency rule, the only senior government official to do so. Nariman sets a high ethical bar, in keeping with his eminence.

He served for many years on the International Commission of Jurists and was its chairperson from 1995 to 1997. Nariman headed a committee to examine how racial discrimination affected the awarding of death penalties in the USA, with the accused not provided with proper legal representation nor a fair jury selection process. He was also the counsel for the Gujarat government against the PIL filed by activists objecting to the increase in the height of the Narmada dam, but returned the brief abruptly when he felt that Christians in the state were being deliberately victimised.

In 1999, after being nominated to the Rajya Sabha, Nariman gave up his flourishing legal practice for his entire six-year term to avoid any conflicts of interest.

The late Soli Sorabjee, a contemporary of Nariman's, made a significant contribution to the interpretation of constitutional law in independent India. He was a champion of free speech and citizens' civil liberties, working pro bono, for instance, to help political prisoners arrested under the MISA law in the Emergency. He also offered his services for free to Sikhs in Delhi after the 1984 riots in which Sikhs were sought out and killed by mobs after the assassination of then prime minister Indira Gandhi by her Sikh bodyguards. Sorabjee was extremely generous in providing free legal assistance when a genuine need arises. Law, he believed, is a profession, not a trading business. 'But today, unfortunately, there is a trend to treat the law as a commercial activity. This is not demand and supply,' he once told me.[11]

Among the precedent-setting cases to which he was a party was the St Xavier's College, Ahmedabad petition against the state which argued for the rights of minority bodies to set up and run their own institutions. In 1979, he represented the government as the additional solicitor general in the Maneka Gandhi passport case where the courts held that a person's fundamental rights entail that he or she cannot be denied a passport without a reason being ascribed. In 1989, he fought the dismissal of the then chief minister of Karnataka, S.R. Bommai, by a hostile central government. The landmark judgement enforced limitations on the president to impose Article 356, which was also open to judicial review. Sorabjee served as the attorney general between 1998 and 2004. He was the special representative to the United Nations Human Rights Commission and served as a member of the Permanent Court of Arbitration at the Hague. Another side to his personality was his deep interest in jazz and English poetry. He was the president of the Delhi Jazz Association for many years.

Another Parsi lawyer who was a renowned expert on the Constitution was the late Homi Seervai, whose interpretation of the Constitution influenced generations of law graduates through his seminal book *Constitutional Law of India*. Palkhivala, Seervai, Nariman, Sorabjee and many other leading Parsi lawyers were trained in the chambers of Sir Jamshedji Kanga, a legendary figure in the Bombay High Court. With his striking height and white priestly turban, Kanga presented a distinguished figure.[13] Born into the priestly Jamasp Asa family, and despite his intimidating persona, Sir Jamshedji was a simple, humble man with great integrity and intellect. He was known among his colleagues to have had an exceptional grasp of the law and a phenomenal memory, often able to cite the exact volume and page on which a particular case was mentioned. He put his own powers of recall down to generations of ancestors who had to memorise religious prayers and verses in Avesta to fulfill their priestly duties.

Supreme Court Justice Rohinton Nariman recalls being taken as a young boy by his father Fali to meet Kanga. Rohinton had just taken his priestly initiation (navar) exam and Kanga, himself an ordained priest, shot some questions at the young boy, trying to gauge what level he'd reached in his studies. Kanga was suitably impressed when he heard that Rohinton had studied thirteen more prayers than he had managed. Rohinton would later use his knowledge of the ancient scriptures to write a popular book on the Gathas, the sacred Avestan hymns.[13]

Kanga never married, largely because his conservative mother was horrified that he had wanted to marry a woman he met in England. Obedient, perhaps to a fault, Kanga did not marry the woman he loved, though he did spend every summer holiday in England. Instead of love, Kanga channelled his energies into his career. Exceptionally generous, Kanga was known for promoting his juniors and recognising ability. Palkhivala, as a tribute to his mentor, insisted on including Kanga's name as a co-author in a book on income tax law that Palkhivala wrote that quickly became the definitive text on the subject at the time. Along with Kanga, the other outstanding legal luminary in the first part of the twentieth century was Sir Dinshaw Mulla who is remembered for his academic contributions to the law. Nariman describes Mulla as a scholar who analysed Hindu and Muslim personal laws in great detail. Among his many books, he co-authored, with the eminent English jurist Sir Frederick Pollock, the standard text on Indian contract law.[14] Mulla reached the pinnacle of his professional success when he was appointed a Privy Counsellor in 1930, a rare honour for an Indian.

Most of these leading Parsi lawyers shared a common love for English literature. Mulla, in fact, was so passionate about writing poetry that he sent some samples of his work to the great English poet Lord Alfred Tennyson as he wanted his opinion on whether he should become a poet or continue as a lawyer. The latter's sage advice: 'Stick to law.'[15] Palkhivala actually became a lawyer by accident. He topped the MA exam in English literature at Bombay University and was confident he would be retained by his college as a lecturer. To his horror, the post was filled by a Parsi woman who was already teaching at the college. Disappointed, Palkhivala thought he would continue with his studies but the only academic course still open at the university was law, for which he enrolled. Such was his gratitude to the woman for indirectly steering him to his true calling, he would take her out every year for a five-star meal.

If the Parsi influence on law in India is much celebrated, the community's contribution to medicine has also been profound. A frayed 1926 group photograph of the students and staff of Bombay's premier institution of medical studies, the Grant Government Medical College, offers telling testimony of the extent to which Parsis dominated the medical profession in western India at the time. The overwhelming majority of the men and women in the photograph are Parsis, each sporting such surnames as Cooper, Doctor, Khambhatta, Adenwala, Engineer, Postwalla and Mistry.[16]

The Parsi doctor, whether a specialist or general practitioner, is a much respected and trusted figure in Mumbai. His or her forte tends to be 'the art behind medicine', a phrase coined by one of the profession's greats, the Parsi doctor Farokh Udwadia, in his insightful 2009 book *The Forgotten Art of Healing*. Udwadia describes this 'art' as the ability to be in sympathetic communication with the patient's spirit.[17] His theory is that medicine is best taught at the bedside, by listening and talking to patients, by touching and examining them, rather than the overly clinical reliance on book-learning and sophisticated gadgetry that characterises the contemporary medical school education. His own gift for diagnosis is, other doctors say, awe-inspiring. Udwadia pays attention to minor symptoms and listens to patients for clues that inform diagnoses that frequently elude other doctors. He sometimes finds himself in Delhi, called for consultations and second opinions by high-ranking politicians and others who turn to him even when the country's finest medical institution, the All India Institute of Medical Sciences, is at their doorstep.

Udwadia is a legend at the Sir J.J. Hospital, where, as a professor of medicine, he taught generations of doctors. Along with the sciences, Udwadia was unusual in suggesting that his students take courses in the humanities to give them as wide a perspective on the spectrum of human behaviour as possible. To his students, Udwadia always stressed the difference between 'curing' and 'healing'. The cure is the scientific intervention necessary to rid a person of disease or infection. Healing, though, involves the patient's entire mind and body. It requires an elevated attention, a connection to the patient as a human being rather than as a case to be solved with the aid of the latest machines.

A renowned pulmonologist, Udwadia's research has resulted in major contributions to the field. He pioneered critical care (and intensive respiratory care, in particular) in India and his research on problems pertaining to critical care in developing countries is internationally acclaimed. He has authored several bestselling books that take in the whole range of his interests, from medicine to history, art and music, showcasing his multifaceted genius.

Singular though Udwadia's contributions might be, he is part of a significant line of Parsi physicians who have displayed a particular genius for patient care. Sir Tehmulji Nariman, who obtained his medical degree in 1872, was one of the founders of the Parsi Lying-in Hospital, the first obstetrical hospital in Bombay. Sohrabjee Mody in 1898, at considerable risk to his life, established a plague hospital for Parsis. In the same year, Hormasji Masina, one of the first Indians to earn the FRCS degree in England, returned to Bombay and founded the Masina Hospital, the first private hospital in the city. Another famous Parsi doctor from the period was Rustom Bomanji Billimoria, who dedicated himself to serve those afflicted with pulomonary tuberculosis which was particularly rampant at the time. In 1912, he opened a sanatorium in Panchgani. In Poona, the diagnostic powers of

Eduljee Coyajee were so legendary that large crowds would gather outside his consulting rooms on Main Street. Rich and poor alike would wait for their audience with Coyajee who offered his services to the needy for free.[18] Coyajee's refusal to charge the poor was in keeping with the belief of many Parsi doctors that one should not enter the temple of science with the heart of a moneylender, that the ability to pay should have nothing to do with every human's right to healthcare.

Among Mahatma Gandhi's doctors was Manchersha Gilder, arguably India's most eminent cardiologist in his time. Gilder's research into human electrocardiography with Sir Thomas Lewis was internationally renowned. So prominent did Gilder become that he, unusually for a Parsi doctor, went into politics, becoming the minister for public health in the Bombay Presidency in the late-1930s. He was by the Mahatma's side when he embarked on a fast unto death at the age of seventy-five. But Gilder was not particularly popular in his own community because he passionately espoused the cause of prohibition, eventually implemented by the Congress government in Bombay State not long after Independence.[19] Many Parsis engaged in the liquor trade lost fortunes and even those Parsis fond of their nightly tipple cursed Gilder for his advocacy of prohibition.

The spirit of selfless dedication in Parsi doctors still continues, as evinced in Mumbai during the coronavirus pandemic. For example, Dr Bohman Dhabar, a renowned medical oncologist in Mumbai, charges a modest fee and continues to see patients at his clinic till 4 a.m. By 9 a.m., he is at the hospital. When the *Indian Express* newspaper, Mumbai did a survey of senior citizen private doctors who continued practising as before and during the corona pandemic continued stepping in and out of hospitals and clinics despite their age, the reporters found a disproportionate number of Parsi doctors. One of the doctors interviewed, Dr R.B. Dastur, sixty-seven years old, explained: 'Even if my age is against me, I cannot not go. This is the time doctors need to step out as it is their duty.'

It is common in Parsi families for one generation of doctors to succeed another. Rustom Soonawala, for instance, was, in his heyday just a few decades ago, the country's leading obstetrician and gynecologist. Many of the country's elite would insist on his presence at the birth of their children. His work on intrauterine contraception has received global recognition. Soonawala's brother, Fardoon, is also a doctor with a specialisation in urology. Indeed, at one point, there were a dozen Soonawalla family members involved in the medical profession. Similarly, the Shroff family of Delhi have been leading ophthalmologists in northern India for four generations. Farokh Udwadia's brother, Tehemton, is a renowned surgeon considered the father of laproscopy of India. Farokh's son, Zarir, is a leading authority on the impact of COVID-19 on patients. Tehemton says his warmth and humaneness as a doctor was something he picked up from his father, Erach, a kindly GP whose patients were mill hands whom he charged only what they could afford. Erach taught his sons the valuable lesson, that a patient is not an anonymous case but a human being.

Under British rule and in the early years of independence, many Parsis were prominent in the civil services and the police forces. They had a national reputation for fair play and honesty. But even elite bureaucratic posts in, for instance, the Indian Administrative Service, no longer appear to attract the Parsi youth. The late Jamsheed Kanga, an IAS officer who was a popular municipal commissioner of Bombay and among the last generation of prominent Parsi civil servants, believed that young Parsis 'do not want to move out of their comfort zone of Bombay and have lost some of the spirit of adventure of their ancestors'. According to Kanga, who died in June 2020, Parsis who joined the civil services tended to come, like himself, from small towns. Bombay Parsis, he argued, were focused on going abroad to further their education, or to become well-remunerated professionals—lawyers, doctors, chartered accountants—in their home city.[20]

Perhaps Kanga's contention—of a safety-first Parsi approach that values urban creature comforts over adventure—could explain why Parsis have also practically disappeared from electoral politics. Before 1946, Parsis were disproportionately represented in both central- and state-level politics. Men such as Dadabhai Naoroji, Dinshaw Wacha, Pherozeshah Mehta, Dhanjishah Cooper and Khurshed Nariman played prominent roles in the Swadeshi movement, the freedom struggle and the effort to uplift the poor and downtrodden.

Of the many pre-independence Parsi stalwarts in public affairs, Dadabhai Naoroji, born 4 September 1825, was undoubtedly a colossus. Termed affectionately 'The Grand Old Man of India', Dadabhai left an indelible stamp as a social reformer, academician and politician from the end of the nineteenth century to the early twentieth century. His greatest legacy was exposing the injustice of colonial rule in India through political activism in London, the capital of the British Empire. His magnum opus *Poverty and UnBritish Rule in India* made the argument that India was monstrously overtaxed and much of its wealth drained away to England, buttressing his thesis with painstakingly collected economic data. It was a theme which he expounded on in many of his writings and speeches.

Dadabhai came from a poor priestly family of Navsari. His academic brilliance was recognised early in life. A scholarship student at the Elphinstone Institute in Bombay, he later became the first Indian appointed as a professor; his subjects were mathematics and natural philosophy. Dadabhai helped encourage women's education and in the process, came in touch with Khurshedji Cama who persuaded him to join the family business, Cama and Company, as a partner and he helped set up the firm's branches in England. This was a first for an Indian company. Dadabhai's entry into business was short-lived, but as a consequence he eventually relocated to England for many years.

He stood as the Liberal candidate from the Holborn constituency in London and was defeated with Prime Minister Lord Salisbury remarking scornfully that England was not ready to elect a 'black man'. But Dadabhai persevered nonetheless and was elected as the Liberal candidate from the working-class seat of Central Finsbury in 1892. He was the first Asian to be elected to the British House of Commons and there was much jubilation in India at news of his victory. Dadabhai devoted his time in the House of Commons to furthering the interests of the Indian people and also supporting such liberal causes as votes for women, Irish home rule and the abolition of the House of Lords.

Through innumerable societies and organisations with which he was associated, Dadabhai contributed enormously in shaping public opinion. He was India's unofficial ambassador who voiced the grievances and aspirations of the Indian people, both at home and to the world at large. Dadabhai was one of the founders of the Indian National Congress and was thrice elected president of the party. A staunch moderate within the Congress, he was mentor to later nationalists Bal Gangadhar Tilak, Gopal Krishna Gokhale and Mahatma Gandhi.

But since Independence, Parsi involvement in active politics has dwindled at an alarming speed. Only four Parsis have been elected to the Lok Sabha: Minoo Masani and Piloo Mody, both multiple-time MPs from the right-of-centre Swatantra Party, Homi Daji from the Communist Party of India and the Congress party's Feroze Gandhi.

Masani, who started out as a left-leaning member of the Congress Socialist Party, grew disillusioned with Soviet-style communism and ended up as an ideologue for the right. He was the leader of the Swatantra Party in the late 1960s when it emerged as the second-largest party, with forty-four seats, in a parliament dominated by the Congress. Piloo, son of Sir Homi and brother of Russi Mody, was president of the Swatantra Party when it merged in 1974 with Charan Singh's Bharatiya Kranti Dal party. A gentleman politician, the large and jovial Piloo Mody was renowned for his wit and the elegant force of his arguments. He held no malice towards anyone, not even Indira Gandhi who had jailed him during the Emergency. When her followers dubbed her critics as American agents, he mocked their paranoia by wearing a badge with 'CIA' emblazoned across it.

Ironically, the Parsi MP who made the most impact in the Lok Sabha is seldom remembered for his role as a parliamentarian. Feroze Gandhi's legacy in the Lok Sabha is overshadowed by his marriage into India's first family in politics. He was the son-in-law of India's first prime minister, the husband of arguably India's most controversial and charismatic prime minister, and the father of yet another prime minister, Rajiv Gandhi, who bore an uncanny resemblance to his father, both in looks and temperament. His grandson Rahul Gandhi is the leader of the Congress party and possibly a future prime minister.

The Gandhi dynasty, which continues to dominate Indian politics, bears Feroze's surname even if Feroze himself is a footnote in the family history. The Congress party prefers to focus on the fact that the family is descended from Moti Lal Nehru and Pandit Nehru. By a fortuitous coincidence, Feroze's surname happened to be the same as the father of the nation, Mahatma Gandhi, a fact which confused many, both in India and abroad. The name 'Gandhi' in Gujarati means grocer, though the Parsi 'Ghandys' generally spell their surname in the anglicised fashion. But Feroze changed his surname's spelling at some point.

While Parsis, with an inborn sense of their own superiority, are generally reluctant to accept the offspring of those who marry outside the community and whose descendants do not adhere to Zoroastrian customs, this aloofness does not hold true for the Gandhis. When Rajiv Gandhi became prime minister, a normally orthodox Parsi dowager gushed proudly to me: 'An astrologer foretold that a Parsi would one day rule India.' An aunt of Rajiv's confessed to me that though he visited his Bombay relatives regularly when he worked as a pilot, he had asked them not to give interviews and to keep a low profile during the 1984 general election. Given the size of the Hindu majority in India, the Congress was keen to downplay any Parsi ancestry.

Many years back when I visited Allahabad, home to both the Nehrus and Feroze himself, I was struck by the contrast. Tourists made a beeline for Anand Bhawan, Moti Lal Nehru's mansion, which has been gifted to the nation, but almost no one, including family members, bothered to pay their respects at the neglected Parsi cemetery where Feroze's grave lies. His brothers and sister erected a gravestone over the ground in which an urn containing some of his ashes is buried. But Feroze's funeral was conducted with full Hindu rites and his two sons, Rajiv and Sanjay, lit the funeral pyre. The only concession to his Parsi roots was that a Zoroastrian priest was first permitted to read the Gatha prayers over the body with only members of the community and his sons present.[22]

The marriage of Indira and Feroze seemed to be a mismatch from the start. Indira was shy, reserved, secretive, dignifed and discreet, with a sense of the importance of her family's place in history. Feroze was gregarious, good-hearted, loud, fun-loving and slightly feckless. When he was courting Indira, he was totally in awe of the Nehrus. Feroze had been adopted by his mother's sister, Shirin Commissariat—one of the first women surgeons in the country—at Lady Dufferin Hospital in Allahabad. Feroze was the son of Jehangir Gandhi, a marine engineer, and his wife Ratti. Both were from middle-class families in Gujarat who settled in Bombay. Feroze was the couple's fifth child and the unmarried

Shirin asked to be allowed to take charge of her nephew's upbringing and education. After Jehangir's untimely death, Ratti and her children spent a large part of their time in Allahabad. (A rumour that Feroze was the love child of Shirin and a prominent Punjabi lawyer based in Allahabad is not backed by any evidence other than small-town gossip.)

As a schoolboy, Feroze came in contact with Indira's ailing mother Kamala Nehru, to whom he was devoted. Kamala in turn was fond of the helpful youth who was always ready to offer his services and give company to the lonely invalid. Partly because of his fascination with the Nehrus, Feroze took part enthusiastically in the freedom movement, much to the dismay of his Parsi family. They complained both to Mahatma Gandhi and Pandit Nehru that Feroze was ruining his future. Shirin even threatened that she would not fund his education in England if he continued to chase after the Nehrus.

Feroze was smitten by Indira from the time she was sixteen, but she had many admirers and suitors and did not give him any hint that she favoured him over the others.[23] Both were students in England together, Indira at Oxford and Feroze at the London School of Economics. It was evident to a few close friends that in London their friendship had slowly blossomed into a passionate romance, but Indira did not breathe a word of it to her father. When the self-willed Indira, on her return to India, informed her father that she intended to marry Feroze, Pandit Nehru was shocked and displeased. In an attempt to prevaricate, he asked her to meet with the Mahatma. Seeing that Indira was determined, Gandhiji gave his blessing. The wedding took place amidst the upheaval of the Second World War, sandwiched between important Congress party meetings.[24] Even as wedding preparations were underway, Nehru got cold feet because of the violent indignation among some people that the bride and groom were of different religions. (In north India, few even knew what

a Parsi was; to them, the name 'Feroze' sounded Muslim.) Indira
Gandhi's biographer, Katherine Frank, wrote that the prospect of
the marriage upset Nehru because Feroze lacked the pedigree and
the connections that Nehru valued. He would not have been so
opposed had Feroze come from one of the patrician Parsi families
of Bombay. Feroze had not completed his university education,
had no professional qualifications and no prospect of a steady
income. Eventually, they married in a Vedic ceremony. The only
Zoroastrian touch was that Feroze's mother, Ratti, persuaded him
to wear his kusti under his khadi sherwani.[25]

But this was only a token assertion of Feroze's Parsi roots and
suitably clandestine. He neither mixed in Parsi society nor followed
any Zoroastrian customs. Unlike most Parsis, his upbringing
in Allahabad meant that he spoke flawless Hindi and was even
known to recite passages from the Gita with some expertise. The
couple had two children: Rajiv, who became prime minister, and
Sanjay, who was his mother's key adviser during the Emergency
and remained her trusted sounding board till his death in an air
crash in 1980 at the age of just thirty-three.

Feroze and Indira drifted apart a few years into their marriage.
One reason was that Nehru was possessive of his daughter and
he insisted that she move to Delhi to serve as his official hostess
when he was made prime minister of India. Feroze, whose
easygoing nature concealed surprising reserves of pride, remained
in Lucknow where he was the director of the *National Herald*
newspaper. Some in the Congress viewed Feroze as a lightweight.
He was fond of gossiping in coffee houses and had a reputation
as a womaniser. He was adept with his hands and had a knack
for gadgets. It was a skill that both his sons inherited and perhaps
manifested itself in Sanjay's enormous enthusiasm for setting up
the Maruti factory to manufacture a small Indian car. Despite
the generally cool relationship between Nehru and his son-in-law,
the former helped Feroze get jobs, first at the *National Herald*

newspaper in Lucknow and then as the general manager of the *Indian Express* in Delhi.

Feroze was elected for three terms as a member of Parliament from Rai Bareilly and was also a member of the constituent assembly. At the start of his parliamentary career, he was a backbencher who listened rather than participated. He came into his own gradually, making a famous maiden speech on 6 December 1955. He took aim at the Bharat Insurance Company, run by industrialist Ramkrishna Dalmia, and exposed the widespread misuse of funds. As a result of Feroze's findings, Dalmia, then the richest man in India, was sentenced to two years in prison. The insurance industry was nationalised. Feroze's greatest scalp as a crusader against corruption was that of the powerful Finance Minister T.T. Krishnamachari (TTK). In one of the first financial scandals of independent India, Krishnamachari was a casualty of the decision by the nationalized Life Insurance Corporation of India, at the behest of Haridas Mundhra, a shady businessman, to invest a huge sum of money in six ailing companies in which Mundhra owned a significant number of shares. Feroze established that the finance minister was not being strictly truthful when he said that the investments, made by sidestepping normal LIC procedure, were made to prop up the stock market. The LIC investments, Feroze revealed, were made on a day when the stock exchanges were closed and that it had every appearance of a bailout for Mundhra.[26] Feroze's accusations were confirmed by a commission of enquiry headed by the retired Bombay High Court Justice, M.C. Chagla. TTK, a good friend of Nehru's, had perforce to resign. The prime minister was livid. (TTK was made finance minister again six years after his resignation.)

But his 'feckless' son-in-law had shown a reporter's nose for a story and the instinct and zeal to execute an investigation. He was willing to undertake long hours of research to make sure he was on firm footing and was also willing to take on his own party in the interests of the truth, not least his own father-in-law. Feroze was not just muckraker-in-chief; he was responsible for getting the Protection of Publication bill passed by the Lok Sabha. The bill sought to protect journalists covering parliamentary proceedings from prosecution. Ironically, nineteen years later, during the Emergency, Indira Gandhi quashed her own husband's law protecting press freedoms.

Even when Feroze moved to Delhi from Lucknow, he continued to live separately from his wife in his MP's quarters, though he did eat breakfast every morning at the prime minister's residence and was close to his sons. The estrangement with his wife, though, was so total that at one stage Feroze wanted to formally divorce Indira so that he could marry a beautiful young woman from a prominent Muslim family in Lucknow.[27] Nehru put his foot down as he did not want the family name to be besmirched by scandal. He asked his friend Ramnath Goenka to find Feroze a job at the *Indian Express* in Delhi. Incidentally, after Feroze broke the Mundhra scandal in Parliament, he was relieved of his job and office car almost overnight.[28]

Disillusioned with the party, his marriage over for all intents and purposes, Feroze became a bitter and frustrated man towards the end of his life. A heavy smoker and drinker, he refused to give up his habits even after his first heart attack. On 7 September 1960, Feroze suffered his third heart attack. His wife, by then the president of the Congress, was away in Kerala at a conference. She returned to Delhi immediately when she heard her husband was in hospital but was tired and chose to go home from the airport. Feroze was alone in hospital when he died, four days short of his forty-eighth birthday.[29] It came as a surprise to Nehru to discover that Feroze had a considerable following as an anti-corruption crusader. The streets were lined with people all along the 3-kilometre funeral route. Feroze had proven in Parliament that he had integrity; so overwhelming was the Congress's majority that it could be argued that Feroze, the Congress MP and prime minister's son-in-law, was the de facto voice of the opposition.

Though Indira may have informally separated from her husband, she always retained a soft spot for the community of her in-laws. In November 1976, she even acceded to an extraordinary request from the Parsis that an empty Air India Boeing 707 with an all-Parsi crew and some priests be requisitioned to transport the sacred live burning fire from an old fire temple in Aden to India. The fire was eventually installed at a temple in Lonavala. The small community of Parsis who had settled in the Yemeni city, once a British protectorate, at the end of the nineteenth century had returned to India by 1967 when the British left.[30]

* * *

While Parsis have usually made a name for themselves in conventional professions, they are certainly no philistines, but lovers of music, both Western and Indian, and the arts. Some have even carved out successful careers in what was once uncharted territory in India. For instance, Dadi Pudumjee was fascinated by puppets since his childhood, and despite the odds became an internationally renowned puppeteer, and the first non-European to head the eighty-year-old international puppetry forum Union International De La Marionette (UNIMA). He stepped down in 2021 after three terms as president. The late Astad Deboo was a pioneer of modern dance in India who performed across the world with artists like Pina Bausch, Alison Becker Chase and Pink Floyd.

8

Trailblazing Women

No account of the Parsis in the professions would be complete without mention of the achievements of the remarkable Parsi women. They were trailblazers in many spheres. As far as women's literacy and emancipation, Parsis were considerably more progressive than their fellow Indians from other communities. While in 1842, Sir Jamsetjee Jejeebhoy had to have his daughters educated in the utmost secrecy, already by 1870, over 1000 Parsi girls were enrolled in secondary schools in Bombay. By the nineteenth century, Parsi merchants shrewdly surmised that the advantage of socialising when accompanied by their womenfolk, as the British did, would get them further in colonial India than behaving like their Hindu counterparts. Sir Jamsetjee Jejeebhoy set an example by taking his wife and daughters-in-law to balls, or to the opening ceremonies of various institutions that they had endowed.[1] Wealthy Parsis also began to open Gujarati schools for Parsi girls.

Bhikhaiji Cama, who is discussed in greater detail in a later chapter, is probably the best-known Parsi woman and exemplified two important characteristics seen in many Parsi women: empowerment and a deep social conscience. But even before Bhikhaiji, Parsi women occupied important roles within their families and were not restricted to domestic chores. Some of the women in the Wadia and Readymoney families, for instance, helped run the family businesses. Bhikhaiji played a major role in the freedom struggle, but she was not the only one. True, the revolutionary instinct of many Parsi women was snuffed out by their families whenever possible. Dhanbai Petit, for instance, came down to breakfast in a khadi sari, only to be ordered by her mother, Maneckbai, to go back and change. Maneckbai told her daughter that the Petits were a family loyal to the king and that if Dhanbai wanted to follow Gandhi, she might think about leaving home and moving to his ashram. Dhanbai obediently went upstairs and changed.

But another aristocratic Petit girl, Mithuben, defied her family rather than renounce her principles.[2] The granddaughter of the first Baronet Sir Dinshaw Petit, Mithuben had followed Mahatma Gandhi since his return from South Africa. She stood behind Gandhiji at Dandi (then Navsari) on 6 April 1930 when he broke the British Raj's salt laws. (Mithuben is one of the main figures in Deviprasad Roychowdhury's iconic sculpture in Delhi depicting the march to Dandi.) Two years earlier, she participated in a campaign headed by Sardar Patel against taxes imposed by the British. Mithuben took up social work full time and opened an ashram in Maroli, Gujarat, for poor tribal and scheduled caste children. She taught them useful skills, from handling sewing machines to leather work and dairy farming. She also opened a hospital for the mentally ill.

* * *

Progressive Parsi women can take the credit for breaking many glass ceilings for Indian women. Cornelia Sorabji, who came from a Parsi family that converted to Christianity, was the first woman to graduate from Bombay University, passing the exams with flying colours. She went on to study law at Oxford University in 1892; in those days, Oxford did not grant women degrees, so when she returned to India, Cornelia did her LLB from Bombay University. It took until 1923 for her to be admitted to the Bar after the law was changed to allow women to enter the profession. She practiced in the Allahabad High Court, but she worked mostly with purdahnashins, women who observed purdah and as a result were ignorant of their legal rights in India, including their shares in the estates of fathers and husbands who had died. She wrote several books on her experiences and two autobiographies.

Technically, though, the honour of being the first Indian woman barrister goes to another Parsi, Mithan Jamshed Lam (née Tata), who studied law at Lincoln's Inn, London when women had just begun to be permitted to practise as barristers. In fact, in 1923, Mithan had the distinction of being the first woman ever called to the Bar from Lincoln's Inn, as well as the first Indian woman to be called to the Bar in Britain.

Mithan's interest in law was aroused because of her championship of the suffragette movement. She and her mother Herabai Tata, while on a holiday in Kashmir in 1911, had a chance encounter with Sophie Duleep Singh, a feminist who proudly flaunted the badge 'Votes for Women'. Both Mithan and her mother were drawn to the cause, despite reservations from some in the freedom movement who felt that fighting for independence from colonial rule should be the priority. The struggle for gender equality should in the meanwhile take a backseat. Mithan saw no contradiction between the two demands. 'Men say Home Rule is our birthright. We say the right to vote is our birthright and we want it,' she declared in 1918, paraphrasing Gandhiji's famous words. Mithan and her mother were selected by women's groups in Bombay to represent their view before the British parliament, which was considering a package of reforms later to become known as the Montagu-Chelmsford Reforms.[3] While unsuccessful in the immediate goal, the British parliament did leave the issue to the discretion of individual Indian provinces. In 1921, both Madras and Bombay presidencies granted limited women's franchise.

While in London to plead the women's cause, Mithan also pursued a legal education and a master's degree in economics from the London School of Economics. When she returned to India, she found herself the sole female lawyer in the all-male Bombay High Court. 'I felt like a new animal in the zoo,' she recalled. According to court lore, she got her first case because the client had instructed the solicitor to engage the only woman lawyer as it would be a double humiliation for his opponent when he lost. However, she soon built up a formidable reputation on the strength of her legal skills. Her cases ranged from prosecuting currency counterfeiters to defending the validity of a Jewish betrothal.[4]

Apart from her work as a lawyer, Mithan helped frame legislation for marriage and inheritance and was a staunch advocate for women and child rights. She worked at the grassroots, in slums, to better infrastructure and health facilities and helped resettle refugees during the Partition. She mentored generations of Indian lawyers and was an active member of the All India Women's Conference. After Independence, she added another first to her credit: she became the first woman sheriff in India.[5]

Another Parsi, Freany K.R. Cama, was the first woman to become a licentiate of medicine and surgery at Bombay University in 1892; she went to Belgium and Britain for further training and worked for some time at the Pasteur Institute in Paris before returning to Bombay and joining the Cama and Albless Hospital.[6] Freany Cama was one of the first two women selected to study abroad as J.N. Tata scholars, having been chosen personally by Jamsetji Tata himself. Banoo Jilla, who qualified in 1936, was among the country's first women dental surgeons and Perin Jamsetji Mistry Bhiwandiwala may well have been the first Indian woman architect.

Enterprising Parsi girls were eager to explore unchartered territory. Homai Vyarawalla, for instance, was India's first female photojournalist. A graduate of the Sir J.J. School of Art, Homai learnt photography from her husband Maneckshaw, who worked for the *Times of India*. She began taking photographs in the 1930s but was so low-key that, initially, she published her photographs in the *Illustrated Weekly* under her husband's byline. Later, she adopted the unusual pseudonym 'Dalda13', the number plate of her car. She covered the Second World War in Burma and then moved to Delhi, where she worked for the British Information Service. The only woman in a crowd of male photojournalists, Homai worked on being unobtrusive, blending into the background so that her subjects were not conscious of the lens being focused on them. She became known for her candid shots of leading political figures during the last years of the British rule in India and the first years of Independence. Her pictures of Jawaharlal Nehru caught the public imagination, as did the ones she took for *Time* magazine of the young Dalai Lama's entry into India. With characteristic modesty, she attributed her success to the fact that she happened to be in the right place at the right time. In 1970, shortly after her husband's death, Homai decided to give up her profession, upset by the pushing and shoving and general unruliness of the new generation of Indian photographers.[7]

Rati Petit (not to be confused with 'Ruttie' Petit who married Mohammed Ali Jinnah) was another gifted photographer and artist. Schooled in England before being sent to finishing school in Paris, Rati took a deep interest in the artists of the Bengal School upon her return to India. After the breakup of her first marriage with the well-known criminal lawyer Karl Khandalavala, Rati lived in Shantiniketan, Bengal for twelve years where she studied art, music and dance. She was the last pupil of the famous painter Abanindranath Tagore (a nephew of Rabindranath). At Shantiniketan she met Ernst Hoffman, a German professor of philosophy at the Vishwa Bharati University who had converted to Buddhism and taken the name 'Lama Angarika Govinda'. She married him and took the name 'Li Gotami Govinda'.

Li Gotami and her husband undertook two dangerous expeditions to western and central Tibet between 1947 and 1949. She was accorded the singular honour of being permitted to photograph, sketch and study monastic life in all its aspects. Her extensive collection of photographs and fresco tracings brought to the world's attention the vanishing art and culture of the golden age of Tibetan Buddhism in the eleventh century.[8]

This line of globally recognised Parsi women photographers continues into the present day with Sooni Taraporevala, a contemporary photographer who has an international reputation for her solid body of work. Apart from her perceptive and eye-catching pictures of her own community, she has written screenplays for award-winning films such as *Salaam Bombay*, *Mississippi Masala* and *Such a Long Journey*. This last film, incidentally, is based on the novel by Rohinton Mistry, a Parsi who lives in Canada and counts the Booker Prize among his many awards. The main characters of Mistry's bestselling novels, *Family Matters* and *Such a Long Journey*, are Bombay Parsis, as he once was.

If some Parsi women have been recognised for taking pictures, others have been recognised for being the subject of pictures. Among the first Indian women to make their presence felt in Hollywood was Persis Khambatta, a beauty queen, model and actor in Bombay who later moved to Los Angeles. Most of her film roles in the West were minor, but she caused a sensation as the shaven-headed Lieutenant Ilia in the *Star Trek: The Motion Picture* (1979). Another Parsi beauty, Katy Mirza, was discovered by a *Playboy* talent scout when she was working at the desk of London's Hilton's hotel. Katy agreed to strip for the magazine's centrefold, earning both publicity and considerable notoriety in straitlaced 1970s' India. Another trendsetter in the 1960s and 1970s was dancer Uttara Asha Coorlawala who travelled to the United States to study at Smith College. She learnt from and collaborated with avant-garde choreographers such as Martha Graham and Ted Shawn and went on to evolve her own fusion-infected style. She started her own company and tutored many in her evolving style of dance from American modern to Indian new age.

Incidentally, the first woman of colour to marry into the snobbish British aristocracy was a Parsi, Bapsy Pavry, who, in 1952, wed Henry Paulet, the sixteenth Marquess of Winchester, a title created in the sixteenth century. This was more than half a century before the British tabloids were agog over a girl of part-African blood, Emma McQuiston, marrying Viscount Thynne, heir to the Marquess of Bath, and actress Meghan Markle, also of mixed race, marrying Prince Harry. The Marchioness of Winchester was an intrepid social climber who hustled her way into an alliance with the sixteenth Marquess of Winchester. The only snag in Bapsy's matrimonial triumph was that the marquess was ninety years old, twice divorced and in love with someone else. Within days of the wedding, he left her for his mistress. The fifty-one-year-old Bapsy successfully sued her rival, his former fiancée Eve Fleming—the mother of author Ian Fleming, the creator of James Bond—on the grounds of the alienation of her husband's affections. But she lost her case in appeal. She exacted her revenge by bequeathing £500,000 to the city of Winchester, provided the community centre at the Winchester Guildhall was named after her and featured her portrait prominently on the premises. The civic authorities of the city of Winchester, which had actually nothing to do with the Winchester title and family, prevaricated for years. But when the legacy swelled to over a million pounds, they fell in line.[9]

Duncan Fallowell recounts Bapsy's strange tale in his book on misfits who once made the headlines and then abruptly disappeared. He salutes her social-climbing skills, noting that 'in a world of good manners, it is amazing what pushy people can achieve'. Bapsy and her brother Dr Jal Pavry worked as a team, sending off letters on one pretext or the other to the crowned heads of Europe as well as other luminaries such as the Viceroy of India, Shah of Iran, Crown Prince of Saudi Arabia and former British prime minister Neville Chamberlain. She got courteous replies from many of them and even managed to meet several grandees. The daughter of a Zoroastrian high priest, Bapsy lived in England and was presented as a debutante at the court of King George V and Queen Mary.[10]

Ordinarily, being a scholarly high priest of Navsari is not the sort of role that pays well. But Bapsy's family had large estates in Baroda and considerable wealth which enabled her to travel around the world. Fallowell's portrait though, does not present the complete picture. She may have been a social climber and one of the first Parsi debutantes at court, but she also graduated in 1925 with a degree in Indo-Iranian languages from Columbia University in New York. She did a master's thesis in Avesta and the literature of India and Persia. She also regularly attended international conferences on religion and peace. In her will, apart from a bequest to Winchester town, Bapsy funded an international peace prize in the name of her brother Jal Pavry at her alma mater. She also left money for two annual lectures in her name and that of her brother at Oxford University.[11]

Another Bapsy who made waves in society, albeit closer to home, was Bapsy Sabavala, the daughter of the second Cowasji Jehangir baronet. Bapsy was highly individualistic, eccentric and deeply committed to various social causes. She was among the pioneering suffragettes in India and a great animal rights advocate. Among her many campaigns, she began a chain of cooperative stores where poor Parsis could find employment and opened a home for battered wives.

Unfortunately, Bapsy's eccentricities often overshadowed her considerable humanitarian efforts. Tales about her were legion and were a regular source of entertainment in the Parsi society of her day. Bapsy had a huge collection of dolls of all sorts and sizes and she often had them chauffeur-driven to her friends' houses to spend the day. A close friend of hers, Zenobia Lord, recalls how once, when a doll was left with her for the day, Bapsy was furious to find that it had been left carelessly unattended on top of a cupboard. She was considered a terror by the drivers plying their buggies on Malabar Hill who knew she was liable to snatch their whips and even give them a hiding if she felt they were mistreating the horses. She once ran up a huge bill at a fancy hotel in Montreaux, Switzerland, where she had stayed for several months in the 1930s with her two sons. Her father, who supported her extravagances up to a point, ordered her to return to India. When, after a month, no payment was forthcoming from Bombay, Bapsy suggested to the hotel owner that she would leave her sons behind as surety. The proprietor, who did not want to be saddled with two weeping children, told her firmly to take her sons and leave. He knew that the baronet would eventually cough up.[12]

Incidentally, Bapsy was also the matchmaker who brought together Kekoo and Khorshed Gandhy by inviting them to one of her charity balls. This remarkable Parsi couple opened Chemould Gallery, a fulcrum for the Progressive Art Group in India. The talented husband-and-wife team were the catalysts in the 1960s for the careers of some of the biggest names in the art world, including S.H. Raza, M.F. Husain and F.N. Souza.

Bapsy's own marriage was unhappy. Her husband, Ardeshir Sabavala, came from a respectable Surat family but not from the kind of wealth to which Bapsy was accustomed. Inevitably henpecked, Ardeshir nonetheless made a name for himself in civic affairs and also worked for the Tatas for many years. Still, his wife would not let up. She once brought a horse up the stairs of the Taj Mahal hotel, of which Sabavala was then general manager, just to embarrass him. Eventually, Bapsy demanded a formal divorce from her husband. She insisted on arguing the case herself before the Parsi divorce court and invited all her friends to witness the proceedings. After Bapsy's death, it was discovered that she had sold off all the heirloom jewellery she'd inherited from her mother to finance her many causes, particularly animal shelters. She had fakes made of the Readymoney jewels before she sold them so that her family and others wouldn't become suspicious. Her two sons had perforce to put out notices disassociating themselves from her debts, so that they would not be left bankrupt.

To turn to a less colourful but perhaps equally controversial figure, the Parsi feminist and social activist Avabai Wadia tirelessly propagated family planning and contraception at a time when Indian society was extremely resistant to the idea. Born into an affluent family from Ceylon, she was educated in London, where she obtained her LLB in 1934 from the University of London. Though she started her professional life as a lawyer in London and Colombo, it was only after her move to Bombay that Avabai discovered her vocation. She joined the All India Women's Conference in the early 1940s and soon discovered that she was ideologically committed to popularising contraception, particularly among those unable to afford large families. In 1949, using her inheritance, she set up the Family Planning Association of India, and was its president for thirty-four years. She was also one of the international suffragettes who founded the International Planned Parenthood Federation and was president of the association twice. It was thanks to her efforts and connections with Jawaharlal Nehru that family planning was included as one of the targets in the government's First Five Year Plan. Avabai was a respected name who was appointed to numerous government committees and commissions, where she used her position to promote the causes in which she believed.[13]

In the twenty-first century, the social-activism baton has been picked up by another high-profile Parsi woman whose work in particular areas has helped shape government policy. Anu Aga (her full name is 'Arnawaz' but, as with many Parsis, she prefers to go by her pet name) was formerly the chairperson of the large multinational engineering firm Thermax, which specialises in environment and energy equipment. Anu is regularly listed as one of the richest women in India. Forced to take over the reins of the firm when her husband Rohinton died prematurely, Anu rose to meet the challenge despite her inexperience. But she is known for more than just her success in business. In 2002, as the chairperson of the western region of the CII, she created a stir by criticising then Gujarat chief minister Narendra Modi's government for its callous treatment of Muslim refugees left homeless by communal riots. Few Indian businesspersons have the courage to speak out so openly against state governments for fear of reprisal for their companies. There were immediate repercussions—other Gujarati businessmen threatened to quit the CII and the director general of the confederation, Tarun Das, eventually visited Ahmedabad to apologise. Though she was treated as a persona non grata by the CII, Anu was unfazed. Her fellow team members on the committee, Cyrus Guzder and Rahul Bajaj, stood by her. A few years later, when the Congress came to power in Delhi, the CII wanted to make her its first woman president. But she, wisely, declined a poisoned chalice, saying she had retired from her business career at the age of sixty and wanted to set a precedent by not clinging to office.

Retirement, though, only meant that Anu was preparing to throw herself into her causes. The Manmohan Singh government, impressed by her record, appointed her as a member of the powerful National Advisory Council, chaired by Sonia Gandhi, on which Anu served for a decade. The NAC was responsible for several key bills passed by the UPA government, including the Right to Information Act and the Food Security Act. In 2012, Anu was nominated to the Rajya Sabha by the Congress government.

Anu's father, Ardeshir Bhathena, was an unusual Parsi. He wanted to join Gandhiji in the independence struggle, but at the insistence of his father, a doctor, he accepted a job with Godrej & Boyce instead. Later, he set up his own company, dealing in steel and sterilisation equipment. He lived frugally; the family had a one-bedroom flat between Dadar and Matunga, though they could afford a much larger space and a fancier address.

But Ardeshir ploughed everything he earned back into the business.[14] His spartan lifestyle rubbed off on his daughter who, despite her wealth, lives extremely simply. At an early age, Anu demonstrated that she had a mind of her own, walking out of the house for a while when her father objected to her then choice of boyfriend. After a BA in Economics, Anu went on to do an MA in social work from TISS, topping her class in both years. But she points out, 'Not once was it suggested to me that I could join the family business. That was for my brothers.' She won a Fulbright scholarship. This was around the time she met her future husband, Rohinton Aga, a good friend of one of her brothers.

Rohinton had a degree from Cambridge University and well-paid work at a British firm in Calcutta. But when he and Anu met, he was on the verge of giving up his cushy boxwallah job because he did not believe he could grow to his full potential as an executive at a foreign company. Ardeshir had started his own company, Wanson, after falling out with his partners. Eventually, when he and Anu, married now, moved to Poona, Rohinton joined Anu's father to fill the gap left by Anu's brothers. With two children to look after and an ailing mother-in-law, Anu confesses that she was content to socialise and play cards, even though her husband encouraged her to find a job. Differences cropped up between her father and husband, though, and eventually Anu's father decided to sell his company to Rohinton. In 1980, the company was renamed 'Thermax'. Just as Rohinton's company was beginning to take off, though, he suffered a massive heart attack, followed by a stroke.

The brilliant, driven businessman lost his memory and could no longer remember the alphabet or recognise his wife. It took Anu two years of devoted nursing, with speech and physiotherapy, to get Rohinton back on his feet and return to his old self. Fourteen years later, in 1996, after successfully taking Thermax public, Rohinton suffered a second heart attack and passed away. The company board met two days after Rohinton's death. It insisted that a reluctant Anu take over as the executive chairperson since the family owned 62 per cent of the company's stock. (After her husband's first heart attack, Anu had begun working in Thermax's HR department.) She had little time to mourn. Then, a little over a year later, her only son, Kurush, who had returned home from abroad shortly before his father's death, died in a car accident. On the advice of a friend, she took a Vipassana meditation course, which she feels gave her the inner strength and positivity to carry on. 'Once I start things, I am never a quitter,' she said to me.

When Anu was appointed the chairperson of Thermax, the Indian economy was doing poorly and the company fared badly. The share price fell from Rs 400 to Rs 36 in a year. She received an anonymous letter from a furious shareholder, lambasting her for allowing the company's fortunes to dissipate. The criticism affected her deeply. She pulled herself together and took some tough measures. Despite the board's protests, for instance, she hired a pricey multinational consulting firm to help her figure out how to revamp the company, insisting, 'Can we afford not to hire the consultancy firm?' By the time she retired at the age of sixty in 2004 and handed over the reins to her daughter, Meher Pudumjee, Thermax was not just back on track but doing better than when it went public.[15]

After her son's death, Anu decided to donate one-third of the family's dividends to worthwhile causes. As a trained social worker, she had clear ideas of where she wanted the money to go. Anu singled out two charities, Akansha and Teach for India, both NGOs started by Shaheen Mistri, a fellow Parsi. Anu is the chairperson of the Teach for India Foundation. The foundation has set up a network of college graduates and highly qualified professionals who volunteer to serve as fulltime teachers for two years at low-income schools. In 2012, the Congress government selected her to Parliament in the nominated members category meant for outstanding achievers.

A Parsi woman who is a role model in the sports world is Diana Edulji. She dominated women's cricket in India for decades and made a name for herself internationally as well. Diana is the best-known Indian woman cricketer. *Indian Express*'s sports editor, Sandeep Dwivedi, compares her standing in the sport to that of Sunil Gavaskar's in men's cricket. Diana set a global record by becoming the first woman cricketer to take hundred Test wickets. A dynamic all-rounder, Diana was an outstanding left-arm spinner as well as a hefty hitter of the ball.[16] She captained the Indian World Cup team in 1978 and once again in 1993. She represented the country in cricket for a very long spell and made such a mark that many young women were attracted to a sport which had been considered a male preserve.

It was thanks to the enthusiasm and dedication of another Parsi lady, Aloo Bamji, with the encouragement of a few male cricketers, notably Vijay Merchant, that in 1970 the first woman's cricket club in Mumbai was formed. The club was known as the Albees Cricket Club after Aloo. When Diana was growing up in the railway quarters at Badhwar Park, Mumbai, she was the only girl in the neighbourhood cricket eleven. The boys could not ignore her since she was more than a match for any of them. A natural sportswoman, Diana was also keen on table tennis and basketball but the competition was tough and she decided to enroll in the Albees club almost from its inception. In 1974, she took part in the first Indian nationals. And a year later, the Australian team came to play in India.

At that time, the women's team was run by a separate federation from the Board of Cricket Control in India (BCCI) and the players had to make a lot of sacrifices. Unlike male cricketers who were accorded five-star luxury, perks and star status, there were no sponsorships and no money whatsoever in the women's game. When the Indian women's team visited Australia, they were lodged in the homes of NRI families. In domestic cricket, women players were expected to travel on unreserved railway tickets and were not provided any hotel accommodation. They were put up in cheap guest houses and government institutions. During summer practice sessions in Delhi, they found the dorms at the stadium so hot at night that they regularly dragged their mattresses onto the playing field, where they would be woken up in the morning by dogs licking their faces. 'We struggled a lot,' Diana told me, 'but we played with passion and even put in our own money.' Indeed, to play in the World Cup, the women on the team were expected to chip in Rs 10,000 each. The Maharashtra contingent applied to then chief minister Abdul Antulay for assistance.[17]

It was thanks to the inspiring example of the pioneers in the game, particularly the outspoken and forceful Diana, that more young girls took to the sport. In 2006, the BCCI finally agreed to administer women's cricket. Diana was part of the delegation that approached the BCCI, asking for women's cricket to be run by the same federation as the men. Since the inclusion of women's cricket in the BCCI ambit, things finally began to change for Indian women cricket players. Tournaments and facilities were upgraded and the players started earning some money. Before this, women players had to rely on jobs with the Indian Railways to see them through. The then railways minister Madhavrao Scindia was a supporter of the team and, on Diana's recommendation, had offered jobs to female players with a future in the sport. Her contribution in promoting women's cricket was not restricted to her performances on the field. Her work with the Indian Railways included recruiting and training promising talent. It was thanks to Diana's efforts that for many years the overwhelming majority of players in the Indian team were from Indian Railways.

In 2017, the Supreme Court appointed a four-member committee of administrators to implement the Lodha Committee report and hold elections in the BCCI, a body tainted with scandal because of the high stakes involved. Diana was the only sportsperson on the committee. She played an important role in shaping cricket policy even if she occasionally had sharp differences with her male colleagues. 'That's the way I am,' she says. 'I wanted to ensure that the body is run as per its constitution.' When she disagreed over policy, she put her foot down even if it meant antagonising fellow members. For instance, she refused to brush sexual harassment charges levelled against the then BCCI CEO under the carpet. 'I believe in calling a spade a spade. As long as I am following the right path,' she says frankly. Even if that path made the boys club of Indian cricket uncomfortable.

During her term as administrator, Diana managed to give Indian women's cricket a big push. There is a newfound respect for the sport and women are now winning lucrative endorsements. The increased money, prospects and fame has impacted performances for the better. In the last four World Cups, Indian women have made it to two finals and one semifinal.

* * *

The story of enterprising Parsi women continues. A recent example is Kainaz Messman who opened a bakery in a disused doctor's clinic, and within fifteen years built up a national chain of over fifty outlets located in Mumbai, Pune, Delhi, NOIDA and Gurgaon. The professionally run patisserie chain, Theobroma, is known for its mouth-watering brownies, mava cakes and lemon tarts as well as other tea-time snacks. It was established by Kainaz along with her sister Tina. The sisters inherited some of their recipes from their mother, as also her flair for cooking and baking.

9

Pioneers in Cricket, Theatre and Cinema

Young Parsi boys started playing cricket at a time the rest of India preferred to be mere spectators and watch British soldiers and civilians compete against each other in this very English sport. For the adventurous Parsis, cricket offered yet another opportunity to imitate the British rulers and explore new avenues. Initially other Indians held back, perhaps partly because of fears of violating social norms. The late author and cricketer Vasant Raiji writes that Parsi schoolboys were receiving instructions in cricket as far back as 1839 and the game was initially referred to simply as 'bat ball'.[1] When the boys grew up they formed the first Parsi club in Bombay in 1848, named the Oriental Cricket Club. Initially, the Parsis played the game in their flimsy muslin sudrehs. But the religious undergarments were impractical, with the sudrehs flapping in the wind and the ball sometimes getting entangled in the kasti (girdle). Soon players were wearing shirts over the undergarment.

In 1876, Ardesher Patel founded the Parsee Cricket Club and he yearned to test his team's mettle against British players. Before the Parsee Cricket Club, cricket clubs in India were open only to Europeans. (The first club in India was the Calcutta Cricket Club formed in 1792.) In 1877 Patel arranged for the Parsi team to play against the whites-only Bombay Gymkhana team. Though the Parsi team lost to the Bombay Gymkhana by sixty-three runs, Patel's appetite was whetted and he was determined to take a Parsi team to England. The English were tickled that this was one group of natives that had enthusiastically embraced their nation's favourite sport and the *London Graphic* newspaper wrote approvingly of the possibility of 'descendants of the Fire Worshippers of Persia' competing with the English county teams. The visit got delayed and interest in the Indian press and the British media mounted.[2] The tour was held up for a few years because of a dispute between Patel and one Kaikhoshru Kabraji, which led to a libel suit. (As mentioned earlier, Parsis being extremely litigious by nature, instances of them slapping libel suits to defend their honour is not uncommon.) The members of the team which finally visited England in 1886 were selected not merely for their prowess in the sport, but also for being affluent enough to pay for the voyage. A Surrey professional was engaged as a coach.

Expectedly, the Parsis were thrashed on their first English tour, losing nineteen matches, drawing eight and winning only one. But there was considerable interest in Britain over the tour and applause for the spirit of the visiting team. *Cricket Chat*, in a feature on the tour, observed, 'Anything which can tend to promote an assimilation of tastes and habits between the English and the native subjects of our Empress Queen cannot fail to conduce to the solidity of the British empire. The Parsee fraternity is the most intelligent as well as the most loyal of the races scattered over our Indian possessions.'[3] The last match was played at Cumberland Lodge, Windsor Great Park, at the express desire of Queen Victoria. Two royal princes were part of the opposing team. In 1888, a second Parsi team visited England and the Parsis displayed a marked improvement in their skills.

In 1889–90, G.F. Vernon led the first English team of amateurs to tour India. By the time they reached Bombay, they had won six matches and drawn one. They defeated the Bombay Gymkhana by an innings and the Parsi team was expected to meet the same fate. The team captain, J.M. Framjee Patel, provided a delightful account of this encounter in his book *Stray Thoughts on Indian Cricket*.[4] Patel believed that the golden age of Parsi cricket began on 30 January 1890, with the match with Vernon's team. The entire city was very excited over the game. Businesses came to a standstill on the two days of the match. A crowd of some 12,000 descended on the Azad Maidan. The elite of Bombay sat in canvas tents and many Parsi women showed up as well. Zoroastrian priests in their white robes recited special chants invoking blessings for the victory of their co-religionists.

Against all odds and predictions, the Parsis won the match. Two Parsi fast bowlers, Machliwalla and Meherwanji Pavri, were the heroes of the hour. Sir Dinshaw Petit and Sir Jamsetjee Jejeebhoy hosted lavish receptions for both teams. Exuberance over the victory was immense. Sorabji Bengali was so elated that he declared that this was an avenge for the battle of Nahavand, where centuries earlier the Zoroastrians were badly beaten by the Arabs and had to flee. While most of England and the native press praised the team for their unexpected win, some unsporting Englishmen blamed the defeat on the lavish lunch arranged by Jamsetji Tata at his mansion during the game. The tour stimulated much interest in cricket and soon other Indians also took to the sport.

A second British visiting team led by Lord Hawke toured India in 1892–93. The Parsis in Bombay once again won the match by 109 runs. The *Bombay Gazette* wrote, 'The success which the Parsees achieved by their superior fielding and bowling was greeted with thunders of applause.' At the reception at the Yacht Club, Lord Hawke admitted he had prepared a speech on the assumption that his team would be victorious. While Hawke and his players were sporting about their defeat, by then, some Britishers in India were infuriated that the natives were besting their colonial masters at their own game. A few spoilsports even tried to ban the general public from practicing cricket on the Azad maidan on the pretext that the ground should be reserved instead for playing polo.

After forming India's first cricket team, the Parsis' next step was to open a sports club of their own on the lines of the Bombay Gymkhana. A group of sports enthusiasts met at the venerable Parsi Ripon Club (it remains exclusively for Parsis even today though women are now admitted as associate members) in the Fort area. A committee was formed to organize a sports pavilion and start a gymkhana, with Jamsetji Tata as chairman, his son Dorab as honorary secretary and several important members of the community included. A prime site was selected at Kennedy Sea Face opposite Marine Drive; within three years land was obtained and a handsome pavilion came up.

The much improved Parsi team soon began to beat the European teams of the Bombay Gymkhana and Poona Gymkhana quite regularly. With the matches fairly one-sided, the governor of Bombay, Lord Harris, a famous cricketer himself and patron of the sport who played a major role in popularizing cricket in the Bombay Presidency, suggested that the Parsis should compete against a combined team of Englishmen selected from the Bombay Presidency. The first Presidency match was played in Bombay in July 1892 and is remembered as the 'fire engine' match as the fire brigade had to be summoned to drain out the rain water from the ground. The match had eventually to be abandoned because of the slushy conditions. But the Presidency matches became a popular annual feature until 1906.

Cricket was increasingly becoming a popular sport for both the classes and the masses. Between 1892 and 1906, twenty-six matches were played; the Parsis won eleven, the Europeans (Presidency) ten and five matches were drawn. The matches evoked enormous public interest and cricket fever soon reached other parts of the country. Lord Harris acknowledged the role of Parsis in popularizing the sport. The fame of the Parsi cricketers had spread beyond the British empire. In 1903, when Jamsetji Tata met American President Theodore Roosevelt in connection with setting up a steel plant in India, Roosevelt enquired 'How is Parsi cricket getting on?' He sent a message of encouragement.[5]

While some dubbed the Parsis toadies for imitating the Brits, in fact the Parsis fought fiercely in cricket for equal rights. For example, initially only Englishmen were permitted to be umpires for the Presidency matches. After objections, a concession was made that the Parsis could chose one of the two English umpires. The secretary of the Parsee Gymkhana, J.M. Divecha, turned down the offer, pointing out that it was difficult to select English umpires since 'our acquaintances with such people is very limited. Times have changed and many Parsi cricketers have the background and experience to be an umpire.' The European Gymkhana, while agreeing in principle, insisted on putting obstacles in the way of selections from a potential panel of Parsi umpires. In retaliation, the Parsee Gymkhana decided to stop selecting players for the Parsi team for the Presidency matches. Finally, Dorab Tata intervened to end the stalemate. By the turn of the century, Parsis were accepted not only as cricketers but also as umpires.[6]

Undoubtedly, the best Parsi captain in those early days was Meherwanji E. Pavri, and as long as he was in charge, his team won most matches. A medical doctor by training, he also played for English county teams while training in the UK. Incidentally, even among the Parsis, some orthodox elements were initially opposed to the game. Pavri recalls his conservative grandfather threw his bat into the fire because he didn't want Pavri to play. Pavri simply went to the timber yard of his uncle, a contractor, and helped himself to a huge log of wood. He instructed the carpenter to shape a bat. The value of the whole log was ten times the cost of the bat to be made out of it and Pavri's furious uncle gave him a beating, but he also ensured that no one burnt the bats in future.[7] Pavri can be counted as the first in a long line of India's iconic greats in the sport. He played for the Parsis for twenty-eight years and captained the side for twenty-four years. He was an all-rounder, a resourceful leader with his massive physique and impressive bearing. Veteran sports editor and author Gulu Ezekiel counts him as the country's first great fast bowler.[8]

At the start of the twentieth century, the Hindus taking inspiration from the Parsis had not only taken up cricket in a big way but had also set up their own Hindu Gymkhana next to the Parsi Gymkhana. This was followed by gymkhanas for the Muslims and the Christians. As the other teams joined the highly competitive cricket tournaments, the Presidency matches became known as the Triangulars, the Quadrangulars and finally the Pentangulars. These tournaments were the predecessors of the Ranji Trophy and today's IPL. (Incidentally, the practice of teams being formed on the basis of religion was finally ended at the urging of Mahatma Gandhi. Popular Parsi cricket commentator A.F.S. Talyarkhan also campaigned to discontinue the communal Pentangular matches, which were against the spirit of secularism.)

With others in the country taking to cricket, inevitably the Parsis lost their dominant position. But it is to the credit of the community that for years they continued to throw up outstanding players. Eleven Parsis have represented India in Test cricket. In the 1950s and early 1960s, three Parsis in a team was not uncommon.[9] Rusi Modi, who played in both pre- and post-independent India, was a phenomenon with several records to his credit. In the 1944–45 season, Modi became the first to accumulate over 1,000 runs in a season in the Ranji Trophy, totalling 1,008 runs in just five matches at a phenomenal average of 201.00. The record stood for forty-four years.[10]

Parsi cricket after Independence reached its zenith when Nari Contractor led the Indian team to the West Indies in 1962. The Indian Eleven for the first and second Tests included four Parsis—Contractor, the opening batsman; Polly Umrigar, a former captain nicknamed the 'palm-tree hitter' in the Caribbean; Farrokh Engineer, wicket-keeper and dashing batsman; and Rusi Surti, stylish left-handed all rounder. For a community which barely comprised 0.02 per cent of the total Indian population to contribute 36.4 per cent of the players in the cricket team was a truly stupendous feat.[11]

It was on this tour that Contractor came close to death when an express delivery from Charlie Griffith—the fast bowler with a controversial action—fractured his skull. After two life-saving operations, Contractor was able to play the game once again but never made it back to the Indian team.

Polly (Pahlan) Umrigar stands out among all the latter-day Parsi players. He played 59 Test matches, scoring 3,631 runs at an average of 42.22. He was a shrewd captain and studied the weaknesses of his opponents. A brilliant fielder, his greatness lay in the effortless ease with which he made impossible catches look easy. He was certainly the most effective player of his time. Sunil Gavaskar paid tribute to Umrigar, observing, 'If there is one cricketer who lives, breathes, dreams cricket, it is Polly Kaka.' Rusi Modi described him as 'certainly the most effective player of his time'.[12]

Engineer played for English county Lancashire from 1968 to 1976, the longest county stint by an Indian professional. He also had the honour of being the only Indian to be chosen for the prestigious World XI team both against England in 1970 and against Australia in 1971–72. He is the only Parsi cricketer to have represented India in the World Cup (first Prudential World Cup in England in 1975) and toured England three times (1967, 1971, 1974) as well as West Indies, Australia and New Zealand. Surti was the star performer for India on the twin tours of Australia and New Zealand in 1967–68 and became the first Indian cricketer to play domestic cricket in Australia, representing Queensland in the Sheffield Shield competition. He is one of the few to end his Test career with a high Test score of 99 and was an outstanding fielder.

Since 1974–75, when Engineer retired, no Parsi man has played for India. In fact, the last Parsi to play Test cricket was Ronnie Irani in the 1990s. Irani played for England and not for India since he was born in the UK, his father having migrated from Bombay. In 2021, there was excitement in the Parsi sports world when Arzan Nagwaswalla, a left-arm pace bowler from Surat, was included in the Indian touring squad as a standby in the series against England that year. Though he did not get a chance to play a Test match, he is still a good prospect for Gujarat in the Ranji Trophy.

Sadly, today the Parsi Gymkhana, which trained generations of Parsi cricketers, and the Zoroastrian Gymkhana see few Parsi youths on the playing fields. Diana Edulji, former India woman's cricket team member, bemoans, 'Parsi youngsters are no longer coming forward to take part in sports. Maybe youngsters have other interests such as education and the social media and of course our population is also dwindling.'[13]

Apart from cricket, Parsis also made a name for themselves behind the scenes in sports administration, on selection panels, as umpires, authors and media personalities. One of the most legendary sports commentators in India was A.F.S. Talyarkhan, whose pet name was Bobby. His lively five-to-six-hour-long uninterrupted commentaries on All India Radio in the 1930s and 1940s made him a household name. He quit when AIR wanted him to share the commentary slot with others. AFST also wrote a very popular sports column in the *Times of India*, his signature last line being, 'Do you Get me Steve.'

In yesteryears, Parsis stood out in several other sports too. But in recent times, there are rare mentions of Parsi achievers in the sports pages. Jehan Daruwala is an exception, who has made a breakthrough as a racing-car driver competing in FIA Formula 2 championships. The brilliant jockey Pesi Shroff, often rated the best in India, has won 106 Classics and the Indian Deby numerous times. Karl Umrigar and Kaikhushroo Irani were other great jockeys who lived up to the Parsi tradition of excellence in horsemanship. Tragically, both died prematurely because of injuries on the racetrack. And long before Cyrus and Zavereh Poonawalla were known for their vaccines, they were recognised in horsing circles for producing star racehorses at their stud farms, some of which have been exported to other countries for racing.

No write-up of the Parsi community's contribution to sports in India would be complete without recalling the role of Sir Dorabji Tata, who was the man behind facilitating India's early participation in the Olympics. In 1919, Dorabji, the second chairperson of the Tata group, was chief guest at the annual sports meet of the Deccan Gymkhana in Poona. He noticed that most of the participants were poor farmers from the nearby villages who ran barefoot but were clocking timings which were close to European standards. (Sir Dorabji was himself a dedicated athlete who during his two years at the University of Cambridge distinguished himself at sport, winning colours at Gonville and Caius college in cricket, rugby and football. He also played tennis for his college, coxed his college boat, won a number of sprint events and was a good horseman.) Seeing the spirit of these peasant athletes, Sir Dorabji aspired to organise an Indian team which could participate in the Olympics, the most prestigious sporting event in the world.

The Tata chief persuaded Sir Lloyd George, then Governor of Bombay, to obtain affiliation for India with the International

Olympic body at Antwerp in 1920. Since there was no official Indian team, he set up a committee on his own to select the most promising athletes and supervise their training and diet. He believed that with proper food and training under English coaches, the athletes would make India proud and he financed their travel and stay. Thanks to his efforts, the Indian team, comprising four athletes and two wrestlers, marched proudly at Antwerp Stadium. The athletes selected from all over the country came from humble backgrounds and were chosen for their natural talents. Though the team did not win any medals, they began the glorious tradition of India's participation at every Olympics since.[14]

Sir Dorabji returned from Antwerp fired with the enthusiasm that the country nurture a sports culture. He hired a physical director from the YMCA to visit every part of the country to spread the message and launch a sports talent hunt. In 1924, for the Paris Olympics, Sir Dorabji once again bore a share of the expenses for the Indian team. But by now his campaign for spreading an Olympic spirit had caught on and the national team was also funded by various Indian states. The Indian Olympics Association (IOA) was formed in 1927 with Sir Dorabji as its first president. The IOA selected India's team to the 1928 Amsterdam Olympics. This time around, the contingent also included a men's hockey team, championed by the Indian Hockey Federation. Nine nations competed in hockey, and India was the only non-European team. The Indian team excelled and beat the Netherlands in the final to claim its first ever Olympic gold medal, a historic moment for India. (Incidentally, the British, who had one of the best hockey teams in the world, stopped sending a hockey team to the Olympics after India started participating.) Sir Dorabji was also selected a member of the International Olympic Committee. Dorabji, incidentally, was one of the founders of some of Bombay's first sports clubs, including the Parsi Gymkhana, the Willingdon Sports Club and the Cricket Club of India.

* * *

The early Indian cinema industry is actually a direct descendant of Parsi theatre. In the mid-nineteenth century, Parsis took to theatre as a commercial venture and also as a forum for showcasing their literary and cultural talents. They were inspired to enter this new medium after watching English touring theatre companies perform in Calcutta and Bombay. While theatre in India may be traced back to the Sanskrit dramatist Kalidasa's plays, it was only with the Parsi Natak Mandalis that commercial theatre came into its own in the country. Rashna Nicholson, assistant professor of Theatre Studies at the University of Hong Kong, specifies that 'the social history of the modern South Asian theatre and cinema is intimately bound with the Parsi community. From its inception in 1853, Parsi theatre grew in 40 short years into the subcontinent's primary form of visual entertainment that catered to the needs of a new Indian middle class and industrial working class.'[15]

When Parsi theatre first began, there was nothing particularly Parsi about the content and its influence extended far beyond the community. It took its name because it was the brainchild of the commercially minded community which operated several travelling theatre groups and handled all the roles from acting to play writing, from composing the music to fashioning the screen props. The theatre groups were often started by amateurs who later turned full-fledged professionals, backed by Parsi businessmen. The language spoken in the first plays was largely Gujarati. But as travelling theatre groups moved all over the country, the Parsis realized that the most easily understood common language was Hindustani and Urdu and they switched accordingly.

The first 'natak' (as the plays were called) was *Roostum Zabooli and Sohrab* in 1853, staged by the company Parsi Natak Mandali, owned and directed by Gustadji Dalal, who had the support of the city's Parsi intellectuals, including Dadabhai Naoroji, K.R. Cama and Ardeshir Moose. The play was an adaptation of a Persian epic, the tragic story of King Rustom and his son Sohrab, written by the Persian poet Ferdowsi. More than a dozen other theatre companies soon cropped up with names such as the Zoroastrian Theatre Club, the Student Amateur Club, the Empress Victoria Theatrical Company and the Alfred Natak Mandali.[16]

Initially, the plays were largely Persian legends, adaptations of Shakespearean plays and comedies from folk tradition. In 1857, there was a special performance of the *Taming of the Shrew* for women, which sanctioned the entry of women into public spaces. Initially, however, the female roles were all played by good-looking young boys and occasionally professional female singers and dancers. An Englishwoman, Mary Fenton, was also a prominent actress. Even the relatively emancipated Parsis had some reservations about women appearing on stage at the start.[17]

Between 1853 and 1860, many drama companies sprang up and several also shut down after going bust. There were only a few theatre houses in Bombay, so Parsi theatrical companies frequently toured the country, including Gujarat, Bengal, Tamil Nadu and Uttar Pradesh. Some, like the Victoria Theatrical Company founded by famed theatre artist Khurshedji Balliwala, even travelled to places as far away as Rangoon, Singapore and London.

Since the theatre groups travelled frequently in north India, they often employed Muslim writers for preparing scripts in Urdu. Indo-Persian and Islamic culture was a major influence because of the use of lilting Urdu poetry. By now audiences had increased substantially and comprised all sections of society, including labourers, domestic servants and sailors. The intellectual class could not dictate tastes and the new populist trends were not to the liking of the respectable Parsi reformists who first encouraged the theatre movement.

To inject more meaning and respectability, Kekhusro Kabraji, in 1875 established the Society for Amelioration of Drama with the idea of uplifting the content of the plays. He popularised a move to revive Hindi literature and produce plays shorn of spectacle, gimmicks and elaborate costumes. Kabraji staged the play *Harishchandra*, translating Sanskrit into pure (shudh) Gujarati as opposed to the free-wheeling colloquial Parsi Gujarati which incorporated words from English and other languages. The play was a huge success.

Several of the Hindu mythological themes of plays were of virtuous and long-suffering heroines being victimized and later being vindicated by emerging triumphant through a trial by fire. Women came in large numbers to watch these tear-jerkers and Kabraji even provided cots in the playhouse yard for children to sleep while the play was on. Nicholson argues that while some plays demonstrated loyalty to the imperial project (for example, during the Indian Uprising of 1857), others that glorified a Hindu mythological past helped indirectly fuel the nationalist movement. From the mid-1870s the theatre provided icons and motifs for what would come to be understood as Hindu revivalism. She notes that performances depicting female mythological characters helped gestate the figure of Bharat Mata, thereby inadvertently visualising a nation long before elite discourses of political revolution and national awakening came to the fore.[18]

Parsi theatre in those days was known for its melodrama and entertainment, incorporating numerous songs, hybrid music borrowed from both the West and India. The proprietors spent lavishly on stage sets, borrowing European traditions in use of backdrops, curtains and Western props. They also imitated the English practice of staging small farces side by side with the main storyline. The influence of Parsi theatre spread across much of India.

The early Indian films, with their sub-plots, dialogue, song and dance sequences and fate-driven themes, reveal very clearly the influence of the playwrights of Parsi theatre.[19] The first silent movie in India, *Raja Harishchandra*, produced by Dadasaheb Phalke (1913), is basically a screen version of the stage play which had such enormous appeal. Most of the Parsi actors and directors simply switched to films from plays, particularly after sound recording techniques enabled filmmakers to produce talkies. Incidentally, the first Indian sound film in 1931, *Alam Ara*, was directed by a Parsi, Ardeshir Irani. He also produced the country's first colour film, *Kisan Kanya*. Irani was a low-key, little-known figure. The prints of his original film have been lost and even the publicity material for *Alam Ara* mentions only the names of the actors Zubeida, Master Vithal and Prithiviraj Kapoor. The *Arabian Nights*-type fantasy moved away from mythologies. Irani, whose family members were fairly recent migrants to India, made 145 silent films before his first sound film. He admitted to getting the idea of producing a talkie after watching at the Excelsior theatre in 1929 the Bollywood movie *Show Boat*, a film which had 40 per cent sound.[20]

Among the early entrants to the film world was Jamshed Wadia (generally known by his initials JBH), who set up the company Wadia Movietone in 1931. JBH was a pioneer of many film forms. He produced India's first documentary newsreel, the first Indian movie to be filmed in English, *The Court Dancer*, and the country's first TV series *Hotel Taj Mahal*. JBH's background was unusual for the film industry. He was the aristocratic descendant of the Wadia shipbuilding family and was expected to take up an approved career in law, finance or the civil services. He was, however, hooked on cinema from his school days when he watched Hollywood action movies, serials and thrillers whenever he could.

After graduating in English literature, JBH applied for entrance to the Indian Civil Service. He was rejected because of his poor eyesight. His father died around this time, so perforce he became the family's sole breadwinner and took up a fellowship tutoring English as well as working in a bank. On the sidelines, he wrote scripts for Bombay film producers. He began personally making films in 1928, towards the close of the silent era. His first film was *Vasant Leela*, a silent film with a social theme.

JBH was a fan of stunt films and was fascinated by Douglas Fairbanks's film *Mark of Zorro*. After he started his own company, his first film was *Thunderbolt* or *Diler Daku*, inspired by Zorro. His brother Homi, who had joined JBH in the movie business as a cameraman, helped direct the film. After *Diler Daku*, JBH produced *Toofan Mail*, a railroad thriller, borrowing the cliffhanging technique he had closely observed in American movies. JBH then embarked on making a series of action movies and, unusually for those times, he selected a female actress, Miss Padma, to play the rescuer rather than the stereotypical heroine acting the damsel in distress. Miss Padma was very beautiful but rather delicate. And JBH finally found the female role model he was looking for in his action movies in an Australian girl, Mary Ann Evans, who had grown up in India and had an athletic build. His new heroine was an expert swimmer and rider and, most importantly, she had also worked as an acrobat in a circus. She was rechristened Fearless Nadia and the movie in which the whip-yielding sprightly actress wearing tight pants and sporting dark glasses starred was *Hunterwali*, which became a runaway hit. It led to a series of successful films with Fearless Nadia as the heroine. JBH had introduced the concept of empowered womanhood into films.

JBH experimented with different genres: action movies, thrillers, historicals and mythologies. He even made a film without a single song, an unheard of concept in those days. It was a feature film in Sindhi on Hindu–Muslim unity to help promote secularism. He sought to educate audiences through entertainment. JBH was an intellectual who was very politically aware; the guests at his residence in Worli included not just India's leading freedom fighters but also internationally renowned revolutionaries such as Vladmir Lenin and Mexican revolutionary Emiliano Zapata. He was a close friend of M.N. Roy, the founder of Radical Humanism, and JBH was a believer in Roy's philosophy.

JBH and Homi had professional differences and Homi eventually formed a separate film company, Basant Pictures, which made the rest of the Nadia series of movies. Homi was a businessman and stuck to sure-shot money-spinners such as action movies and mythologies, while JBH was more creative and experimental. However, the brothers remained personally close and Homi usually directed JBH's movies. Homi eventually married his heroine Nadia after decades. Initially, he hesitated in making his relationship official because of the firm disapproval of his extended family, though JBH supported him throughout and told him not to be bothered by social conventions. Both brothers worked well into their seventies and introduced many film stars to the screen.

Another icon of the early Indian cinema is Sohrab Modi. He was a well-known Parsi Shakespearian play actor who eventually gravitated to the cinema world. He occupies a special place in the history of Indian cinema for his grand cinematographic creations and interpretations of medieval and modern Indian history. A perfectionist and an idealist, Modi was an outstanding actor, director and producer, whose company, Minerva Movietones, produced films such as *Pukar*, *Sikandar*, *Jhansi ki Rani*, and *Khoon ka Khoon*. Modi is best known for his grandiose historical themes, but he was also deeply committed to producing socially relevant films. His early films dealt with such contemporary social issues such as alcoholism, *Meetha Zahar* (1938) and divorce, *Talaaq* (1938). He also acted in other director's films. His last film was Kamal Amrohi's *Razia Sultana* (1983). Modi's perfectionism and spell-binding voice were his USP. (Modi was not a particularly good student and when he asked his school principal for advice as to what profession to take up, the principal replied, 'With your voice, you should either be an actor or a politician.'[21] *The Maharashtra Herald* described him in his obituary as 'the grand old man of the film industry'.

The best-known Parsi actor today is Boman Irani, a hilarious comic who entered Bollywood only after he had crossed forty. He started helping out in his family's potato chips and hospitality business when he was young. For ten years he acted on the stage, winning accolades for his acting talent, before he finally got his first break in the film world. His second film in 2003, *Munna Bhai MBBS*, was a smash hit and his role earned him a Filmfare nomination for best actor in a comic role. Since then he has not looked back, acting in numerous hits including *Three Idiots* and *Lage Raho Munna Bhai*. The multi-talented Irani is also a photographer and script writer and plans on directing movies after he has completed his acting commitments. The old-fashioned logo of his new production house, Irani Movietone, is designed to resemble the Parsi production houses of the past, Wadia Movietone, Minerva Movietone et al.[22]

The Parsi influence on Indian cinema was not just on the artistic side. In the early days of the movie business, many of the cinema theatres and distribution rights were owned by Parsis. Even outside Bombay, it was common for a large town's main cinema hall to be owned by a Parsi. Sohrab Modi's family, for instance, had distribution rights in Gwalior and later, his younger brother Keki expanded to the whole of western India. Besides this, Keki owned a chain of twenty-seven theatres in ten cities, including Bombay. He was nicknamed 'Mr Hollywood of India' since he represented all the major film companies from the USA.

With the arrival of the talkies, inevitably Parsi theatre was much diminished, since many transferred to the new medium. Parsi theatre, however, experienced a revival in the 1950s. Modern Parsi theatre was based on contemporary themes, generally laced with much humour and often parodying and targeting the idiosyncrasies of the community. Humour is one of the Parsis' defining characteristics and quintessentially Parsi jokes are usually directed at their own community. Several Parsis made a name for themselves in Gujarati and English theatre, but none matched the popularity and sparkling genius of Adi Marzban.

Marzban entertained Bombay audiences for almost five decades with the rib-tickling Parsi Gujarati plays he wrote and produced independently. Though he helped run his family newspaper *Jam-e-Jamshed* and was editor for many years, he was completely immersed in Bombay's theatre movement, staging both English and Gujarati plays. A UNESCO scholarship gave him a chance to study theatre at the Pasadena Playhouse in California, USA. On his return to Bombay, he switched entirely to Parsi theatre and played the dominant role in modernizing and popularizing Parsi plays. His play *Piroja Bhavan* is considered a milestone in the birth of modern Parsi theatre.

For generations of Parsis, no Navroze celebration was complete without watching one of Marzban's plays. He felt that, discarding the pretensions of many Bombay theatre persons who imitated Western drama, 'theatre must spring from the Indian way of life'.[23] Some critics felt that Marzban's light-hearted humour and rib-tickling jokes detracted from serious theatre. Marzban believed that his farcical, sometimes risqué, plays with urban settings were a 'slice of life'.[24] The multifaceted genius who wrote around 100 Parsi-Gujarati plays and produced some 5,000 radio and television scripts was a major influence on a whole generation of English and Gujarati theatre talent in Bombay. Apart from theatre and journalism, Marzban also played several musical instruments and was a gifted painter. He set the template for the characterisation of a typical Parsi Bawa in Bollywood films, a frequent figure of fun for his eccentricities.

10

The Iconic Four

Among the galaxy of Parsi achievers in contemporary India, at least four have achieved iconic status. (Five, if you include Nani Palkhiwala.) The two best-known Parsis in independent India are Homi Bhabha and Field Marshal Sam Manekshaw. If a poll were taken outside the country, though, the honours would go to the celebrated conductor Zubin Mehta and the fabulous Freddie Mercury (Farrokh Bulsara), lead singer of Queen, who died in 1991 but remains in the view of many perhaps the greatest ever frontman of a rock band.

Homi Bhabha laid the foundations for Indian science in the new postcolonial nation. He led India towards the development of atomic energy, thus paving the way for the country to become a nuclear power as part of its goal of self-reliance. Manekshaw, just five years younger, gave India her greatest military victory in modern times. Bhabha and Manekshaw had very different temperaments and upbringings, but were similarly patriotic and driven to achieve excellence. Bhabha was a Parsi aristocrat from Bombay: versatile, sophisticated and knowledgeable in many fields, not just in his core areas of science and engineering. Doors had been opened for him all his life because of his privileged position and his genius. The earthy, outspoken Manekshaw, an upcountry Parsi boy, was cut from a very different cloth. Despite his outstanding military record, his career was stymied at one point by a vengeful politician. Had fate not intervened in the forms of the Chinese invasion and later the war with Pakistan, in which India fought to secure East Pakistan its independence as Bangladesh, Manekshaw might have been forgotten by future generations.

Ten years apart in age, Zubin Mehta and Freddie Mercury did not come from very different backgrounds but were miles apart in temperament and lifestyle. Zubin proudly wears his heritage on his sleeve. Although a 'citizen of the world', a cosmopolitan as comfortable in the capitals of Europe as he is in Israel, North America or South East Asia, he never stops reminding people that he is an Indian passport holder and a proud Parsi. In turn, Parsis glory in his achievements, referring to him possessively as 'apro Zubin' (our Zubin). Freddie, in contrast, appeared uncomfortable, or uninterested, in his ethnic origin. He hid his original nationality, religion and roots. His impact on the world was as a British, rather than Parsi, rock star. So much so, in fact, that in 2005 when a prestigious Parsi publication compiled an encyclopedia of eminent Parsis of the twentieth century, it did not mention Freddie, while listing a large number of lesser-known musicians and music industry figures.

If Zubin, now in his eighties, can look back in contentment at a very fulfilled life surrounded by family and friends, a tormented Freddie before his premature death at the age of forty-five from bronchial pneumonia, connected to the AIDS he might have been suffering for nearly a decade, once remarked bitterly: 'You can have everything in the world and still be the loneliest man. And that is the most bitter type of loneliness. Success has prevented me from having the one thing we all need: A loving ongoing relationship.'

The two great musicians never met, but Zubin said in a 2012 interview in Israel that he 'loved Freddie Mercury because he was a Parsi like me, he had that little Parsi belly. He's one of us.'[1]

Of these four outstanding Parsis, only Homi Bhabha was not solidly middle class. Bhabha was born into the rarefied atmosphere of the Parsi upper crust. On his mother's side, he was a descendant of the baronet Sir Dinshaw Petit and from his father's side he was a nephew of Sir Dorab Tata, the chairman of the Tata Group through the first three decades of the twentieth century. The paternal side of Bhabha's family was known for its scholarship. His grandfather was the Inspector General of Education in Mysore while his father, Jehangir Bhabha, was a barrister from London with an MA from Oxford who joined the Tata group as a legal adviser and rose to be a director.[2] Bhabha was one of fortune's favourites. When introducing him at the annual meeting of the Indian Academy of Science, held in Nagpur in 1941, the physicist and Nobel laureate C.V. Raman described Bhabha as a 'great lover of music, a gifted artist, a brilliant engineer and an outstanding scientist—he is the modern equivalent of Leonardo da Vinci'. Raman at that stage did not realize that Bhabha's multidimensional personality had still other facets, by which eventually he would be best remembered by a grateful nation. He was a visionary who built and administered institutions and was responsible for India's great leap forward in science, particularly in atomic research, at the dawn of Independence.

Born into wealth and culture, the infant prodigy attended one of Bombay's leading schools, The Cathedral and John Connon School, the de rigueur institution for the children of Bombay high society. As stimulating as school, if not more so, would have been the intellectual atmosphere at home. His musical talents were nurtured by his maternal aunt, Cooma Panday, and his paternal aunt, Lady Tata, an accomplished pianist. Bhabha took painting lessons from the well-regarded artist Jehangir Lalkaka, and at the age of seventeen, Bhabha's self-portrait won a prize at the Bombay Art Society exhibition. Two years earlier, at just fifteen, Bhabha was said to have had a good grasp of Einstein's theory of relativity.

His privileged childhood meant that he was exposed to the conversations of his parents' prominent dinner party guests, including politicians and industrialists. When still a boy, he was already familiar with such luminaries as Mahatma Gandhi, Sardar Patel, Jawaharlal Nehru and his father, Moti Lal, among the many other fine minds who would shape independent India. Bhabha's father, aware of his son's mathematical abilities, wanted him to take up engineering and hoped that he might eventually join the Jamshedpur steel works. But when Homi arrived at Cambridge University, he was clear that his first love was not engineering but physics. He pleaded with his father 'Physics is my line, business or a job as an engineer is not the thing for me.'[3] Father and son reached an understanding. If Bhabha obtained a first class in his Engineering Tripos, he could stay on at Cambridge and read for the Mathematics Tripos. Homi passed both examinations with flying colours before plunging into research for a doctorate in physics.

Exciting breakthroughs in physics in Europe had brought about a major revolution in the field during this period. Cambridge University's Cavendish Laboratory was one of the epicentres of the recent, rapid developments in physics, particularly on the experimental side. Ernest Rutherford, the 'father of nuclear physics', headed the institution and Bhabha wanted to be part of its pioneering research. While on a travelling studentship, he visited Neils Bohr's Institute for Theoretical Physics at the University of Copenhagen, another centre of dizzying scientific progress. Bhabha interacted with many of the great names in the field such as Wolfgang Pauli, Enrico Fermi and Paul Dirac. There was peer appreciation for Bhabha's own award-winning research at the cutting edge of physics, particularly electrodynamics to which his most notable contributions include the 'Bhabha scattering' and the theory of electrodynamic cosmic ray showers.[4] Bhabha would probably have stayed on and continued his research in the charmed academic ambience of Cambridge but for a quirk of fate.

He took a short vacation to visit his family in 1939 but while he was in India, the Second World War broke out. During the war, most academic research in England came to a standstill; scientists were either enlisted for war duty or switched to war-related research. Bhabha had perforce to remain in India and shuttled between Bombay and Bangalore, where he joined the IISc. His princely lifestyle was disconcerting for some of the other scientists. He stayed in the posh West End Hotel, would arrive at the institute in a limousine and moved in glamorous, intellectually and culturally influential circles, most with a left-socialist bent of mind. But Bhabha also worked late into the night and produced several well-received research papers. In 1941, he was elected a Fellow of the Royal Society, London. He was the eighth Indian to be so honoured and the fifth, and youngest, to have achieved the distinction in his lifetime.

Bhabha realised that opportunities for scientific research in his homeland were limited, but after the war, he made a deliberate choice to remain in India. He believed fervently that if the right facilities were provided, Indian scientists could compete with the best in the world. To realise this dream, he turned to the Sir Dorab Tata Trust, which since 1942 had been funding his post as a full professor at the IISc. Bhabha took advantage of his close relationship to the Tatas and informally sounded out JRD, who remained chairman of the group for over half a century, about putting a proposal before the Sir Dorab Trust to bankroll a research centre for theoretical and experimental physics comparable to the best in the world. While an eminence like C.V. Raman might have had similar ambitions, he did not have Bhabha's enviable contacts. The Tata trustees agreed to finance the proposed scientific centre and, as it was supposed to be located in Bombay, the state government and Bombay University also chipped in with financial and administrative support.

TIFR was formally inaugurated on 19 December 1945, and marked the beginning of modern scientific research in India, creating the talent pool that would ultimately lead India into the nuclear age.[5] Bhabha went about building his institution with single-minded determination, meticulous attention to detail and flair. He visited different research centres abroad to see and experience for himself the latest developments in fundamental research, particularly atomic and nuclear science in the wake of the atomic bomb. He also undertook a recruitment drive of promising Indians working in foreign institutions.

Bhabha foresaw that atomic energy would play an important role in the economy and industry of nations and that if India was not to be left behind, it was imperative to pay heed to this branch of science. He inspired his close friend Jawaharlal Nehru with his vision and a Board of Research on Atomic Energy was set up up barely eleven days after Independence, with Bhabha as the automatic choice for chairman.[6]

Undoubtedly Bhabha, throughout his life, enjoyed opportunities that would have been denied to others less well connected. His proximity to Nehru was a great advantage. Indira Gandhi once said that Nehru had given standing instructions that if Bhabha called, the phone was to be given to him immediately. The two men shared the same aristocratic background, tastes and value system. Bhabha treated Nehru as a friend and colleague rather than as a prime minister, addressing him informally in his letters as 'Bhai'.

When Bhabha wanted to expand the TIFR to build a campus, he coveted an area on the southern tip of Bombay in Colaba, which belonged to the navy. Though Krishna Menon, the defence minister, objected strongly, Bhabha approached Nehru directly and got his way. Privately nicknamed the 'maharaja' by his fellow scientists because of his expensive and fastidious tastes, Bhabha had an impeccable eye for aesthetics and abhorred the drab post-Independence architecture of most government buildings. He set his institutions in scenic surrounds instead, creating a harmonious working environment. Bhabha even got Nehru to agree that 1 per cent of the budget would be spent on acquiring Indian art, an amazing luxury when the government's mantra was frugal socialism. (The TIFR, thanks to Bhabha, today has one of the finest collections of contemporary Indian art in the country.) It was not paintings and building plans alone that Bhabha selected with great care; he also personally looked into every detail of the layout of the gardens and replanting trees. He provided a work atmosphere for his scientists which was very different from the normal government offices, where even the smartest of buildings turned grimy over time. In addition, he ensured that the scientists had opportunities to visit advanced centres abroad, that the best facilities be made available to them in India and a generous policy on sabbaticals be followed, giving scientists time to publish, do research and bring new knowledge and experience back to TIFR.[7]

Some resented Bhabha's cocksure approach and apparent arrogance. Once, Wolfgang Pauli and other foreign scientists were infuriated to discover that they were travelling to a conference in India on a bus, while Bhabha followed in his private chauffeur-driven car. But Bhabha was no spendthrift dandy; he was a caring, benevolent aristocrat whose staff adored him because he always went out of his way to help them through any personal difficulties.[8]

He was a man of tremendous verve and vitality who believed in packing as much as he could into his life. In 1934, Bhabha, then twenty-five, wrote to a female friend: 'Since I cannot increase the content of life by increasing its duration, I will increase it by increasing its intensity. Art, music, poetry and everything else that

I do will have this one purpose—increasing the intensity of my consciousness and life.'[9]

The handsome bachelor Bhabha, with his charm, background and obvious importance, was a magnet for the opposite sex. He developed some close friendships with women but his most constant companion, whose striking face he captured often in his paintings, was Pheroza Wadia. Known in Bombay society by her pet name 'Pipsy', she was a trendsetter and leading member of the Time & Talents Club. During the Chinese aggression in 1962, Bhabha, off his own bat, allotted a corner of the compound of his official offices in the Old Yacht Club at Apollo Bunder for the Time & Talents Club to open a popular restaurant, Victory Stall, where home-cooked Parsi meals were served and the funds donated for the welfare of jawans.

By 1954, a separate Department of Atomic Energy was set up directly under Nehru, with Bhabha appointed as the secretary to the Government of India, DAE. Along with heading the DAE, he continued as the director at TIFR. Bhabha had convinced Nehru of his vision to develop a comprehensive programme for atomic energy, extending over a wide spectrum. In inter-governmental negotiations, Bhabha generally managed to get very favourable terms for himself because of his charisma, self-confidence and old friendships in the international scientific community. For instance, it was thanks to Bhabha's friendship with Wilfrid Bennet Lewis, the prominent Canadian nuclear scientist and Bhabha's old rowing teammate at Cambridge, that the Canadian government funded the setting up, in the 1950s, of the Cirus nuclear reactor, only the second in the country. Though set up for research purposes alone, the plutonium generated by the reactor's fuel rods was secretly used to make India's first nuclear bomb.[10]

Because of Bhabha's closeness to Nehru, the powerful Indian bureaucracy, which generally stymied the growth of the government's technical and specialised institutions, dared not interfere in Bhabha's domain. Which is why the first nuclear reactor was commissioned in Asia at Trombay, the headquarters of the Atomic Energy Establishment, as early as 1956 and, by the time of Bhabha's death in 1966, the Tarapur atomic power station had been built and India's atomic energy programme had developed a wide base. Bhabha made it clear that nuclear disarmament could not be separated from general disarmament. A staunch nationalist, he realised the importance of India being strong and self-reliant and was in favour of the country acquiring nuclear capabilities for defensive purposes. Nehru, as a leader of the Non-Aligned Movement, could not support Bhabha's views openly, but he nevertheless sanctioned plans for Bhabha to set up the infrastructure necessary to make nuclear weapons.[11] Bhabha was responsible for the spadework that made the Pokharan implosions in 1974 and Pokharan II in 1998 possible. It was his protégé and fellow Parsi, Homi Sethna, who would eventually take over as chairman of the Atomic Energy Establishment, renamed Bhabha Atomic Research Centre, who completed the task. Sethna was by Indira Gandhi's side at Pokharan when the first nuclear tests were conducted in May 1974. The far-sighted Bhabha also understood that space would become an important field of research for Indian scientists.

Tragically, Bhabha died before his time. He was only fifty-seven and on a routine fight to Geneva on 23 January 1966, when the Air India plane *Kanchenjunga*, in which he was travelling, crashed into Mont Blanc in the Swiss Alps. The country and the world mourned his loss. The *Guardian* newspaper wrote that 'India has lost a prophet and a guide in Dr Bhabha who single-handedly at the start, set the nation's sight on the highest peak of technology.'[12] If Bhabha had remained in Europe and continued with his research, he could well have ended up with a Nobel Prize, but the institutions he left behind were of far greater significance to his country. They laid the scientific foundation for the new republic. Bhabha was the most powerful man in Indian science for nearly three decades after Independence and his influence continues to bear fruit.

Field Marshal Sam Manekshaw, nicknamed 'Sam Bahadur' (Sam the Brave), is loved not just because he led India to its greatest military triumph as an independent nation—defeating Pakistan decisively in 1971 and enabling the creation of Bangladesh—but because of his colourful, larger-than-life persona. Manekshaw is often described as a 'solider's soldier': a commander whom the troops adored because of his bravery, gentlemanly conduct, humour, candour and genuine concern for his men. Sam fiercely guarded the dignity of the army and resisted any attempt at interference or undermining the functioning of the defence forces by the political classes. Whether his outspokenness and lack of guile would have helped him rise to a similar stature in today's far more politicised army is questionable. It was a combination of his remarkable qualities as a military man and destiny, the luck of being born in the right place at the right time, that put Sam on the pedestal he still occupies. Statues of the field marshal in cantonments throughout India continue to serve as a source of inspiration for our jawans.

Sam grew up in Amritsar, Punjab's religious and cultural capital, and his daughter Maja Daruwala feels that his upbringing in a small town helped mould his personality. 'He was,' she says, 'an upcountry Parsi. Had he been brought up in Bombay, he might have been completely different. Possibly he would have loved music, art and poetry, but he wouldn't have been the daredevil he was, a robust and hardy man who spoke fluent Punjabi. He became cosmopolitan only with seniority, when he began to be posted abroad and interacted with people from different countries.'[13]

Sam came from middle-class stock. His grandfather was a school teacher in Valsad, a small town in Gujarat. Morarji

Desai, India's fourth prime minister, was one of his students. It was Sam's father, Hormusji, who bettered the family's finances by graduating as a medical doctor from Bombay. But when his practice did not take off in Bombay, Hormusji was advised to try his luck in Lahore. On the train to Lahore, his wife Hilla and he broke their journey in Amritsar and decided to stay on and make a go of it in the town. There were almost no Parsis in Amritsar and perhaps in part because of his novelty, Hormusji quickly became a popular doctor. He had six children and the four boys were sent to Sherwood, a well-known boarding school in Nainital. All six children became successful professionals.[14] Sam was a top student and dreamed of studying to be a doctor in England. Since he was only sixteen when he graduated, his father, who had earlier promised Sam that he could go abroad to study, asked him to wait for two years. Finances were tight as both Sam's elder brothers were already in the UK studying engineering. While biding his time at the Hindu Sabha College, Sam happened to see a government advertisement inviting applications for the first-ever course at the newly opened Indian Military Academy in Dehradun. (Earlier, Indian officers were trained at the Royal Military Academy at Sandhurst, England.) Of the 1,200 hopefuls who applied in 1930, Sam was one of just sixteen to be selected.

Before being commissioned in 1932 to the Frontier Force Regiment, Sam was attached to a British Regiment. Critics of the British government felt that training in British regiments was designed to make brown sahibs of Indian officers. In the Second World War, Sam was a captain in charge of a Sikh company. In Burma, he displayed exceptional bravery while trying to prevent the Japanese from capturing the Sittang Bridge across the Chindwin river. He continued to command his troops even after receiving bullet wounds in the abdomen. Sam owed his life to his Gurkha orderly Sher Singh who carried him on his back to the medical-aid post. When the doctor suggested that Sam was too far gone to be treated, Sher Singh threatened the doctor with his pistol, saying, 'Please treat him or I will shoot you.' The British commanding officer and brigade commander, in recognition of Sam's valour, immediately dispatched a signal to headquarters recommending him for the Military Cross. It was feared that his chances of survival were slim and the medal could not be awarded posthumously.[15]

In September 1946, Sam was promoted to lieutenant colonel and assigned to General Headquarters in the Military Operations Directorate where, ironically, Yahya Khan, Pakistan's military commander in 1971 and Manekshaw's direct counterpart, was also posted. Sam knew him well. During Partition, Sam had a ringside view of the annexation of the princely states, since he was directed by Sardar Vallabhbhai Patel, the deputy prime minister, to accompany his secretary V.P. Menon, who was in charge of ensuring accession. Sam witnessed firsthand the accession of Kashmir. And in 1948, Sam, by then a brigadier, signed the ceasefire in Kashmir on behalf of the commander-in-chief, General Roy Bucher, albeit reluctantly since the raiders had retained the northwestern part of the state. General Bucher described Sam as one of the best staff officers he had ever met.

It was during Sam's tenure as a major general in Jammu in 1958 that he had his first run-in with the then defence minister, Krishna Menon, a left-wing politician who believed that the army chief should be subservient to his political bosses. He asked Sam for his opinion of General K.S. Thimayya, the army's chief of staff, with whom Menon had differences. Sam, who held Thimayya in high regard, gave Menon a blunt response: 'Mr Minister, I am not allowed to think about him, he is my chief. Tomorrow you will ask my brigadiers and colonels what they think of me. It's the surest way to ruin discipline in the army. Don't do it in future.'[16] Menon flew into a rage and accused Sam of retaining his British slave mentality. Sam crossed Menon again by refusing to allow soldiers to be assigned to the building of a housing complex as if they were construction labourers. The slow-burning feud with Menon was soon common knowledge.

In 1959, Sam was posted as the commander of the Defence Services Staff College in Wellington, in the Nilgiris in Tamil Nadu, where he impressed with his strategic vision and his extensive professional knowledge. Menon, though, was interested in promoting Lt General B.M. Kaul, who was reportedly close to Nehru. Kaul aspired to be the next army chief, although he had no combat experience. Menon and Kaul colluded to effectively try and destroy Sam's career and reputation. He was accused of being an Anglophile and anti-Indian. Kaul initiated a court of inquiry against Sam on the basis of petty canards spread by Kaul's own henchmen. One of the charges was that Sam had restored and hung portraits of Robert Clive and Warren Hastings in his office. Another accusation was that Sam was prejudiced and had made a disparaging remark about dark-skinned Indians. Fortunately for Sam, another lieutenant general, Daulat Singh, the presiding officer of the court of inquiry, was a man of integrity and exonerated Sam of all charges. He also gave the tale-tellers a mouthful for trying to besmirch Sam's character. An infuriated Menon then wrote a strong letter expressing his severe displeasure with Sam and putting it in his official record.[17] Sam, in turn, sent a stiff rejoinder.

At this point of impasse with Menon, Sam's career might have been summarily ended. His promotion to the rank of lieutenant general was held in abeyance for eighteen months because of the court of inquiry. Indeed, had China not invaded India, perhaps Sam wouldn't have been able to resurrect his career. The army, controlled by Menon, Kaul and their underlings, was caught completely off-guard by the Chinese. In the aftermath of the military debacle, with angry questions being asked in Parliament, Kaul was relieved of his command. General Pran Nath Thapar, the army chief of staff, resigned and Menon was removed as minister. Sam was sent to take charge of 4 Corps from Kaul. 'It was the Chinese who came to my rescue,' he quipped in private.[18] He told the demoralised 4 Corps soldiers in no uncertain terms: 'There will be no more withdrawals.'[19] Sam's authority and confidence instantly lifted the morale of the troops who had been humiliated by the Chinese advances.

Sam's style of command was informal. Giving short shrift to protocol, he would often pick up the phone and speak directly to a commanding officer in a forward area. But Sam was unforgiving and ruthless in dealing with dishonesty and deception. Brigadier Behram Panthaki, who was Sam's longtime aide-de-camp and wrote his biography, has said that Sam had the memory of an elephant and could repeat verbatim what had been said to him months earlier. His most abiding quality as a leader was that he cared deeply for his soldiers, especially those posted to forward areas. Sam was appointed army chief in April 1969, though Menon's successor as defence minister, Swaran Singh, was lobbying for General Harbaksh Singh, a fellow Sikh. Indira Gandhi had a high opinion of Sam's capabilities, even if he had once slightly offended her by denying her entry into the control room, when she accompanied her father to the Chinese border, because she held no official position in the government. By early 1971, it was clear that trouble was brewing on India's borders once Pakistan's General Yahya Khan ordered a military crackdown in East Pakistan because of mounting civil disobedience following the refusal to allow Bengali leader Sheikh Mujibur Rehman to form the government. He had won the 1970 Pakistan general election by sweeping the country's eastern half, winning about double the seats mustered in the western half by Zulfikar Ali Bhutto's Pakistan People's Party. Mujib was eventually arrested and a civil war erupted with lakh of refugees from East Pakistan crossing over into India. In April 1971, Sam was summoned to a cabinet meeting. Indira Gandhi wanted him to launch an immediate offensive against Pakistan. Sam, who had done his homework before the meeting, said firmly that it would be a fatal mistake to jump the gun. He needed time to mobilise the troops and trains would have to be requisitioned, which would lead to a hold up in the movement of grain and result in food shortages. Roads would have to be built near the border and the monsoon, Sam said, was not the right season to launch an offensive. Visibility for planes would be poor. The mountain passes were open so there was a chance that the Chinese could open up a third front along the northern border. East Pakistan would be taken in less than a month, he promised Indira, but only if he was given a free hand over when to launch the offensive and had to report to only one political master. The autocratic Indira was not used to being crossed. Sensing her anger, Sam offered to send in his resignation citing health reasons.[20] Surprisingly, though, Indira conceded, giving Sam control though some 10 million refugees had already crossed over from East Pakistan, creating a major problem for her government. Jagjivan Ram, who had become defence minister a year earlier, was particularly hostile to a proposal in which he was effectively sidelined. Describing the tension years later at a lecture, Sam joked that 'there is a very thin line between being dismissed and becoming a field marshal'.[21]

With Indira's acquiescence, Sam got the time he needed to plan a brilliant strategic campaign. On 3 December 1971, the Pakistan Air Force struck Indian airports on the Western Front but the damage was contained. There was now a legitimate reason for the well-prepared Indian army to launch a three-pronged attack, along with Mukti Bahini fighters, on East Pakistan. The enemy was outnumbered and outflanked with India launching a coordinated assault by land, sea and air on West Pakistani forces in East Pakistan. The lightning speed of the operations in the east led to the fall of Dhaka. Pakistani army casualties numbered around 6000 men, while India's were a third of that number. It took not a month, as Sam had promised, but just two weeks to win the war. The then Pakistani lieutenant general A.A.K. Niazi surrendered on 16 December 1971, with 93,000 of his soldiers taken prisoner. Under intense US and UN pressure, India agreed to a ceasefire on the following day. Indira asked Sam to proceed to Dhaka, the capital of the new nation of Bangladesh, to accept the surrender of the Pakistani forces, but he declined the honour. He said that the privilege should go to the eastern army commander, Lt General Jagjit Singh Aurora. It was the sort of generous gesture that marked Sam out as a great leader.

After leading India to such a decisive victory, the already popular general became a legend. A jaunty military march, *Sam Bahadur*, especially composed in his honour is a staple at military functions such as the annual 'Beating Retreat' ceremony in the capital. Politicians became increasingly suspicious of Sam, whose showmanship and style, accentuated by his handsome profile, signature handlebar moustache and razor-sharp wit, captured the public imagination and made him a favourite of both the armed forces and the media. Rumours of potential military coups and martial law being enforced cropped up sporadically. Even Indira Gandhi once asked Sam about his intentions. He guffawed and assured her that though he had the characteristic long Parsi nose, he never interfered in business that did not concern him. He had no political ambitions and a coup was bad for the country and the army.

In January 1973, Indira made Sam the first Indian army officer to be promoted to the largely ceremonial rank of field marshal, despite the objections of the still smarting defence minister, Jagjivan Ram. But almost as soon as Sam reached the pinnacle of his glory, he fell from grace. In a moment of weakness, he allowed his puckish sense of humour to get the better of his common sense and the dignity of his high office. He was asked by a young woman reporter at a Dak bungalow what would have been the outcome of the 1971 war if, at Partition, Sam had opted to go with his regiment, the Frontier Force, to Pakistan rather than remain in India. He joked that Pakistan might have won. His enemies, in any case fed up of all the adoration and positive publicity surrounding Sam, used these poorly chosen words to strike back at him. Though the interview was published in late January 1973, the controversy around his joke erupted much later when Sam was in the UK and unable to defend himself.[22]

Jagjivan Ram ensured that embarrassing questions were asked in the Lok Sabha about Sam's remarks. No one, including Indira, offered any defence of the field marshal. Later, she asked him, in exasperation: 'How many people can I defend in Parliament?'

The Ministry of Defence seized the opportunity to strip Sam of some of his perks and privileges.[23] Even when Sam left Delhi to retire in Coonoor, a hill station in the Nilgiris, there was no military escort to see him off to the airport. Perhaps because he had rubbed up too many the wrong way, but also because he did not want to accept any position that would compromise his standing as field marshal, Sam did not receive any plum post-retirement appointments, as the governor of a state, say, or an ambassador in some sought-after location. Indeed, Sam was even denied the benefits and status due to a field marshal. It was not until 2006–07, when President Abdul Kalam made a personal effort and visited Sam in hospital, that he finally got his long-pending dues. In less than a year, though, Sam was dead.

Throughout his career, Sam was totally immersed in his work. His only recreation was relaxing with family and close friends. His daughter, Maja Daruwala, says those times were always special: 'He was a lovely charismatic man, very funny, full of charm . . . you couldn't be in a room with him without feeling alive and merry.'[24] Stories about Sam's wit abound. When he was replaced by the government as a director on the Escorts company board by a man named 'Naik', he joked that it was the first time a Naik (corporal) had replaced a field marshal.[25]

Sam married Silloo Bode, a Bombay girl and a graduate of the J.J. School of Art, whom he had first met in 1937 at a social gathering in Lahore. They had two lively and talented daughters, Sherry (short for 'Sherna') and Maja. He enjoyed joking that one daughter had married a Batlivala (bottle seller) and the other a Daruwala (liquor vendor), and that he had a daughter named Sherry and a granddaughter nicknamed 'Brandy'. Maja says her mother in her quiet way was as remarkable as her father. Indeed, on occasion, Silloo could outdo her husband for directness. At a function, when Sam was chief of staff, the couple encountered his one-time nemesis, Krishna Menon. 'Darling, you remember Mr Menon,' Sam said by way of polite introduction. 'No,' said Silloo sharply, 'I don't.'[26]

Even in death, the government's behaviour towards Sam was shabby. The then defence minister, A.K. Antony, did not fly to Coonoor for the funeral and neither did any of the three military chiefs. The army did not bring Sam's body to Delhi for a State funeral, as might have been expected at the passing of a field marshal. A few years later, celebrating the centenary of his birth, the government tried to make amends but it was too little too late. The Indian government may not have given Sam his due in his lifetime, but for soldiers and military enthusiasts he will remain an inspiration.

Zubin Mehta and Freddie Mercury have dazzled audiences throughout the world with their performances and are counted among the all-time greats in music. They rose to be international celebrities in rock and classical music though Bombay, where they grew up, was a cultural backwater for Western music. Zubin's contribution in shaping today's music world is immense. He was the music director for over half a century to some of the world's leading orchestras and opera houses, encompassing three continents. He has been described as the rightful heir to such legendary conductors as Arturo Toscanini and Wilhelm Furtwangler.

Zubin did have a good start, though, growing up in a warm, traditional, very musical Parsi family. He says, only half-jokingly, that he is not certain whether he learnt musical notes before he learnt to speak in Gujarati, his mother tongue. Zubin's father, Mehli Mehta, was a remarkable individual. He had trained to be an accountant and was expected to join the family business as a cotton miller. At the time, few Western classical musicians bothered to visit Bombay but Mehli was fortunate enough to hear the renowned violinist Jascha Heifetz play a recital in the city on his way to Shanghai. So spellbound was Mehli by Heifetz's performance that he painstakingly taught himself how to play the violin.

At home, Zubin was surrounded by music, accustomed to his father either practicing the violin in the living room or listening endlessly to records on the gramophone. In 1935, a year before Zubin was born, Mehli founded the Bombay Symphony Orchestra, made up of an assortment of colourful amateurs of varying standards, and the Bombay String Quartet. Some years later, Mehli also decided to travel to the United States and take lessons from a qualified violin teacher. His quest was sponsored by several Parsi charities, including the Tata Endowment Fund, and he was able to study in the US for four years.[27] Zubin's strong-minded mother Tehmina, who came from a well-to-do family, managed to cope without a steady income, taking in tenants to help ease the cost of running the household.

On his return to Bombay, Mehli did his best to invigorate and enrich the classical music scene. When Zubin was about fifteen, the violinist Yehudi Menuhin came to Bombay and agreed to play with the Bombay Symphony Orchestra. During practice sessions, Mehli would play the solo and Zubin got the chance to conduct for the very first time. Zubin never saw himself as a musician, in the sense of playing an instrument, admitting that at the time he was more involved with cricket than the piano. After school, he submitted obediently to the family demand that he should study medicine. But within a term or two of his pre-med course Zubin realised that it was music rather than dissecting dogfish that was his true calling. Though his family wanted to see him take up a conventional profession, they were supportive of his decision to set out for uncharted territory, when they realised that he had made up his mind. Using half the money he was left by his maternal grandfather, he was able, at the age of eighteen, to travel to Vienna to study conducting with the renowned conductor and teacher Hans Swarowsky.[28]

Zubin never forgot the uplifting moment when he heard the Vienna Philharmonic play for the first time. The sound emanating from one of the world's most beautiful auditoriums was entirely different from the scratchy records he grew up listening to. It was in Vienna, too, that he developed a lifelong friendship with another student, Daniel Barenboim, a child prodigy who was barely thirteen. Barenboim grew up to be a renowned conductor and pianist.

In 1958, at the age of twenty-two, having graduated but still struggling to make a living, Zubin won the International Conducting Competition in Liverpool and, shortly thereafter, the second prize at a prestigious competition held by the Tanglewood Music Center in Massachusetts. His success earned him an appointment as the assistant conductor and then music director of the Royal Liverpool Philharmonic. He caught the attention of some of the big names in the music industry, including the agent Siegfried Hearst. The world began to open up to Zubin. In 1961, several famous conductors happened to either fall ill or cancelled their performances and Zubin took their place. A year earlier, he had been invited to Montreal to stand in for a conductor who had cancelled at short notice. To his surprise, shortly afterwards, he was offered the job of the musical director of the Montreal orchestra.[29]

Prized assignments kept falling into the lap of the dashing conductor, whose fame continued to spread. At one concert, the formidable Dorothy Chandler, wife of the owner of the *Los Angeles Times* and chairperson of the Los Angeles Philharmonic, was so bowled over by Zubin's performance, she immediately offered him the post of associate conductor. But the main conductor, Georg Solti, took offence that he had not been consulted and resigned in a huff. Zubin ended up getting Solti's job. From being practically unemployed for nearly two years after graduation, Zubin now, at the age of twenty-five, had two prestigious permanent jobs in his pocket. *Time* magazine, which featured Zubin on the cover in January 1968, noted that he had 'precociously stormed the most daunting redoubts of European music', having become one of the youngest men to conduct both the Berlin and Vienna Philharmonics.[30]

But while his professional life flourished, Zubin's personal life fell apart. He had married a Canadian singing student, Carmen Lasky, while still in Vienna and they had already had two children by the time Zubin's career took off. As his work and travel commitments increased, his marriage floundered under the strain. In a twist, Zubin's brother Zarin, who had moved to Montreal, had developed serious feelings for his ex-sister-in-law and vice versa. By 1966, they were married, a year after Zubin and Lasky had divorced.[31]

As Zubin became single again, the media frequently began to refer to him as 'the playboy Parsi'. He was linked with a series of beautiful women, including the soprano Teresa Stratas. In 1967, he became a father to another daughter, Alexandra, though the relationship with her mother was fleeting. A year later, Zubin met Nancy Kovack, a voluptuous blonde model and television actress with striking looks and a cerebral bent of mind. Nancy had a deep fascination for Iran, having spent nearly three years in the country making two movies and learning the culture. They were married in 1969 and she gave up a successful career. Their bond has survived Zubin's frenetic lifestyle and even the birth of his son Ori in 1991 with a woman in Israel.[32]

Despite having a green card, Zubin has hung onto his Indian passport. It shows the depth of his attachment to his roots. When he first moved to the USA, he was comforted by the knowledge that his parents too had settled in Philadelphia. Mehli had joined the Curtis String Quartet, performing in venues across the States. He later taught at UCLA and founded the American Youth Symphony, based in Los Angeles (and still going strong over fifty-six years later). Zubin, who had moved to Los Angeles two years before his father, quit the city's philharmonic orchestra after sixteen years to take over as the music director, in 1978, of the New York Philharmonic. He held the post for thirteen years, the longest tenure in the orchestra's history. The NYP gave Zubin an opportunity to experiment with new ideas. From New York, Zubin moved to Florence as the conductor of the Orchestra del Maggio Musicale Fiorentino. He has also worked as the music director in Munich for both the Bavarian State Opera and the Bavarian State Orchestra.

Zubin is noted for having given more opportunities to young artists, soloists, conductors and composers in debut performances than arguably any other conductor of his stature. He has also experimented with fusion music, premiering Ravi Shankar's *Sitar Concerto No.* 2 with the New York Philharmonic and conducting compositions by the Indian violinist and composer L. Subramaniam. At a concert in Srinagar in 2013, Zubin led the Bavarian State Opera together with Kashmiri musicians and artists from Delhi, bridging the gap between two entirely different musical worlds.

Zubin made recording history when he conducted the 'Three Tenors Concert' in Rome in 1990, on the eve of the FIFA World Cup final. The World Cup had brought together Luciano Pavarotti, Placido Domingo and Jose Carreras and the concert, at the ancient Baths of Caracalla, included both classical arias and a medley of popular songs. It has gone on to be the bestselling classical music album in history. Spanish tenor Carreras had made a miraculous recovery from leukemia to join his compatriot Domingo and the Italian Pavarotti, perhaps the most famous of them all; together they formed an operatic supergroup that sold records and drew crowds in numbers more familiar to the likes of Madonna and Michael Jackson than classical musicians. Zubin was chosen to conduct the trio, in part because his orchestra in Florence accompanied the tenors, but also because he had the charisma and star wattage to share the spotlight with Pavarotti, Domingo and Carreras.

But among all the orchestras Zubin has worked with, it is the Israel Philharmonic that holds a special place in his heart. A bond developed after he played there in 1961 for the first time. It was strengthened by the 'Six Day War' in 1967, when the conductor then in residence with the philharmonic fled Israel. Zubin, to show solidarity, cancelled two engagements and rushed halfway around the world to make it to war-torn Israel. For the last leg of his journey, he boarded a special El Al flight, sitting on crates filled with guns and ammunition and only one other passenger. Zubin had the honour of conducting the first victory concert in Jerusalem after the brief war ended.[33] Some years later, Zubin was made music director of the Israel Philharmonic for life, an active post he finally relinquished in October 2019 after fifty years, holding an emotional farewell concert at the age of eighty-three; he is now the orchestra's music director emeritus.

Zubin's relationship with Israel is very close and he was furious when in 1978 the Indian government, which did not recognize Israel at that point, refused him permission to bring the Israel Philharmonic to Bombay. He played a role in establishing a cultural dialogue between the two countries and in 1994, Zubin was able to fulfil his dream of bringing the orchestra to India. Zubin has often used his music as a message for peace, whether it is in Israel, Palestine, Sarajevo or Kashmir. He has always emphasised that the causes he supports are humanitarian, not political. Being born in a community which was originally of migrant stock, he empathises with the travails of those who have been forced out of their homeland. Throughout his career he has been an example of music's unique capacity to bring countries and cultures together. Some years back, he set up the Mehli Mehta Music Foundation, in honour of his father, as a non-profit trust to help increase awareness of Western classical music in Mumbai. Apart from the MMMF, the two major organisations that sponsor Western music recitals in his home city are also run by Parsis: the pioneering Time & Talents Club and the Tata Trust's National Centre for the Performing Arts.

India has always been on Zubin's performance itinerary whenever he travels in this part of the world with an orchestra. He is passionate about bringing his music to his country. On every visit to Bombay, he is fussed over and feted as if he were royalty, especially by Parsis. But the unpretentious Zubin has always seemed to remain himself—warm, friendly and unaffected by all the adulation.

Zubin's style is steeped in his characteristic passion, labelled flamboyant by some. He stuns his audience with his volcanic zest and fiery passion, clearly glorying in what he is doing on stage. Acclaimed violinist Itzhak Perlman described the Zubin magic to CBS News: 'There are many conductors who are fine musicians . . . but that little element which is the communication between the musician and the conductor sometimes is missing . . . And then you have somebody like Zubin, you know, he goes in and he just goes like that and it catches you.' The late, celebrated cellist Jacqueline du Pre, when she was herself a young musician, is widely quoted as saying 'playing with Zubin is like riding a magic carpet'. Of all the many awards and accolades Zubin has won, including the Padma Vibhushan, perhaps the most meaningful was when the Austrian conductor Karl Bohm described the Bombay-born Parsi Zubin Mehta as 'the bearer of the Wagner tradition'. In his will, Bohm left Zubin a ring which had been left to Bohm by the conductor Arthur Nikisch, as if to welcome Zubin to the fraternity.[34]

Freddie Mercury was not a one-of-a-kind Parsi; he was unique by any standard. And the legend of the outrageous showman of rock who lit up the stage with his magnetic presence has only grown with time. Inducted into the Rock and Roll Hall of Fame and the Songwriters Hall of Fame, Freddie has consistently been voted one of the greatest singers in the history of popular music. He may have died in 1991 but Freddie was included in a 2002 BBC list of the '100 Greatest Britons' and a 2007 Japanese national survey of the '100 Most Influential Heroes'. According to Billboard, the Mercury-fronted Queen's *Greatest Hits* album is the bestselling album in UK history, outselling even the Beatles and ABBA. Two Queen songs, written by Mercury, *We are the Champions* and *Bohemaian Rhapsody*, are routinely voted as the 'greatest song of all time' in major polls. There are numerous monuments in different parts of the world dedicated to Freddie but the most memorable is a bronze statue overlooking Lake Geneva, of the singer in his classic pose: legs akimbo, hip jutting, one clenched fist raised to the skies, a microphone dangling from the other hand at a rakish angle.

Despite dozens of books and a major biopic, *Bohemian Rhapsody*, which won four Oscars including 'Best Actor' for Rami Malek's uncanny portrayal of Freddie Mercury, there is still a haze of mystery around the singer. Freddie assiduously guarded his privacy, gave few interviews and kept his life so compartmentalised that his mother Jer Bulsara claims not to have known her son was gay until after his death. Long after he became famous, no one knew his real name or where he came from, least of all the religion he was brought up in by his orthodox family. An old schoolmate of his, Subash Shah, remembers Freddie as shy: 'But he was also "a born show-off" and his entire personality would transform once he was performing.'[35]

Freddie was a dual personality—the introvert who became a flashy prima donna on stage. There was much he kept hidden. He was not homosexual, as widely assumed, but bisexual. Though for public consumption, till the very end, he would parade Mary Austin around as his girlfriend. She supposedly inspired the Queen song *Love of My Life*, though he reportedly ended any physical relationship between them fourteen years before his death. Their strangely close friendship endured though, with Freddie leaving Mary his home and half his fortune in his will. In his sex life and in his drug habit, there were no holds barred, yet Freddie made it a point not to smoke a cigarette in front of his father since it offended his Zoroastrian sensibilities. Smoking is forbidden by the religion because it is seen as a desecration of fire. Out of filial respect, he also hid his homosexuality from his parents. While some biographies of the singer make out that homosexuality is deeply abhorrent to the Zoroastrian religion, it is more likely that his parents, like most Parsis of that era, were brought up with Victorian-bequeathed values that condemned homosexuality as an unnatural act. (Jokes about homosexuality and Parsis are sometimes cracked, not because there is evidence of a higher percentage of homosexuals among Parsis than other communities but because high-profile men such as Russi Modi and Edulji Dinshaw chose not to hide their sexuality at a time when it was considered taboo.)

Freddie was not a stereotypical pop musician. He was a deeply cultured individual, with refined tastes and was knowledgeable about art, antiques, Dresden china, good food and vintage wines. He enjoyed the opera and the ballet. But in his private life, his considerable appetite for one-night stands was usually sated by picking up rougher men, archetypes of unreconstructed masculinity. One of his many biographers described his preferred partners as 'unwashed truck drivers'.

Freddie's background was conventional and middle class. He was born Farrokh Bulsara in Zanzibar (now part of Tanzania). His father Bomi and mother Jer were originally from Gujarat; the surname suggests that their origins were in Balsar/Valsad. And they were devout Zoroastrians. Before Mercury was born, Bomi took a job at the Zanzibar High Court. The family lived comfortably, in a large house with several domestic servants. Like most Parsis, the Bulsaras placed a premium on good education. When he was seven, they sent him off to boarding school in India while his baby sister Kashmira remained behind with their parents.[36]

Once he entered the music industry, Freddie avoided mentioning that he was born in Zanzibar or that his parents were originally from India. Some excuse his desire to erase his past by pointing out that Freddie's Britain, or more specifically England, was the country of Enoch Powell, the National Front and casual racism towards 'Asians' was rife. But his sister Kashmira Cook denies that he went out of his way to deny his roots. 'Colour and religion didn't matter to him,' she says. 'He didn't deny his origins, he never said anything—that he was a Parsi—because nobody asked him.' She pointed out that in England, in those days, few even knew what a Parsi was and if you were Asian, you were automatically classified as Indian.[37] But some of his biographers continue to believe that there was a deeper compulsion for Freddie to keep his past secret. Certainly, he never discussed his ethnic or religious background with journalists. The closest he came to doing so was in response to a question about his outlandish persona. 'That's something inbred, it's a part of me,' he said, 'I will always walk around like a Persian popinjay.'[38] Persian, perhaps, was an oblique reference to his Indian Parsi background.

Freddie's Indian boarding school was St Peter's, located in the hill station of Panchgani, near Bombay. It was patterned on a British public school with an emphasis on sports as well as academics. Being separated at such a young age from his mother was probably emotionally traumatic for him, though he would later claim, matter-of-factly, that 'boarding school helps you fend for yourself.' Sometimes, Freddie would spend holidays with his aunt Sheroo in Bombay or even at school, because of the distance from India to Zanzibar by ship. In a rare revelation, he once confided to a friend's son that he missed out on the 'homely side of family life as a child'.[39] The stoic and reserved Balsaras may not have been overly demonstrative in their affections but they clearly adored their children and were very proud of Freddie's success. Despite their objections to his opting for such an uncertain career and unconventional lifestyle, his mother says that they loyally attended one of his first major concerts in 1973 at the Hammersmith Odeon in 1973.[40] Even when he was famous, Jer made it a point to try and attend every concert of his that she could. She would bake his favourite cheese biscuits and pack them for him when he went on trips.

It was clear from early on that Freddie had musical ability. His cousin Jehangir recalls that if Freddie heard a song even once, he could go back to his aunt Sheroo's home in Bombay and play it on the piano.[41] His mother Jer, who died in 2016 at the age of ninety-four, said that Freddie started piano lessons in Bombay because one of his teachers at boarding school had told his parents that he was very gifted.[42] Freddie joined the school choir and with his close friends formed his first band, 'The Hectics'. They had many fans in the girls' school next door. He was nicknamed 'Freddie' almost from the start of school life, as is typical for Parsi boys named Farrokh, just as Jamshed inevitably becomes 'Jimmie' and Rustom becomes 'Russie'.

When Zanzibar became violent in the early 1960s, as revolutionaries fought to liberate the country first from British control and then from the sultan, the Bulsaras decided to leave for England. They had British passports and already had family in the country. The family moved into a modest semi-detached house in Feltham, a nondescript suburb of London. The move was something of a cultural and financial shock for the Bulsaras. Both parents had to take jobs, Bomi as a cashier and Jer as a shop assistant at Marks & Spencer. Even after Freddie became super-rich, his proudly independent parents refused their son's offer to buy them a house and continued to work for a living.

When Freddie joined his parents in England, he was expected to continue with his education by opting for a conventional profession like law or accountancy, as his cousins had done. But his grades were not great and instead he chose to work towards a diploma in graphic art and design at the Ealing College of Art. As a student in London, Freddie, an ardent Jimi Hendrix fan, was in his element. The immigrant boy began to acquire some urban, bohemian sophistication. The Bulsaras were upset to find their son increasingly restless and rebellious and keen to be part of a band. They considered his choices unrealistic.

But Freddie had blind ambition and determination. He hung around an amateur student band called 'Smile' and convinced two of their members, Brian May and Roger Taylor, whose academic backgrounds were incidentally impressive, unlike Freddie's, to allow him to join. The band which took on a fourth member, John Deacon, was renamed 'Queen'. Unsurprisingly, the name was Freddie's idea. He was slowly emerging from the sidelines to become the driving force of the group and played a major role in moulding the band's character. His instinct was to shock, to be different, to make himself, with his wigs, heels and lurid, shiny bodysuits, a kind of visual assault. More importantly, Freddie had natural presence. He was able, with some ease, to hold an audience in the palm of his hand. His vocal range went from bass to soprano. He also, with Brian May, wrote most of the songs. Freddie could put a song together in minutes, conjuring melodies sometimes out of thin air seated at a piano.[43]

'Nothing is typical of my work,' he once commented. The proof of the pudding was *Bohemian Rhapsody*—a song that defied all the conventional and commercial wisdom of how to write popular music. At nearly six minutes, it was far too long for most radio stations to play in its entirety and the song veered wildly from acappella singing to piano music to squalling, thrashing guitars; from rock and roll to mock opera to classical pastiche. The lyrics are at once yearning, menacing, overblown, comic—it is a song that leaves you always a little off-kilter, unsure what to expect next.[44] The song is today universally acclaimed as a masterpiece but at its inception there were many doubters, including from within the band. Some now interpret it as Freddie's coming out song; the song's magnificence though defies easy reductions and pat conclusions. *Bohemian Rhapsody* gave Queen its first UK number one single.

World tours, hysterical fans, private jets and extravagant aftershow parties became Freddie's new normal. Japan was among the first countries to recognise Queen as a major force in music. On a South American tour, Queen was seen by over half a million people, many of whom were unfamiliar with rock concerts.[45] In São Paulo, where few spoke English, there were riot police posted everywhere as more than a 1,00,000 fans sang along to *Love of my Life*. In Mexico, the audience threw cans at the stage since they viewed the song *I Want to Break Free* as a cry for liberation from dictatorship and did not like Freddie singing it while dressed in women's clothing.

Queen's most memorable concert, though, was probably their appearance on 13 July 1985 as part of the 'Live Aid' show at Wembley Stadium in London. Many people had written off Queen as a band in decline. Freddie was in poor health. He had a bad throat and many already speculated that he had contracted the HIV virus. The musician and activist fundraiser Bob Geldof had invited the band to appear at the sixteen-hour marathon he was organising, featuring the likes of Bob Dylan, Tina Turner, Bryan Adams, Paul McCartney and Dire Straits, to raise money for relief efforts in Ethiopia where a famine had been raging through the country for nearly two years, killing hundreds of thousands of people. The concert was to be broadcast live to over 1 billion people worldwide.[46] Queen stole the show, delivering a punchy medley of their greatest hits. Freddie gave a performance of passion and bravado, looking out onto a sea of ecstatic, swaying arms. It was perhaps the greatest of the many hundreds of shows they had performed in every corner of the globe. Only one country was never on Queen's tour schedule though—India, where Freddie's people once belonged.

With his lifestyle, it was simply a matter of time before Freddie was exposed to the HIV virus. In the 1980s, AIDS had reached epidemic proportions, particularly among homosexuals. After the Hollywood star Rock Hudson died of the dreaded disease, the tabloids had a field day and the gay community was badly shaken. Freddie must have suspected that he was in the eye of the storm. Two of his former partners had died of AIDS. There were telltale signs of the disease, from the strange blemishes on his face to the lesions on his body, but he refused to acknowledge the possibility that he had contracted the virus. He remained in denial, insisting that he had tested HIV negative.

But Freddie was making lifestyle changes. He abruptly quit Hamburg, the famously louche city in Germany where he had been living for years, leaving behind close companion and sometime sex partner Barbara Valentin, a moderately famous actress, as well as Winfried Kirchberger, an aggressively uncouth restauranteur, who was also one of Freddie's on-again, off-again lovers. In the unconventional Barbara, dubbed 'Germany's Jayne Mansfeld', Freddie had found a confidant, someone he could talk to, not just count on to join him in a threesome. Barbara, like Freddie, hid some aspects of her personal life from her family. But if Freddie could confide in Barbara, in Kirchberger he thought for a time that he had discovered true love. In Hamburg, his life was filled with night clubs, casual sex, multiple partners and drugs. But after he moved back to London and the sanctuary of his beautiful home, Garden Lodge, once owned by a banking family named 'Hoares'—an open goal for Freddie who dubbed his mansion 'Whore's House'—Freddie's frenetic lifestyle slowed down. His 1970s' Bohemian dress style was eventually replaced by a bristly moustache, closely cropped hair, a muscular upper body and tight denim jeans. Though not monogamous exactly, towards the end of his life he had a steady partner in Jim Hutton, an Irish hairdresser, whom he turned to on the rebound from Kirchberger, who refused to leave Germany. Hutton remained devoted to Freddie and was by his side till the end, though he used to be introduced as the gardener when the Bulsaras came to visit. Back in London, Freddie reconnected with his parents and visited them nearly every week in their modest Feltham home. One of his last songs was an experimental collaboration with the Spanish opera diva Montserrat Caballe, whom he hugely admired. She persuaded him to write a duet for her home town Barcelona which was to be the venue for the 1992 Olympic games.

But as HIV made its painful progress through his body, Freddie's suffering was immense. There were occasional bouts of blindness and night sweats, skin and mouth sores and he had difficulty breathing. He could barely speak, had lost the use of his muscles and was surviving on a liquid diet. After years of obsessive secrecy about his illness, Freddie finally instructed Queen's public relations team to make an official statement that he was suffering from AIDS. Most of the world's front pages carried the news on 23 November 1991, that Freddie had AIDS. A day later, he was dead, the first major rock star to succumb to what was becoming the AIDS pandemic.

It was Freddie's desire to be cremated. Only a few close friends, including Elton John and Elizabeth Taylor, Freddie's family and some thirty relatives were present. Two Zoroastrian priests, in their white robes, chanted the traditional prayers for the dead. This was followed by gospel music sung by Aretha Franklin and a Verdi aria sung by Montserrat Caballe, as Freddie had wished. The location where Freddie's ashes were placed remains a secret. But a Parsi school friend of Freddie's, Gita Choksi, who was visiting her father's grave in a dedicated Parsi plot in Surrey's Brookwood Cemetery, says she was told by a caretaker that Freddie's ashes are buried there.[47] If this is true, then Freddie's ashes lie close to those of several other distinguished Parsis, including Jamsetji Tata, his son Ratanji, and Shapoorji Saklatvala. Freddie would have, at the end, returned to his roots.

11

Two Rebels a Century Apart

The loyalty of Parsis to their rulers is evident throughout their history in India. In the fifteenth century, when Sanjan was attacked by invaders from Ghazni, the Parsis, under their leader Ardeshir, rallied together and fought side by side with the local king. Ardeshir and many of his men died in the bloody battle. Sanjan was sacked, but the Parsis managed to escape with the sacred Iranshah fire. Another Parsi legend is that of Rustom Nanabhoy who raised a militia to save Bombay from an Abyssinian attack in the 1690s, when the British had temporarily evacuated their new acquisition because of a plague that had infected the city.[1] During colonial rule, the majority of Parsis were loyal subjects of the crown. Many Parsis fought, and some died, for the Allied cause in both World Wars; an exclusively Parsi battalion with a strength of 1,051 officers and men was formed during the First World War and as many as forty-six Parsis were killed in action. In 1926, a war column in Khareghat Colony on Hughes Road in Bombay was erected in their memory.

In the early years of independent India, Parsis were represented in much greater strength in the armed forces than their proportion

249

of the actual population would suggest. Several made a name for themselves. Parsis have, at different times, been chiefs of the Army, Navy, Air Force, Coast Guards and Border Security Force. In fact, it was a Parsi police officer, Khusro Faramurz Rustamji, who founded the BSF. The courage shown by Lieutenant Colonel Ardeshir Tarapore in the 1965 war with Pakistan won him the Param Vir Chakra, India's highest military decoration. Despite being severely injured, Tarapore refused to be evacuated from the battlefield. He had been mortally wounded during an exchange of fire with Pakistani soldiers but his regiment, inspired by his example, continued to fight and in a memorable victory, was able to destroy sixty enemy tanks, while losing only nine of its own. Today, though, few Parsis enlist for the armed forces, preferring to take up more lucrative professions.

As a migrant community, Parsis have usually stayed on the right side of the establishment. But there have always been some ready to speak out against the government of the day. During British rule, Dadabhai Naoroji, Pherozeshah Mehta, Khurshed Nariman, Feroze Gandhi and many others fought for Swaraj and independence. But their battles were fought more formally, with the use of democratic outlets of dissent, such as the media, the legislature and politics, rather than on the streets. This remained the case in independent India. During the Emergency, for instance, lawyers like Nani Palkhivala, Fali Nariman and Soli Sorabjee were not afraid of making public their opposition to Indira Gandhi's authoritarian regime. Politicians such as Piloo Mody and Minoo Masani also challenged the government in their time, but always with civility and within the confines of the law.

There are, however, examples of Parsis who believed that their particular causes were worth any cost and sacrifice. The most notable such nonconformist among the Parsis was, of course, Madame Bhikhaiji Cama. An ardent revolutionary and socialist, she endorsed the use of physical force to overthrow the colonial British government.

For decades after her death, the Parsis remained ambivalent about Madame Cama, an iconic figure of the freedom movement. A trailblazer, she entered politics ahead of stalwarts like Sarojini Naidu and Annie Besant. As if to underline her revolutionary credentials, Cama is best known as the first person to raise the Indian flag on foreign land, hoisting the earliest version of the tricolour (green, yellow, red, with a crescent moon, a sun and eight lotuses to represent each province of British India) forty years before Independence at a socialist conference in Stuttgart in Germany. The crusading lawyer and freedom fighter, Khursheed F. Nariman, himself considered something of a rebel by the Parsi community, described Cama as 'a revolutionary volcano who struck terror in the mighty British Empire'. He noted sadly that, after years of lonely exile in Europe, she died in the Parsi General Hospital in Bombay in straitened circumstances, 'unsung and unwept by her ungrateful countrymen'.[2] Nariman's bitter rebuke seems to have been directed largely at his own community.

By the twenty-first century, Madame Cama's place in Indian history was well established. In Mumbai, a major road next to the state government secretariat has been named after her, while in Delhi, a large office complex bears her name, even if it is misspelt. A stamp too has been issued in her honour. But not all Parsis are convinced that Bhikhaiji Cama is a worthy example for emulation. The late Muncherji Cama, a member of her husband's family once observed disapprovingly about his illustrious relation, 'She was a born anarchist. Not someone we are particularly proud of. Her heroes were men like Lenin and Savarkar.'[3] (Incidentally, when I met him Cama's mobile ringtone was *God Save the Queen*, and he confessed that he has the Union Jack firmly entrenched in his heart.) When Bhikhaiji's birth centenary was to be celebrated in 2006, the Indian government approached the K.R. Cama

Oriental Institute, named after her father-in-law, Khurshedji Cama, a renowned scholar of Avesta and the Zoroastrian religion, to hang a portrait in her memory. The Cama Institute politely declined. In an obituary, poet, dramatist and actor Harindranath Chattopadhyaya, Sarojini Naidu's younger brother, wrote, 'It is amusing that an average little girl-volunteer who has been arrested once and served a pretty little sentence in gaol should be acclaimed more than a mighty personality of history, such as Madame Cama was.' Chattopadhyaya wondered why the Parsi community was not as proud of her as they were of Dadabhai Naoroji and others. And why they did not consider erecting a memorial to one of the 'greatest, finest and most beloved women this country has produced'.

Dadabhai's pre-eminence was undisputed. In 1917, over 15,000 people followed his funeral procession to the Tower of Silence.[4] But Bhikhaiji Cama, many Parsis believed, had consorted with, and saw as allies, the wrong people. She was, they pointed out, an ardent supporter of Vinayak Damodar Savarkar, the Hindutva demagogue who was bitterly opposed to Mahatma Gandhi. It also irked the Parsis, that the British saw fit to intern Bhikhaiji; for a community accustomed to being looked upon with special benevolence by the colonial rulers, she was a disgrace.

Nothing in Bhikhaiji's early years hinted at the rebellious path she was to take in later life. She came from a very wealthy business family that was loyal to the Raj. In the family's stately drawing room, along with Chinese jars, crystal chandeliers and other bric-a-brac, a portrait of the British king and queen hung in solitary splendour on a central wall.[5] Her father, Sorabjee Patel, founded the firms Wallace and Company and Framji Sons and Co. He had the franchise for Singer Sewing Machines in India. Sorabjee took an active interest in public affairs and charitable work, including promoting education for girls. He was a member of the BPP.[6] Despite Sorabjee's commitment to the education of girls, he was more conventional when it came to bequeathing his fortune to his children: his two sons inherited trust funds of Rs 13 lakh each, while his eight daughters received Rs 1 lakh apiece. Bhikhaiji attended the Parsi-run Alexandra Girls' English Institution and the independent-minded young girl was married at the relatively late age of twenty-four. By then, she had already developed the sort of social conscience that would see her work day and night to nurse the sick and dying during the 1896 outbreak of plague in Bombay despite the risks to herself and her family. She empathised with the problems faced by less well-to-do Indians under British rule, and vowed to do what she could to alleviate their suffering. Her eminently suitable groom, Rustom Cama, was a handsome lawyer from one of the leading Parsi families, pioneers in the China trade.[7]

Most biographies of Bhikhaiji depict her marriage as a failure from the start, with the conservative Camas disapproving of her unconventional behaviour and interest in public affairs. According to one account, the Camas demanded that the Patels rein in the boisterous, even hoydenish behaviour of their free-spirited daughter.[8]

But these tales seem designed to burnish Bhikhaiji's legend, rather than as accurate portrayals of her marriage or relationship with the Camas. For a start, the latter could hardly be described as a 'conservative' family. Muncherjee Cama recalls the adventures of a female relative, Pirojbai Cama, who once travelled on an open sleigh from Moscow to Vladivostok, which showed that Cama women hardly lacked spirit themselves. Pirojbai was in the Philippines on a world cruise in 1903 when she received a telegram that her father was on his deathbed. She did not turn back, pointing out practically that her father would have passed away by the time she reached India. Nor is it correct that Bhikhaiji's husband objected to her nationalistic views. In fact, Rustom was a member of a 'ginger group' within the Congress, pushing it to consider more radical ideas and action. Between 1888 and 1915, he was also an official delegate of the Bombay Presidency Association, in some ways a precursor to the Congress in its political aims and ambitions.[9]

Nawaz Mody, her biographer, says that contrary to the stories that Bhikhaiji left her husband over their political differences, it was more likely that their marriage fell apart due to a more conventional source of domestic discord. Rustom Cama had an ongoing relationship with another woman. Bhikhaiji refused to accept the humiliation of her husband's infidelity and returned to her maternal home. The couple separated but were never formally divorced.[10] In 1902, Bhikhaiji moved to England on medical grounds and would not return home for thirty-three years.

She had travelled across Europe before settling in England, where she assisted Dadabhai Naoroji in his work with the Congress and became virtually an unpaid secretary. Dadabhai, incidentally, was a close friend of her husband and the Cama family. He had even represented the Camas' firm in England as a partner. After she left India, Bhikhaiji opted for the title 'Madame Cama' over the plainer, more conventional 'Mrs Cama'. Perhaps she partly identified with the French Republican tradition or was influenced by Irish nationalist women who adopted the title 'Madame'. In addition, it was an act of feminist assertion, since her marital status was unclear.[11]

Through Dadabhai, Bhikhaiji came into contact with several Indians involved in the freedom struggle, including Sardarsinhji Ravaji Rana and Shyamji Krishna Varma, who in 1905, founded the Indian Home Rule Society. Bhikhaiji gradually moved from the moderate views of her original mentor, Dadabhai, to the extremist views of her new friends. She was a regular contributor to Shyamji's *Indian Sociologist*, and came in contact with Savarkar who was staying at India House in London. Savarkar made a deep impression on her, and she was converted to his viewpoint that violence was the only way to free India from British shackles and that Hindi in the Devanagari script should be the national language of a free India. She enlisted as an active member of Savarkar's radical Abhinav Bharat Society and helped spread revolutionary literature. Along the way, Bhikhaiji developed close links with the radical press, Irish revolutionaries, socialists and freedom fighters from many countries.

When Savarkar was implicated in the 'Nasik Conspiracy case', in which twenty Browning automatic pistols and ammunition were smuggled into India, Bhikhaiji did her best to save him from arrest at her own cost. She signed a statement in the British consulate in Paris, taking the blame for smuggling the pistols into India. Bhikhaiji was a generous contributor to the movement and also funded Savarkar's legal battles and sent money home to his family. Little wonder then that the militant Hindu nationalist Savarkar always had the highest praise for the Parsis, in contrast to his views on other minorities in India.

The British authorities were keeping a watchful eye on Bhikhaiji and her revolutionary activities, and so in 1907, she moved her base to Paris. Her home in the French capital became a meeting place for revolutionaries with nationalist aspirations, not just from India but those involved in liberation struggles all over the world. Some affectionately called her the 'Mother of the Indian Revolution' since she nurtured, sponsored and supported a number of young Indian freedom fighters. She also financed and wrote regularly for the virulently anti-British journal *Bande Mataram*, which was launched in 1909 by Bhikhaiji and Har Dayal and published from Geneva for distribution to other centres. She had a keen understanding of internationalism and had great faith in socialist ideals. Bhikhaiji was very impressed by Lenin, with whom she corresponded regularly as she did with many revolutionaries. Her shining moment was on 22 August 1907 when, at the second International Socialist Congress in

Stuttgart, she unfurled India's first national flag—a move aimed at enlisting the support for India's freedom struggle throughout the world. At the end of her fiery speech, she mooted a resolution calling for complete independence for India.[12] (Bhikhaiji managed to gain admission to the conference even though there was no official Indian delegation.) Her critics, including some members of her husband's family, sought to detract from her heroic action by dubbing Bhikhaiji an exhibitionist who had simply cut off one of her sari pallus and flown it as a flag. In fact, her flag was very carefully conceived and stitched together. It was a tricolour with stripes of red, yellow and green. The words 'Vande Mataram' were on it, as were a sun and crescent moon, symbols of Hindus and Muslims. The flag was supposedly inspired by one hoisted in Calcutta on Boycott Day, 7 August 1906. The tricolour that Bhikhaiji unfurled in Stuttgart was the original model for the Indian flag.

Bhikhaiji's fiery, radical energy got her into hot water with the British authorities even in Paris. When the First World War began, she addressed Indian troops in France and urged them to lay down their arms, declaring that Indians should not be involved in a European war. She was held by the French government after pressure from the British authorities. Upon her release, Bhikhaiji was allowed to stay on in the country only because of the efforts of her socialist French and Russian friends.

Even if some of Bhikhaiji's Parsi acquaintances and relatives ostracised her, describing her as a dangerous revolutionary, she remained nostalgic about Bombay, her home town. Muncherji Cama recalled that his grandfather would relate how every time he met her in Paris, he found her homesick. She would quiz him in detail about the latest Parsi gossip and clap her hands in delight when he had a particularly scurrilous scandal to report. She corresponded in Gujarati with several family members and was generally abreast of the news from Bombay, including the fact that her husband had suffered a major financial downturn. Bhikhaiji retained links with many prominent Parsi business families, including the Tatas, Petits and Saklatvalas who visited France often, and was very friendly with one of Ardeshir Godrej's brothers who had settled in Paris.[13] Among her best friends were Goshi and Perin Naoroji, Dadabhai's granddaughters. Bhikhaiji invested the money she inherited from her father wisely so that she was able to continue funding the revolutionary movement even after the British deprived her of income from the trust. When she first left for England, her husband also gave her a letter of credit to allow her to withdraw money as she desired.[14] She lived modestly, spent little money on herself and over the years sold off much of her jewellery to support the issues in which she believed. Still, during the war years, with the downslide in the economy, she was forced to cut back on her generous donations.

Her health, always frail, began gradually deteriorating. She fractured her skull in a car accident and later had a stroke which paralysed one side of her face. When asked why she did not return to India, she explained that she had taken an oath not to go back on a foreign passport. In 1935, Sir Cowasji Jehangir met an enfeebled and ageing Bhikhaiji who confessed she wanted to die in India. He took the initiative to collect medical certificates from doctors in Paris and asked her to provide a declaration that she would not take part in political activity. She had refused to give such an undertaking earlier, but her infirmities now ensured she could no longer be active in the freedom struggle. She signed an undertaking saying, 'Being 75 years of age and naturally very feeble, I am anxious to go to India to spend the rest of my days, in my birth land, amongst my numerous relatives and friends. I undertake not to take part in politics, direct or indirect.'

The British government finally permitted the 'notorious seditionist', as she was termed, to return home. When she arrived at the Bombay port in November 1935, she was met by her late sister's husband, Rustom Taleyarkhan, and taken directly to the B.D. Petit Parsee General Hospital. The enfeebled old lady had to be carried down the gangway because she could hardly see, walk or hear. Barring a few friends, such as the Naoroji sisters and the Savarkars, no one called on her. Rustom Cama tried to meet her, but she refused to see him. (Since he had a child out of wedlock, he might have wanted to legalise his companion Shirin Warden's position for the sake of their daughter.[15]) Nine months after she returned to India, Bhikhaiji passed away. She bequeathed what remained of her jewellery, furniture and assets to the Petit Orphanage for Girls. The major share of the remainder of her estate was donated to the family agiary in Mazagaon. Her muktad ceremony (the day when the souls of the departed are believed to make their annual visit) is still performed at the Patel Agiary every year.

If Bhikhaiji was the best-known Parsi revolutionary of the twentieth century, Kobad Ghandy is probably her closest twenty-first century counterpart. The police identified him as a politburo member of the banned Communist Party of India (Maoist); he has had around twenty criminal cases filed against him in different parts of India. His 2009 arrest in Delhi, while being treated for cancer, made headlines all over the country. As if to underline the connection, Kobad was arrested in the Bhikaji Cama complex in Delhi, named after Bhikhaiji whom the British had, of course, branded as a notorious seditionist. Kobad is accused by the authorities of being an extremist, a man who helped foment Maoist guerrilla action against the Indian State. There are similarities between Bhikhaiji and Kobad, even if one supported a far-right Hindutva icon in Savarkar and the other was a far-left idealogue. Kobad himself acknowledged their connection. 'Patriotism was the guiding force for both of us,' he acknowledged to me, 'and we have much in common. Only the times and conditions were different. Marxism was and is only a tool.'[16] As with Bhikhaiji,

Kobad came from a wealthy Parsi family. But unlike her family, his backed him to the hilt. The only member of his immediate family still alive today is his sister, Mahrouk Vevaina, who has loyally stood by him and assisted him during his ten-year-long imprisonment, even though she is not a believer of his ideology. He has also had the solid support of his cousins and the Parsi community, including lawyer Fali Nariman and the Parsi journal *Parsiana*.[17]

Now past seventy, this tall, frail white-haired man, suffering from a multitude of ailments—prostrate problems, a bad knee, slipped disc, arthritis, cervical spondylosis, irritable bowel syndrome, dysentery and fading eyesight—has been shuttled from one jail to another across the country. Though he has not been found guilty in a single case, it took him a decade to finally secure bail, with the authorities deliberately dragging their feet. Kobad was not treated as a political prisoner but housed with common criminals and there was no sympathy for his numerous significant health problems.[18]

A man of deep conviction, discipline and dedication, Kobad explained in a letter to his Doon school friend, Gautam Vohra, that he sought comfort in little things in jail. In maintaining some human contact with his fellow prisoners, in befriending a cat or doing a bit of gardening whenever the jail authorities permitted. Kobad's family was not religious, so he was properly introduced to Zoroastrianism only through Rohinton Nariman's book on the Gathas. The book was given to Kobad by Fali Nariman via the former's lawyer when he was at the Tenughat jail in Chhattisgarh, a state where he knew no one and 'everything and everybody was alien'. Kobad started to read *The Inner Fire* because he had nothing else to do, expecting little more than what he described as essentially religious mumbo-jumbo. But he was astonished that the ancient tenets of the religion into which he had been born reflected his own belief that the path of truth requires one to seek happiness for all. He even reviewed the book for the *Parsiana* magazine from his cell.[19]

Kobad is charged by the State with having handled the publicity wing of the banned CPI (Maoist) group, liaising with fellow revolutionaries abroad, preaching outlawed Maoist doctrine for three decades, organising demonstrations and using a fictitious name. There is little proof of any criminal offence in the numerous charges against him. When he was arrested, police officials conceded privately that Kobad has never been accused of actual violence. Asked in an interview by a journalist two years before his arrest about the use of guns by his organisation, Kobad remarked, 'I can't tell you about the armed wing, since I don't deal with that and don't even know their members.' He did say of the organisation he represents that, 'We believe that a democracy which respects people must be established in this country.' Kobad claims that he split with the People's War Group in 1987 due to personal ideological differences, although he remained broadly a sympathiser, writing economic and social articles and books for their publications wing. Through these years, he also kept in touch with Maoists and other Marxist parties abroad. But, some critics have alleged, the Andhra Police and other state police blew such small pieces of speculative evidence up in the media to make a name for themselves.[20]

Kobad's life story is so romantic and idealistic that it has captured the imagination of many—the rich, educated, sophisticated man who has been rotting in prison for over a decade because of his principles. Actor Om Puri admits that his character in the film *Chakravyuha* in 2012 was modelled on Kobad. Adi Ghandy, Kobad's father, was a senior executive in the multinational pharmaceutical firm Glaxo. The family lived in a large apartment on Worli Sea Face in wealthy, fashionable South Bombay. Kobad was sent to Doon School, the country's leading boarding school and often described as the Indian version of Eton. (He was, in fact, for a time, in class with Sanjay Gandhi.)

The family owned a hotel in the hill station of Mahabaleshwar and a bungalow in another hill resort, Panchgani. The family owned an ice-cream manufacturing business Kentucky, which was famous for introducing whole pieces of fruit embedded in the cream, without the use of artificial favours.[21]

After graduating from St Xavier's College in his home city, Kobad went to London to study to be a chartered accountant. It was the 1960s and a period of great ferment among youth throughout the world. His experience in England transformed Kobad's political outlook. He was deeply perturbed by the racism of the British, and felt that the only ones who took the issue seriously enough were various Marxist groups. He read reams of revolutionary literature and came into contact with sympathisers of the radical left. Kobad returned to Mumbai without his accountancy degree and explained to his father than he wanted to understand his own country better. He started working in the slums of Mumbai where he met his soulmate Anuradha Shanbag. She too came from a well-to-do family that owned coffee plantations in Coorg. Her father was a lawyer in Mumbai who often handled cases pro bono for the underprivileged. Inspired by and besotted with each other, Kobad and Anuradha married in 1983. Along with some like-minded colleagues, the couple founded the Committee for Protection of Democratic Rights in the early 1970s, and were deeply involved in anti-Emergency activities. Later, the couple moved to Nagpur, where they lived in a Dalit basti. Anu, was a sociology professor at a Nagpur college, while Kobad worked for a while as a journalist at the *Hitavada* newspaper. Still, their living quarters were as basic as those of their neighbours. Kobad did all the housework, while his wife went to teach. They took up the causes of tribal rights, women's issues and Dalit empowerment. Anuradha's brother Sunil Shanbag, a well-known theatre personality, recalls, 'They were never narrow-minded ideologues, they were non-judgemental and interacted freely with people from all sections of society.'[22] Kobad was gentle and affectionate and never discussed revolutionary work with them. Jyoti Punwani, a journalist and close friend of Anuradha, calls them the 'most unlikely revolutionaries'. She says, 'They liked to have fun and were always enthusiastic. But he was deeply committed to changing the system.'[23]

In the mid-1990s, the couple left Nagpur and decided to work full time with tribal communities in the jungles of central India. This is when they came into contact with Maoists and had per force to go underground for fear of arrest. Now they seemed to be constantly on the run, with even their families unaware of their whereabouts. They never let the physical and mental hardships weigh them down though, despite often spending months apart. In a moving letter from prison, in 2010, Kobad recalls his wife's 'simplicity, straight forwardness and child-like innocence. Our times together were our most cherished moments.' The jungles took a heavy toll on their health. Anuradha suffered from frequent bouts of malaria and sclerosis, an anti-immune disease. In 2008, she died of cerebral malaria after developing a burning fever that could not be treated properly because she was in hiding. Kobad too had bouts of amoebic dysentery.

Though he obtained bail in all twenty of the cases filed against him in 2019, after a full decade in prison, the ailing Kobad's ordeal is far from over. He has to make routine appearances in courts all over the country until either the charges against him are dismissed or he is convicted. His parents have died and so has his brother. But when Kobad's parents were alive, they were proud of their son and of the causes he fought so valiantly for. His father, indeed, gave up his corporate lifestyle, trading his fancy Mumbai flat for a simple home in Panchgani. He appreciated his son's interpretation of the Zoroastrian prayer, that truth is the most important thing in life and truth means contributing towards the happiness of all.[24]

12

Coda

An Ancient Faith in Modern Times

I began this book with the story of my own family which, in many ways, reflects that of the larger community. We Parsis are a vanishing tribe, perhaps unable even to survive beyond the twenty-first century. From a population of 114,000 in 1941, the number of Parsis in India had dwindled to 57,264 in the 2011 Census, a fall of about 10 to 12 per cent per decade. A low birth rate is one factor that explains the rapidly declining population. Parsis tend to marry late and expect to achieve a high standard of living before they have children. These days, of course, Parsi families rarely have more than one or two kids, unlike their aggressively fertile ancestors, for whom a dozen kids was not unusual. In fact, in 2013, the central government's National Minorities Commission even launched the 'Jiyo Parsi' programme that attempted to help proliferate the Parsi population through medical advice and counselling, with limited success. Only around 500 extra Parsi babies have been born in this period.

But another primary reason for the declining numbers of Parsis remains unaddressed—the children of women who marry outside the community are barred from the religion. According to *Parsiana* magazine, 14 per cent of Parsi marriages in 1988 involved a non-Zoroastrian spouse; by 2015, it had grown exponentially to 37 per cent.[1] 'A dominant section of the community in India seems determined to perpetuate its separateness by insisting on what it deems "racial purity",' says Jehangir Patel, editor of *Parsiana*. He adds, with sorrow and perhaps a touch of anger, that in 'Mumbai, the Parsi population is under 37,000 and 35 per cent are above the age of sixty. People want to join and participate in the religion . . . we must be the only religion that says "please don't."'[2] Vispy Wadia, who formed the Association for the Revival of Zoroastrianism in 2006, as a counter to conservative thinking, says, 'Zoroastrianism is a universal religion. It doesn't treat any race as pure or impure. It also does not discriminate between caste and colour. In Iran, the birthplace of our religion, anyone can enter a fire temple. But in India, they follow different rules.'[3]

These issues of Parsi identity are an old tussle between progressive and orthodox forces within the community. Firoza Punthakey Mistree, a scholar and author, married to Khojeste Mistree, regarded as the standard-bearer for Parsi orthodoxy, sees the debate as one between 'the irreligious rich and the pious and devout middle class who have faith'.[4] Unlike many religions, Zoroastrianism has no central papal authority to lay down the law. In fact, after the Parsis moved to Bombay, the priesthood generally played a secondary role to that of the well-heeled gentry in community matters (since it was the laity who were benefactors and trustees of the religious institutions). Rather than the priesthood, it was often the BPP that was the deciding authority on religious and social norms.

Until the mid-nineteenth century, the BPP was instrumental in defining and shaping Parsi identity in Bombay.[5] The history of the punchayet was linked to the community's evolution in the city. Even before it was formally constituted, the leadership of the community was unofficially in the hands of half-a-dozen Parsi 'shetias' (men of wealth and influence who usually had commercial ties with the British). In 1733, the punchayet leadership evolved into a more organised structure with the encouragement of the British who favoured a system of separate administrative structures for different Indian communities under the overarching colonial authority. The two sons of Rustom Manock, the leading Parsi trader and agent of Surat, were among the five original punchayet members. From 1733 to 1787, the punchayet was a plutocratic body. Membership was restricted to the city's wealthiest families, and very often sons replaced fathers, effectively inheriting their community standing and leadership positions. The organisation was free to take steps such as excommunication and even corporal punishment, including beating with shoes, to keep the community in check and ensure adherence to social mores. Relations between the Bombay Parsis and the priests of Navsari were strained, as the latter resisted the growing power of the laity.[6]

There was also a challenge to Navsari from Udvada, a sleepy hamlet on the Gujarat coast, now home to the Iranshah Atash Behram which contains the most sacred fire, consecrated reportedly on a bed of ashes of a holy fire from one of the fire temples in Iran.[7] Tradition holds that the Iranshah fire has never been extinguished since its inception in Sanjan. When Muslim invaders tore through Gujarat, the flame was whisked away from Sanjan and hidden in the Bahrot caves and then moved to Bandsa. Finally, it came to Navsari, where it remained for three centuries. As part of a long-standing conflict between the priests of Navsari and those who came originally from Sanjan, over who got to perform more ceremonies before the Iranshah fire, the ancient fire was spirited away from Navsari secretly by the Sanjan priests. Udvada became its permanent home in 1742. At the request of some prominent local Parsis, the ruler of Baroda provided soldiers to protect the holy fire in Udvada in the eighteenth century. The guard drawn from the Gaekwad's regiments for this purpose was known as 'Bawaji ni Paltan' (The Parsi Platoon).

By the end of the eighteenth century, the punchayet began to pronounce on social issues such as bigamy. A Parsi man who wanted to take a second wife had to first seek the BPP's permission. Other proscriptions included following any customs and rituals that were alien to Zoroastrianism. Superstitions such as wearing amulets and threads, or frequenting Hindu and Muslim shrines were frowned upon. Among the punchayet's first strictures was banning Parsi women from singing in public on festive occasions. Until the mid-nineteenth century, there was ambiguity over the legitimacy of child marriage, a practice common among other Indian communities.

Then, in 1839, an incident galvanised the community, serving as a catalyst for self-preservation. Revered John Wilson converted a sixteen-year-old Parsi boy, Dhanjibhai Nauroji. Even before this baptism, Christian missionaries, particularly the proselytising Wilson, were busy running down Zoroastrianism and criticising its priests' lack of education. The missionaries dubbed it the religion of 'nature worship' and Parsis were frequently described as 'fire worshippers'. The religion was portrayed as dualistic rather than monotheistic. The conversion of two Parsi boys, including Nauroji, at Dr Wilson's school infuriated the community. The punchayet egged on Nauroji's uncle and guardian to file a writ of habeas corpus in the courts and demand that Wilson be prosecuted for kidnapping. The British courts, not unexpectedly, backed the Christian missionary and dismissed the writ, even though a mob of agitated Parsis gathered at the courthouse, threatening physical force to retrieve their boy from the clutches of Wilson. The latter would go on to make a reputation for himself in his homeland by questioning the Zoroastrian value system and the authenticity of Zoroastrian scriptures. (Incidentally, the well-known Wilson College in Mumbai is named after him.) Back in Bombay though the immediate fallout of the conversion case had an adverse impact on Wilson's fortunes, reducing the number of pupils, primarily Parsi, in his school from some 500 to just sixty. The lawsuit also brought the community together and the number of converts to Christianity has remained minimal ever since.[8]

The uproar around conversion also jolted Parsis into the realisation that their priests had to be better educated and not simply recite prayers by rote. Parsi priests ought to learn the ancient Persian languages of Avesta and Pahlavi, some argued, so that they could understand the meaning of their prayers and put themselves in a position to defend the religion against critics on spiritual issues and the essence of Zoroastrianism. For instance, they could argue that Zarathustra's message is only the Gathas, which makes clear there is only one God, Ahura Mazda. Spiritual beings, yazatas or angels, were introduced into the religion long after the Prophet, claims Rohinton Nariman.[9] A seminary for Parsi priests was founded in Bombay in 1854 and more were to follow. The seminaries became popular and the scion of one of the wealthiest Parsi families, Khurshedji Cama, Madame Cama's father-in-law, opened a school for Parsi Iranistic studies.

Young reformers, influenced by Western thinking, wanted a separation between the essence of Zoroastrian religious content and the customs and practices that were incorporated into religious practice over the years by the priests. They interpreted Zoroastrianism as being strictly monotheistic, with the Gathas as the sole frame of reference. They refused to recite prayers in a language that neither they nor the priests understood and demanded translations into Gujarati or English. The orthodox insisted that the prayers could only be recited in Avesta.[10] It was around this time that a depiction of the prophet Zarathustra with a beard and a halo was executed, and seems to have been inspired by portraits of Jesus Christ. The orthodox dubbed those fighting for reforms as Parsis trying to imitate Protestantism.

The Gathas are 238 verses, hymns sung to the one almighty creator, Ahura Mazda. Whereas the first four Gathas were composed and sung by the Prophet himself as teachings to his people, the last is a coda in which the Prophet's daughter gets married. It explains how great was Zarathustra's success in spreading the faith before he died.[11] The first principle of the Gathas is 'Asha', which is the embodiment of truth. Zoroastrian children are taught to respect truth above all else. The other virtues emphasised are purity of mind and righteousness. In the Gathas, there is no concept of nature worship. According to Justice Nariman, fire was originally perceived simply as a symbol of truth. It wasn't until much later that the reverence for the rest of the elements of nature became an essential part of the religion. The high priest of the Iranshah Atash Behram in Udvada, Dasturji Khurshed Dastoor explains that fire holds a central position in the Zoroastrian belief because it is seen as a living, breathing embodiment of the Supreme Divine and a powerful link between the spiritual and material worlds. In the religion, the word 'fire' denotes much more than literal, physical, burning fire; it denotes all forms of energies.[12] Whatever the original belief, though, fire is today undoubtedly the centre of all Zoroastrian religious rituals.

The real difference of opinion centres on a set of practices followed by Indian Zoroastrians, which are contained in documents known as the 'Vendidad' (Laws against Demons). Are these, in fact, integral to the religion? The Vendidad, a much later document than the Gathas, is believed to have been drawn up by Zoroastrian priests. It contains fragments of purported discussions between Ahura Mazda and Zarathustra. Reformists believe that the Vendidad has no religious value except where it reinforces the spirit of the Gathas. Others insist they are ancient oral traditions, later written down as a book of laws for the

Zoroastrian community. Many diktats of the Vendidad, on purity and penance, healing and disposal of the dead, appear awkward and perverse in modern times. And sceptics question how some of the Vendidad's strictures can be considered sacrosanct, while others are summarily jettisoned by otherwise zealous and dogmatic Parsis.[13]

While their Iranian counterparts have modernised, Parsis have remained frozen in time with their dogged adherence to outdated unscientific calendars that no longer harmonise with the solar calendar. As a consequence, the Parsi New Year keeps varying (currently it occurs during the monsoon). Parsis are deeply divided on the issue of calendars and there are three to choose from: Shenshai, Kadmi and Fasli. The seasonal festival, the Spring Equinox of 21 March is observed by most Parsis as Jamshedi Navroz, rather than simply Navroz (New Year) as it is called by Zoroastrians in Iran and elsewhere.

Iranian Zoroastrians look askance at their Indian counterparts' desire to remain entrenched in the past. In a speech in Mumbai in 2011, Shahin Bekhradnia, president of the World Zoroastrian Organisation, pointed out that while the religion prides itself on being based on rational, enlightened thinking, the Parsis insist on adhering to languages and practices that were meant for different times and different conditions. Iranian Zoroastrians do not wear the sudreh and kusti, and often use a gas cylinder (rather than sandalwood) to keep the flame in the fire temple burning. In any case, sandalwood is available only in India and is probably a practice borrowed from the Hindus as are other auspicious and religious symbols such as chowk, garlands, rice and betel nuts used in rituals. But the biggest difference of opinion between Iranian and Parsi Zoroastrians is on the question of conversion.

From 1830, the importance of the punchayet began to decline. The probity of some of the BPP trustees was in question, since decisions were often influenced by class and nepotistic interests.

And with the establishment of British justice and law in India, its role was greatly diminished. The Parsis were now preoccupied with evolving a Parsi code of laws, concerning succession, inheritance, marriage and divorce. After 1865, the punchayet's role was limited largely to being the chief custodian of Parsi community properties, trusts and the functioning of charitable institutions.[14] Today, the BPP remains the custodian of some hundred-odd community charities and bequests but, according to former trustee Noshir Dadrawala, they are either religious trusts or defunct. 'On paper, the BPP has a lot of land, but it has very little cash flow. It looks after some 6,500 flats, of which roughly 5,000 are part of the Wadia baugs and administered by the punchayet along with the committee set up by the Wadia family.'[15]

One of the punchayet's most important trusteeships is its guardianship of Doongerwadi in Mumbai, known as the Towers of Silence. The dakhmas, or wells, into which Parsi corpses are thrown are situated deep inside forty-six acres of forest full of birds and wailing peacocks atop Malabar Hill in Mumbai. The once thick forest is slightly denuded at the moment since in the last few years many of the old trees have fallen either because of storms or white ants. Until the end of the last century, the bodies in these dakhmas were devoured by vultures. Non-Parsis are not allowed beyond the front portion of the garden, where there is a seating space reserved for those not of the religion to pay their last respects to the dead. Only Parsis are permitted to view a corpse and accompany pall-bearers up the hill to a fire temple in the deep thicket. Beyond a certain boundary only the 'nassessalars', or corpse bearers, are permitted. The unfortunate corpse bearers are victims of terrible discrimination within the community because of their duties. They are not supposed to intermix socially with other Parsis and are expected to remain confined to their homes in the dakhma compound.

* * *

The issue of whether outsiders can be admitted into the fold has preoccupied the Parsis for centuries. In the fifteenth century, Changa Asa, a respected lay leader in Gujarat, was believed to have converted Hindus to increase the size of the community. He did so after first consulting Iranian Zoroastrians for advice. Conscious of the lack of ritual knowledge in his own community, Changa Asa had arranged for a Zoroastrian layman of Broach (Bharuch), Nariman Hosang, to travel to Iran and seek guidance from the Zoroastrian dasturs in Yazd and Kerman. Hosang spent a year in Yazd, learning Persian while earning a living by trading in dates. He brought back information on Zoroastrian belief and practice and provided a glimpse into the discrimination faced by Iranian Zoroastrians under Islamic rule. They were marginalised and forced to adhere to a strict dress code to distinguish them from the majority Muslim population. They also had to pay a jizya tax, levied on non-Muslim permanent residents ('dhimmies') of Islamic states. Hosang brought back the response from Iran to Changa Asa's question. It was that one should not oppose the conversion of slaves or servants, provided the prescribed ceremonies were performed, the conversion was for genuine reasons and did not harm the community.[16]

Such exchanges of information between the two communities, known as 'Rivayat', continued for the next three centuries. However, as the Zoroastrians of India became increasingly prosperous and powerful, they no longer turned to the Zoroastrians of Iran for spiritual guidance. By the mid-nineteenth century, they were focused instead on trying to improve the lot of their marginalised co-religionists in Iran. Largely because of Parsi interventions, the conditions of the Iranian Zoroastrians improved. They even succeeded in abolishing the jizya. Some Iranian Zoroastrians, inspired by the affluence of the Parsis, migrated to India. Several of these immigrants started bakeries and restaurants like those back home, leading to the creation of Bombay's once famous

Irani restaurants and cafes, few of which still survive. Others took to chikoo farming with the encouragement of Sir Dinshaw Petit. The second wave of immigrants from Iran in the late nineteenth and early twentieth centuries became an integral part of India's Zoroastrian community.

Parsis now claim that they abjured proselytising in India because this was a condition of their pact with the Sanjan ruler. But the Parsis probably ended the practice of selectively admitting non-Parsis to the fold only by the seventeenth century. By the nineteenth century, the community had developed a great sense of pride in its exclusivity and identity, and objected entirely to the admission of any outsiders.[17] A contentious issue was that several Parsi men had taken non-Parsi women as their mistresses and were seeking to raise their illegitimate children as Parsis. At a community meeting (anjuman) on 11 August 1830, the punchayet decreed that from that day forth, non-Parsis, including the mistresses of Parsis and their illegitimate children, were not to be accepted as part of the fold. However, the practice could not be eradicated through a simple declaration, and some priests continued to perform the navjotes of illegitimate children without the sanction of the punchayet. Fali Nariman recalls Sir Jamshedji Kanga telling his juniors that up to 1865 it was 'customary' for a Parsi gentleman of substance to have more than one wife and several mistresses and hordes of children, legitimate and illegitimate alike. This illicit proliferation of the community was to cease after 1 September 1865 with the advent of the first Parsi Marriage and Divorce Act. When news got around that the Viceroy's Council was considering an enactment compelling monogamy for Parsis, there was a rush to legitimise 'alliances' and 'families'. It was a field day for the priests, who found themselves in great demand, proficiently performing at hastily arranged wedding ceremonies for high fees right up to midnight on 31 August 1865.[18]

Even in the twenty-first century, the schism is still wide open. On the one side are cosmopolitan and affluent modern-thinking Parsis, whether Indians or emigrants, many of whom have family members who have married out of the community but would like future generations to be brought up as Parsis and have navjotes. The Federation of Zoroastrian Associations of North America (FEZANA), for instance, was started in 1987 with the idea of connecting Parsis from different cities and states and maintaining communal bonds even in a new country. First and second-generation Parsi migrants to the West are conscious that if their offspring do not meet fellow Parsis, they are likely to distance themselves from their culture forever. Foreign Zoroastrian organisations, which include a large number of émigré Iranians, are liberal in their attitude and accepting of intermarriage as well as of non-Parsi spouses as members of the Zoroastrian associations.

But not so in the parochial baugs of Mumbai, where the middle classes live in insulated, rent-controlled Parsi housing colonies. For a girl from such an upbringing to marry outside the community still carries a terrible social stigma. As a consequence, there are more spinsters per capita among Parsis than any other community in India.

There is still a stubborn streak of fundamentalism in a sizeable section of this otherwise liberal and highly educated community. This is in part because of the charisma of the conservative, persuasive lay preacher and scholar, Khojeste Mistree. Most priests may have been unwilling to bend with the times, but their influence was limited, particularly as there were always exceptions in the clergy who were agreeable to performing religious ceremonies for those who did not fall within the strict definition of a Parsi. But Mistree succeeded in impressing his strict standards on the Parsi laity for a considerable time.

Mistree, who grew up in Pune, was drawn to mysticism since childhood. He travelled to England at the age of sixteen to attend a water-divining conference, and stayed on in the country to study accountancy. He qualified as a chartered accountant and was on the brink of making partner in a firm when he became interested in religion. He was admitted to Oxford University to study Zoroastrianism. His guide was Professor Mary Boyce, an acclaimed scholar on Zoroastrianism, affiliated to the School of Oriental and African Studies in London. 'Contact with her,' Mistree told an interviewer about Boyce, 'completely changed my life in terms of knowledge, and in terms of the sensitivity which she had towards the living faith.' Until Boyce, Western scholars had focused mainly on the study of Avesta and middle Persian, translating texts, rather than studying practice. Boyce linked both theology and practice to show a continuity of faith.[19]

Mistree returned to Mumbai in 1980 and was invited to give a series of talks on Zoroastrianism. The auditoriums were packed with Parsis, young and old, keen to learn more about the faith in which they were brought up but about which they knew very little. Mistree became something of a religious pop star, thrilling the crowds with his displays of oratory and learning. The effect those lectures had on the audience persuaded him to launch an institute for Zoroastrian studies, offering structured courses for those who wanted to learn more about the religion. His resistance to any concession to changing times coupled with his fast-growing clout made him a highly divisive figure in the community.

Senior journalist Bachi Karkaria regrets that 'reform is a dirty word in the community for reasons more self-serving than sacred.' She believes that Parsis today have little claim to the characteristics and traits that had won the community such renown and success: 'We simply have lost our sense of adventure, sense of liberalism and sense of humour. The voice of the silent majority is lost in the big racket made by a vocal few.' She cites examples of what she describes as an 'uncalled-for sense of entitlement'—Parsi protests against building a particular metro line in Mumbai on the grounds that it will affect the magnetic circuits below an Atash Behram or asking that a part of the Poonawalla-produced COVID-19 vaccine, Covishield, be set aside for Parsis alone. 'Parsis,' she says, 'all clap for their past glories, but no one wants to talk about the present.' Karkaria explains what she means by quoting the writer and critic Shanta Gokhale's theory that 'threatened minorities are seized by pride and paranoia'.[20]

The late Jamsheed Kanga, former Bombay municipal commissioner and Parsi punchayet trustee, argued that Bombay Parsis in particular had become risk-averse and did not like to leave the comfort zone of Mumbai. So, they no longer competed in the civil service entrance exams or took jobs that required them to leave home. Parsis in small towns were far more willing, he claimed, to experiment with new experiences and a new environment.[21]

At the 1960 World Zoroastrian Congress in Tehran, it was hoped that a global body could be formed to lay down a code for contemporary Zoroastrians. But the plans never fructified because of profound, instinctive resistance from the Parsis of Bombay. Mistree saw any attempt at reform as a threat to the religion. He believes, he once told me, that the 'ethnicity of the true followers is what has kept the faith going for 3,500 years'.[22] In 2004, he formed the World Association of Parsi Iranian Zoroastrians (WAPIZ)—the acronym spells out the world 'return' in Gujarati. Those associated with WAPIZ have often won elections to the BPP, which introduced a system of universal adult franchise only in 2008. Since the majority of Parsis reside in Mumbai, around 37,000 at last count, BPP is the big brother from which most other Parsi punchayets and anjumans scattered across the country take their lead. The Delhi Anjuman and the small Calcutta community are exceptions, where the members active in community affairs have a more progressive outlook.

The differences among BPP trustees, between reformists and conservatives, have led to some unseemly squabbles over the last few decades. Indicative of the divide is the fact that many respected names in the community who were elected as trustees resigned before completing their terms because of the aggression and attitudes of some of the more belligerent and close-minded members. Those who left without completing their terms include the likes of Naval Godrej, Jamsheed Kanga, Shiavax Vakil, Muncherjee Cama and Noshir Dadrawala.

One of the major sources of contention was the functioning of the Towers of Silence at Doongerwadi. According to the Vendidad, Zoroastrianism has a unique system of disposal of the dead—dokhmenishini—because cremation pollutes fire, which is considered sacred, and burial is unhygienic. In ancient Iran, the bodies were left on hilltops in pits so that they could be devoured by wild animals or scavenging birds. In the 1940s, the Iranian monarch, Reza Shah, banned this method of disposing of the dead, but in India, Parsis still cling to this tradition in towns that have dakhmas. Mumbai's Doongerwadi complex was donated over the years by different Parsi benefactors who wanted the ancient practice to continue. A common misconception is that the British government granted land to the Parsis for this purpose. In fact, the first dakhma in Bombay was built in 1672 on land donated by the Ghandy family of Bharuch, says Khojeste Mistree. Subsequently, other families also bestowed parcels of land and built wells. (The underground wells which have steps for placing bodies resemble an amphitheatre.)

The system worked efficiently in Bombay for centuries, thanks to the city's large vulture population which swooped down on the bodies almost as soon as they were relinquished to the dakhmas. But towards the end of the twentieth century, India's vulture population practically vanished. This drastic decline was traced to the anti-infammatory drug Diclofenac, which was frequently fed to cattle and other livestock but also prescribed as a painkiller for human beings.[23] Since the vultures feed primarily on the carcasses of dead cattle and buffaloes, they were slowly poisoned, a syndrome known as 'drooping neck'. The disappearance of vultures had an immediate impact on the dakhmas. People living around Doongerwadi complained about the unpleasant odour emanating from the rotting bodies in the wells. From certain vantage points in the plush high-rises that rimmed the area, apartment-dwellers could catch a glimpse of the decomposing corpses. Somebody even managed to secretly take photographs inside the dakhmas. The ghastly photographs of decaying corpses surfaced to the horror and embarrassment of the community at large and the fury of the orthodox. The cream of the Parsi community, led by eminent doctors, warned that, in the absence of vultures, this ancient method of disposing of the dead was a major health hazard and could lead to an epidemic. Respected Parsi professionals began a campaign for the religion to permit cremation. But high priests and conservative Parsis like Mistree were horrified by the suggestion. Polluting fire with dead matter was an unpardonable sin. Dastur Feroze Kotwal, a learned, pious and stern high priest and, like Mistree, a student of Mary Boyce, described the acceptance of the new norm as 'a strike at the very foundation of our religion'.[24] On his advice, the BPP did not permit the Doongerwadi 'bunglis' to be used to hold prayer ceremonies for corpses that would eventually be cremated.

To regenerate the city's vulture population, Mistree, then a trustee of the BPP, mooted the idea of an aviary. The punchayet flew in a raptor expert, Jemima Perry Jones, director of the National Birds of Prey Centre in Gloucestershire, to help find a solution. But she quickly outstayed her welcome, what with her outspoken comment to a newspaper describing the dakhma system as 'bizarre'and media speculation that she was the first non-Parsi to visit the Towers of Silence. Then, to hasten the process of decomposition, the BPP started using chemicals and solar panels.[25] But the issue remained contentious and divisive. The BPP prohibited two priests, Framroze Mirza and Khushru Madan, from performing any ceremonies at Doongerwadi because they had agreed to conduct funerary prayers for those who had been cremated as well as performing the navjotes of children whose mothers had married out of the community. The trustees claimed they had taken advice from such respected high priests as the late Dastur Kaikhusroo Jamasp Asa and Dastur Kotwal.

The late Jamsheed Kanga and Homi Khushrokhan, a respected senior business executive, filed a lawsuit against the BPP trustees, challenging the right of the punchayet to regulate the performance of religious rites and ceremonies. Most leading Parsi lawyers were ranged on the side of the reformists, and the Bombay High Court delivered a stinging judgement against the BPP. The high priests issued a statement terming this an infringement of the community's religious freedom. When the matter came up before the Supreme Court, the nation's highest court was reluctant to adjudicate on a religious subject and instead referred it to a court-appointed mediator. After years of expensive litigation, neither side was satisfied with the mediator's final order. The agreement prohibited the BPP from banning Parsi priests who wished to work in the Doongerwadi complex and the two fire temples under its jurisdiction even if the priests had committed 'irreligious acts' outside Doongerwadi. Ironically, the two priests on whose behalf the case was originally filed were the only exceptions to the rule.[26]

Khushru Madan put out a public statement refuting the allegations levelled against him by six senior priests, the BPP and Mistree's WAPIZ—they had claimed that Madan was converting people to Zoroastrianism for money. In his statement, the reformist priest, dubbed a 'renegade' by the conservatives, cited numerous translated stanzas from the Gathas and prayers to illustrate that

Zarathustra preached tolerance and, while he did not advocate force to spread the religion, he believed it should be open to all. For the benefit of one of his critics, the late Kaikhusroo Jamasp Asa, he quoted the letter written by Jamasp Asa's grandfather who had performed the navjote of Suzanne Tata and also solemnised her marriage with R.D. Tata as per Zoroastrian rites in 1903. The high priest had written to the then secretary of the BPP in 1901, stating that the religion does not bar the acceptance of non-Zoroastrian converts into the fold.

Interestingly, Madan did not refer to a transgression against orthodox belief that another of his critics, Dastur Kotwal, had condoned—the belated navjotes of wealthy industrialist Neville Wadia and his son Nusli Wadia, both of whom had been baptised as Christians. The liberal lobby and the Parsi press sneered at these double standards—one rule for the rich and another for ordinary folk. The fact that Kotwal was allotted an out-of-turn Cusrow Baug flat by the BPP and the Wadia committee was viewed as a quid pro quo. This was one instance where the ultra-orthodox in the community were not on the same side as some of the orthodox priests.

Many feel the most glaring double standards lie in how Parsi men and women who marry out of the community are treated. The woman is excommunicated if she was married in a non-Zoroastrian religious ceremony. Even if she weds simply under the non religious Special Marriages Act, her children cannot be brought up as Zoroastrians; whereas the offspring of a Zoroastrian man who marries out of the community are permitted to remain in the faith. While some attribute this patriarchal attitude to the influence of Hinduism, Mistree disagrees. 'If you look at Sassanian times and Sassanian law books, you will see patriarchy in matters of inheritance. The line of spirituality goes through the male.'[27] Shahin Bekhradnia, of the London-based World Zoroastrian Organisation, disagrees and says that the Gathas treat men and women equally. In fact, today, among Iranian Zoroastrians, women also practice priestly duties.

In 1990, a group of five feminists, including a scion of the Godrej family, Smita Crishna, formed a group called the Association of Inter-Married Zoroastrians to fight to retain their rights to openly practice their religion. The impetus was the death of a young Parsi woman, Roxanne Shah. A practising Zoroastrian, Roxanne had married a Hindu under the Special Marriage Act, 1954, which is non-religious. She died in a car accident and her family brought her remains to Bombay to be consigned to the dakhma. The BPP trustees consulted the two high priests, Kotwal and Jamasp Asa late at night and decreed that her body could not be placed in the Tower of Silence as she had ceased to be a Zoroastrian. Reformists decried the decision as cruel and inhuman.

While the Roxanne debate was confined largely to the community, the issue of Goolrukh Gupta, a Parsi woman who had also married out, attracted nationwide attention when she moved the Gujarat High Court in 2008, asking for an assurance that she had the right to attend her parents' funeral rites at the Tower of Silence in Valsad. She took the legal route after she saw the plight of two friends who were barred from their parents' funerals. After the Gujarat High Court rejected her plea, Goolrukh moved the Supreme Court in 2013. In 2017, the Supreme Court overturned the high court decision, but it also ordered that the issue be placed before a larger constitutional bench.

Apart from the punchayets, another major influence in the community was the Parsi press. The Gujarati newspapers in western India in the early years were almost exclusively dominated by Parsi journalism.[28] The first Gujarati newspaper and the oldest surviving newspaper in Asia is the *Mumbai Samachar*, started in 1822 by Fardoonji Marzban. Initially, the newspaper provided only commercial and shipping news, but by 1855 it had converted into a daily and included a general news section. Increasingly, it took up the cause of religious and social reform among the Parsis and was often critical of the Bombay Parsi Punchayet. However, though it was owned and edited by a series of Parsis, the newspaper's readership consisted mainly of Gujaratis from other communities. To counter the *Mumbai Samachar*, which often attacked the punchayet, a new weekly, the *Jam-e-Jamshed*, was started in 1838, which carried the viewpoint of the punchayet and the orthodox sentiment.[29] The periodical was anonymously funded by Sir Jamsetjee Jejeebhoy, then head of the punchayet. The *Rast Goftar*, which began publishing in 1838 under the stewardship of Dadabhai Naoroji, represented the Indian nationalist point of view and also crusaded for social reform.

Parsi owners of the publications did not usually interfere with the editorial content even when it differed from their own views. For instance, the *Mumbai Samachar* eventually came into the possession of the Cama family as a settlement for unpaid dues. The newspaper frequently took the side of the freedom struggle, even though the Camas were generally supporters of the Raj. The *Jam-e-Jamshed* changed hands several times. For a long period, it was owned by the Marzbans, a family of writers and journalists. The *Jam-e*'s most famous editor-owner was Adi Marzban, who considered himself an out-and-out liberal, and reportedly did not even wear a sudreh and kusti, but he insisted that his newspaper remain staunchly conservative. He used to say, 'The *Jam-e* will survive only as long as it remains conservative,' recalls Shernaaz Engineer, the present editor of the *Jam-e-Jamshed*.[30]

Competing Parsi periodicals often took diametrically opposite positions. The rivalry between two Bombay-based English language weeklies in the 1950s and 1960s, the *Blitz* and *Current*, run by two colourful Parsi owner-editors, R.K. Karanjia and D.F. Karaka, was legendary. The flamboyant Karanjia was the pioneer of tabloid journalism in the country. He was an unlikely but firm supporter of the Soviet Union, even as he also gushed over the royal reign of the Shah of Iran. *Blitz* was bold and brash, and encouraged investigative reporting, and his exposes often rocked the government. The magazine had a huge circulation. In the famous Kawas Nanavati case, which dominated the headlines in 1959 and the early 1960s, Karanjia campaigned relentlessly to win sympathy for the handsome Parsi naval commander who shot dead his wife's philandering lover, Prembhai Ahuja, in cold blood. *Blitz*'s readership soared and the tabloid certainly influenced public opinion. (Even the BPP called a meeting in support of the naval officer in March 1960.) In a city still dominated by the Parsis, the jury exonerated Nanavati.[33] The Nanavati case was cited as a major reason for abolishing the jury system in India.

The Parsi publication that is taken most seriously by the community today is probably the monthly *Parsiana*, published by the outspoken journalist Jehangir Patel, a liberal who has fought courageously to expose hypocrisy and preach reform within the community, infuriating many. *Parsiana* serves as an important link between Parsis in India and other parts of the world.

* * *

Another contentious issue is whether those who are of non-Parsi and non-Iranian ethnic stock can be Zoroastrians. In the US, in the early 1980s, a twenty-seven-year-old Christian chemical engineer, Joseph Peterson, read up on Zoroastrianism in his local library and was so drawn to the religion that, on his own, he learnt the prayers and started following the rituals, including getting his mother to stitch him a sudreh. The North American Zoroastrian Congress, hearing this story, encouraged him to get initiated in the faith through a navjote ceremony and provided the priests. When news of this navjote reached Mumbai, there was an outcry.

The BPP, Kotwal and Mistree were as usual at the forefront of the protests.

There are others outside India and Iran who may not have had a navjote ceremony but consider themselves Zoroastrian. Ali Jaffrey, a Muslim from Pakistan, migrated to North America and started a movement to spread a Zoroastrianism shorn of the rituals practised by the Indian Parsis. He was funded by some wealthy expatriate Iranian Zoroastrians. His followers included the Swedish pop singer Alexander Bard, a Zoroastrian convert. The conservative Parsis of India had no truck with these flamboyant latter-day evangelists who seemed more interested in the philosophy behind Zoroastrianism than the religious customs.

There has also been a revival of interest in Zoroastrianism in countries that had an ancient connection to the religion before the spread of Islam. The central Asian republics of Tajikistan and Uzbekistan were once part of the greater Persian empire; indeed, Zarathustra is believed by many to have been born in the region and to have first preached in those parts. Excavations dating back to 200 BCE have revealed the remains of fire temples and structures that resemble dakhmas. Some of these practices and festivals still exist today. The spring festival Navroz on 21 March, for instance, is thought to have its roots in pre-Islamic Zoroastrian rituals. In Tajikistan, fire is considered sacred and boys have an initiation ceremony at the age of seven.[34]

A few Parsis were keen to encourage potential converts from these countries. Meher Master-Moos, an intrepid Parsi woman with a range of diverse interests and a trained lawyer, was attracted to alternate medicine and holistic healing. She founded the Zoroastrian College in Sanjan. In August 2010, she invited a Russian, Mikhail Chistyakov, a neo-Zoroastrian, for initiation into priesthood. The news of the planned ceremony spread and a group of Parsis, including the president of the BPP at the time, drove down to Sanjan to prevent what they deemed to be an irreligious stunt. Master-Moos accused the mob of ransacking and vandalising her college and manhandling Chistyakov, who returned to Russia bemused by the intolerance of the Parsis. The priest who was to conduct the ceremony fled. He claimed in an interview that hundreds of people in the former Soviet Union considered themselves Zoroastrians and had been drawn to the faith in the religious revival of the 1990s.[35] Mistree, who was at the forefront of the opposition to this 'publicity-seeking venture', dismissed such neo-Zoroastrians and questioned whether they even knew the basic prayers.

He concedes, however, that the Kurds living largely in the mountainous regions of Iran, Iraq, Syria and Turkey have a much stronger case to be counted as neo-Zoroastrians. 'They seem to be taking on Zoroastrianism in a much more serious manner than those in central Asia,' he acknowledges. 'The region where they live is in a state of turmoil, and they feel that Islam may not have given them the spiritual sustenance that a religion should offer. Many are interested in reviving aspects of the old Zoroastrian faith with which they have clear links in terms of language, culture and customs, even if they do not want to abandon Islam. The Gathas have been translated into the Kurdish language and there are some 10,000 copies of the Gathas in the region.'[36]

Orthodoxy may continue to be dominant in the priesthood and a section of the BPP, but reforms in religious practices have slowly gained ground too, thanks to the efforts of Parsi liberals. In August 2015, a group of Parsi Zoroastrians inaugurated a prayer hall at the Worli municipal crematorium for the families of those who choose not to be interred in Malabar Hill's Towers of Silence. Zoroastrian religious ceremonies are first conducted at the prayer hall. During the last few years around 25 per cent of the Parsi community in Mumbai opted for cremation.[37]

In 2017, the sleepy town of Navsari was astir because trustees of the town's dakhma voted to have a burial ground in a section of the compound, despite the objections of the priesthood. That it happened in Navsari, which is a centre of Zoroastrian culture and religion, came as a particular shock. The same year, in December, India's first open prayer hall for Zoroastrians was started under the umbrella of the Association for the Revival of Zoroastrianism in Pune. The prayer hall was meant for reformist Parsis, including those who had married outside the community, their children and even non-Parsis who wanted to learn more about the religion. Within a few months, the centre had held nine navjotes, three funeral prayer ceremonies and two weddings. Mumbai resident Vispy Wadia, one of the moving forces behind the reformist movement, said he was gratified that the concept had been accepted by many in Pune. 'Zoroastrianism,' he says, 'is a revealed universal religion and there is no scope for discrimination in this noble faith.' In addition to the sacred fire, the centre has a community hall, prayer hall and library.[38]

In 2019, the Bhandara Atash Kadeh temple was inaugurated in Houston, the first fire temple in North America that offered all of Zoroastrianism's major rituals, including the boyhood ordination of its priests. The temple was funded by a prosperous real-estate tycoon, Feroze (known locally as 'Fred') Bhandara, a Pakistani Parsi immigrant whose sister is the well-known author, Bapsi Sidhwa. Of the fifteen thousand or so Zoroastrians in the US, around a thousand live in Houston. 'We must adapt in America,' Bhandara, who funded the temple, points out. 'Otherwise, we risk losing our children to other faiths. What our ancient religion needs,' he believes, 'is more American-style openness and tolerance.'[39]

Minorities Commission Vice Chairman Kersi Deboo expresses optimism that the, 'Future of Parsis is not as bad as we assume and those who have migrated abroad will also help to keep the flame of Zoroastrianism burning.' So while it appears to the world that the continued existence of the Parsi community hangs in the balance, this is not obvious to the Parsis themselves. Most believe that a religion that survived for 3,500 years, despite the odds, will manage somehow to survive in spite of the declining numbers of believers. Back in 1879, James Darmesteter, in his introduction to a translation of the Zend-Avesta, wrote pessimistically, 'As Parsis are ruins of a people, so are their sacred books the ruins of a religion.' The term 'ruins of a people', though Darmesteter perhaps meant this in the context of the religion's fall from its dominance of Persia, was surely inappropriate for a community that has proved its standing in its adopted country through successive generations. Parsi numbers may be declining precipitously but the indomitable spirit of the people and their outsized influence on India cannot be so easily snuffed out.

Acknowledgements

My thanks to all those who so very kindly agreed to be interviewed.

A.K. Bhattacharya
Adi Jehangir
Anu Aga
Bachi Karkaria
Chitra Subramaniam
Cyrus Mistry (Late)
Cyrus Poonawalla
Diana Eduljee
Fali Nariman
Farokh Udwadia
Fram Dinshaw
Gulu Ezekeil
Jamsheed Kanga (Late)
Jehangir Patel
Jimmy Mody
Kersi Deboo
Khojeste Mistree

Kobad Ghandy
Maneck Davar
Maja Daruwala
Mithoo Coorlawala
Late Muncherji Cama
Nawaz Mody
Nirmalya Kumar
Noshir Dadrawala
Nusli Wadia
Pheroza Godrej
Ratan Tata
Rohinton Nariman
Rustomjee Maneckjee (Sir Jamsetjee Jejeebhoy, 8th Baronet)
Late Satinder Lambah
Shernaz Cama
Siloo Mathai
Subramaniam Ramadorai
Sucheta Dalal
Suhel Seth
T.N. Ninan
Vicaiji Taraporevala
Vijay Dhar

In addition, a special thanks to those who extended valuable advice and assistance in helping make this project possible.

Ahmed Patel (Late)
Arun Jaitley (Late)
Jehangir Patel
Khorshed Bharucha
Nawaz Mody
Roxna Swamy

Sucheta Dalal
And my editors
G S Ajitha and Chirag Thakkar

And those who preferred to remain anonymous.

Notes

Prologue: A History of the Parsis

1. Encyclopaedia Iranica, https://www.iranicaonline.org/articles/parsi-communities-i-early-history.
2. All references to people from erstwhile Poona and currently Pune date back to the time when the city had its earlier name of Poona.
3. Encyclopaedia Iranica, https://www.iranicaonline.org/articles/parsi-communities-i-early-history.
4. Author's interview with Mithoo Coorlawala.
5. Fali Nariman's lecture on 'Zoroastrianism—the Faith of the Parsis in India', India International Centre, Delhi, 20 August 1999.
6. Author's interview with Rohinton Nariman.
7. Fali Nariman's lecture on 'Zoroastrianism—the Faith of the Parsis in India', India International Centre, Delhi, 20 August 1999.
8. Rukhsana Shroff & Kerman Mehta, *Joyous Flame: The Parsi Zoroastrians*, Parzor Foundation for Preservation of Vulnerable Human Heritage, Delhi, 2011.
9. Author's interview with Rohinton Nariman.
10. Rukhsana Shroff & Kerman Mehta, *Joyous Flame: The Parsi Zoroastrians*, Parzor Foundation for Preservation of Vulnerable Human Heritage, Delhi, 2011.

11. Author's Interview with Kersi Deboo, Vice Chairperson of the National Commission of Minorities in India.

12. Amitav Ghosh, 'Parsis and the China Trade' in Pheroza Godrej and Firoza Mistree (curators of the exhibition catalogue), *Across Oceans Flowing Silks & No Parsi is an Island*, Spenta, Mumbai, 2013.

13. Prashant Kidambi, 'The "Sporting Parsi" and the Making of Indian Cricket', lecture delivered at the Asiatic Society of Mumbai, 18 April 2017.

14. Piloo Nanavutty, *The Parsis*, National Book Trust, Delhi, 1977.

15. Dinayar Patel, 'How Parsis Shaped India's Taste for Soft Drinks', https:// www.bbc.com/news/world-asia-india-51942067.

16. Author's interview with Shernaz Cama.

17. Aditi Shah, 'Bombay's Riot Over Dogs', https://www.livehistoryindia. com/snapshort-histories/2018/05/09/bombays-riot-over-dogs.

18. Jesse S. Palsetia, Early Commerce and the City of Bombay in *Across Oceans Flowing Silks & No Parsi Is an Island*, Spenta, Mumbai, 2013.

19. Ibid.

20. Usha Mehta. 'The Contribution of the Parsi Community to Western India' in Nawaz Modi (ed.), *The Parsis in Western India, 1818 to 1920* (conference publication), Allied Publishers, Bombay, 1998. (The seminar was organised by Mumbai University on the 150th birth celebrations of Sir Pherozeshah Mehta.)

21. Eckehard Kulke, *The Parsees in India*, Vikas, Delhi, 1978.

22. Author's interview with Muncherjee Cama, a former member of the BPP and a member of the illustrious Cama family, which was one of the early Parsi trading families and now owns the *Mumbai Samachar*.

23. Author's interview with Suhel Seth.

Chapter 1: Battle Which Divided a Community

1. Author's interview with Nusli Wadia.

2. 'In the morning trade, Tata Motors share price fell 3.3 per cent, TCS share price shed 0.6 per cent, Tata Steel share price declined 2.7 per cent and Tata Communications share price slipped 2 per cent. Indian Hotels saw the steepest fall of 10 per cent, while Tata Power share price was down 2.9 per cent and Tata Global share price fell 5.3 per cent.'

https://medium.com/@dynamiclevels/mistry-effect-tata-lose-55-000-cr-in-market-cap-in-3-days-98f38fab1928.

3. Author's interview with Vicaiji Taraporevala.

4. Author's interview with Fali Nariman.

5. Berjis Desai, *Oh! Those Parsis*, Zero Degree Publishers, Chennai, 2019.

6. Fali Nariman's lecture on 'Parsi Lore and Law', *Parsiana*, 1994.

7. Author's interview with Chitra Subramaniam.

8. Author's interview with Maneck Davar.

9. Author's interview with Suhel Seth.

10. Girish Kuber, *The Tatas: How a Family Built a Business and a Nation*, Harper Business, Delhi, 2019.

11. Author's interview with Cyrus Mistry.

12. Author's interview with Sucheta Dalal.

13. Jehangir Pocha, 'Tata Sons: Passing the Baton', *Forbes India*, 12 December 2011, https://www.forbesindia.com/article/boardroom/tata-sons-passing-the-baton/31052/1.

14. Author's interview with Nusli Wadia.

15. Author's interview with Siloo Mathai (Ratan Tata's aunt).

16. Author's interview with Adi Jehangir.

Chapter 2: The House of Tatas

1. Peter Casey, *The Greatest Company in the World?: The Story of TATA*, Portfolio/Penguin, Gurgaon, 2014.

2. Author's interview with Suhel Seth.

3. Ibid.

4. Dev Chatterjee, 'Venkatraman: Caught in the Crossfire between Tata and Mistry.' *Business Standard*, 28 October 2016.

5. Author's interview with Ratan Tata.

6. Ibid.

7. R.M. Lala, *Beyond the Last Blue Mountain: A Life of J.R.D. Tata*, Penguin, Delhi, 2017.

8. Author's interview with Ratan Tata.

9. Ibid.

10. Ibid.

11. Mukund Rajan, *The Brand Custodian: My Years with the Tatas*, Harper Business, Delhi, 2019.

12. Author's interview with Satinder Lambah.

13. Mukund Rajan, *The Brand Custodian: My Years with the Tatas*, Harper Business, Delhi, 2019.

14. Piloo Nanavutty, *The Parsis*, National Book Trust, Delhi, 1977.

15. Ibid.

16. F.R. Harris, *Jamsetji Nusserwanji Tata: A Chronicle of His Life*, Blackie and Sons, Bombay, 1958.

17. R.M. Lala, *The Heartbeat of a Trust: A Story of Sir Dorabji Tata Trust*, Tata Mcgraw-Hill, Delhi, 1998.

18. Bakhtiar K. Dadabhoy, *Sugar in Milk: Lives of Eminent Parsis*, Rupa & Co., Delhi, 2008.

19. Margaret Herdeck, Gita Piramal, *India's Industrialists: Volume 1*, Three Continents Press, Washington DC, 1985.

20. The Mistry Family's Appeal Before National Company Law Tribunal, p. 42.

21. Tata sources.

22. Naval Tata's papers, Tata Archives.

23. Girish Kuber, *The Tatas: How a Family Built a Business and a Nation*, Harper Business, Delhi, 2019.

24. R.M. Lala, *Beyond the Last Blue Mountain: A Life of J.R.D. Tata*, Penguin, Delhi, 2017.

25. Ibid.

26. Ibid.

27. Author's interview with Mithoo Coorlawala, a friend of Rhodabey.

28. Piloo Nanavutty, *The Parsis*, National Book Trust, Delhi, 1977.

29. Zareer Masani, *And All is Said: Memoir of a Home Divided*, Penguin, Delhi, 2012.

30. R.M. Lala, *Beyond the Last Blue Mountain: A Life of J.R.D. Tata*, Penguin, Delhi, 2017.

31. Author's interview with Ratan Tata.

32. Sudha Murthy's tribute to JRD, Tata Archives.

33. Author's interview with Vijay Dhar.

34. Author's interview Maneck Davar.

35. Ramachandra Guha, column in the *Hindustan Times*, 24 September 2017.

36. R.M. Lala, *Beyond the Last Blue Mountain: A Life of J.R.D. Tata*, Penguin, Delhi, 2017.

37. Author's interview with T.N. Ninan.

38. J. Anthony Lukas, 'India is as Indira Does', *The New York Times*, 4 April 1976, https://www.nytimes.com/1976/04/04/archives/india-is-as-indira-does-with-total-censorship-guaranteeing-a-docile.html.

39. Author's interview with T.N. Ninan.

40. Author's interview with Ratan Tata.

41. Author's interview with Jimmy Mody, Russi Mody's nephew.

42. Author's interview with Suhel Seth.

43. Author's interview with Nusli Wadia.

44. Author's interview with Ratan Tata.

45. Ibid.

46. Pravin Kadle, speech at the Y.B. Chavan National Award, 2014.

47. T.N. Ninan, *The Turn of the Tortoise: The Challenge and Promise of India's Future*, Allen Lane, Delhi, 2015.

48. Author's interview with Sucheta Dalal.

49. Krishna Kant, 'TCS Accounts for Two-thirds of Tata Group's Market Value', *Business Standard*, 4 September 2015.

50. Author's interview with S. Ramadorai.

51. Ibid.

52. Subramaniam Ramadorai, *The TCS Story & Beyond*, Penguin, Delhi, 2011.

53. 'I Am Surprised Raja After All You Did For Him Is Playing This Game': Ratan Tata, *Outlook*, https://magazine.outlookindia.com/story/ i-am-surprised-raja-after-all-you-did-for-him-is-playing-this-game/268082.

Chapter 3: The Blue-Blooded Outsider

1. Jesse S. Palsetia, *The Parsis of India: Preservation of Identity in Bombay City*, Brill, Boston, 2001.

2. Ardeshir Ruttonji Wadia, *The Bombay Dockyard and the Wadia Master Builders*, R.A. Wadia, Bombay, 1957.

3. Maneck S. Wadia, 'The Star-Spangled Parsis', https://lifeasahuman. Com/2015/arts-culture/culture/the-star-spangled-parsis/.

4. Mani P. Kamerkar, 'Parsis in Maritime Trade on the Western Coast of India from the Seventeenth to the Nineteenth Century', Nawaz Mody (ed.), *The Contribution of the Parsi Community to Western India between 1818 and 1920*, Allied Publishers, 1998.

5. Records of the Peabody Essex Museum, Salmem, Mass., USA. The records are in the museum mentioned in 'The Wadias of India: Then and Now' (citation below).

6. 'The Wadias of India: Then and Now', Zoroastrian Educational Institute, http://www.zoroastrian.org.uk/vohuman/Article/The%20 Wadias%20 of%20India.htm.

7. Jesse S. Palsetia, *The Parsis of India: Preservation of Identity in Bombay City*, Brill, Boston, 2001.

8. Obituary of Ardaseer Cursetjee, Proceedings of the Society of Civil Engineers, 1878.

9. Mani P. Kamerkar, 'Social Crusaders' in Nawaz B. Mody (ed.), *Enduring Legacy: Parsis of the 20th Century: Volume 1*, published by Nawaz B. Mody, 2005.

10. Omkar Goswami, *Goras and Desis: Managing Agencies and the Making of Corporate*, Penguin Random House India, Gurgaon, 2016.

11. Sam Kerr, 'Bai Jerbai Nusherwanji Wadia (1852-1926): An ordinary lady with an extra-ordinary vision', http://www.avesta.org/kerr/Bai_Jerbai_Nusherwanji_Wadia.pdf.

12. Author's Interview with Jairam Ramesh.

13. Kuldip Singh, 'Obituary: Neville Wadia', https://www.independent.co.uk/news/people/obituaryneville-wadia-1308408.html.

14. Sheela Reddy, *Mr and Mrs Jinnah: The Marriage that Shook India*, Penguin Random House, Gurgaon, 2017.

15. Zenobia Shroff, 'Jeejebhoy Dadabhoy and the Industrialisation of Bombay', Nawaz Mody (ed.), *The Contribution of the Parsi Community to Western India between 1818 and 1920*, Allied Publishers, 1998.

16. Omkar Goswami, *Goras and Desis: Managing Agencies and the Making of Corporate*, Penguin Random House India, Gurgaon, 2016.

17. Sheela Reddy, *Mr and Mrs Jinnah: The Marriage that Shook India*, Penguin Random House, Gurgaon, 2017.

18. M.C. Chagla, *Roses in December: An Autobiography*, Bharatiya Vidya Bhavan, Mumbai, 2012 (12th Ed.).

19. Author's interview with Nusli Wadia.

20. Ibid.

21. Vir Sanghvi, 'Nusli Wadia', https://virsanghvi.com/People-Detail. aspx? Key=11.

22. Ibid.

23. Ibid.

24. Author's interview with Muncherjee Cama.

25. Vir Sanghvi, 'Nusli Wadia', https://virsanghvi.com/People-Detail. aspx? Key=11.

26. Ibid.

27. Ibid.

28. Author's interview with Vijay Dhar.

29. Ibid.

30. Author's interview with Nusli Wadia.

31. Author's interview with Suhel Seth.

32. Vir Sanghvi, 'Creating the Taj', *Hindustan Times Brunch*, 23 April 2017.

33. Ritu Sarin, 'The Tata Tapes', *The Indian Express*, 4–6 October 1997.

34. ENS, 'My stand is vindicated: Mahanta', *The Indian Express*, 6 October 1997, https://indianexpress.com/article/news-archive/my-stand-is-vindicated-mahanta/.

35. Author's interview with Nusli Wadia.

36. Ibid.

37. Shyamal Majumdar and Dev Chatterjee, 'I Missed the Bus because I Didn't Manipulate the System: Nusli Wadia', *Business Standard*, 5 November 2012.

38. Kala Vijayraghavan and Rajesh Mascarenhas, 'The Britannia Way: Wadias to Forsake Executive Roles, Remain Shareholders', *Economic Times*, 7 April 2021, https://economictimes.indiatimes.com/industry/cons-products/fmcg/the-britannia-way-wadias-to-forsake-executive-roles-remain-shareholders/articleshow/81956825.cms.

39. Devendra Pandey, 'Preity Zinta, Ness Wadia Fought over Front Row Seats', *The Indian Express*, 17 June 2014, https://indianexpress.com/article/entertainment/bollywood/preity-zinta-ness-wadia-fought-over-front-row-seats/.

40. Author's interview with Fram Dinshaw, FE's great-grand-nephew.

41. Source requests anonymity.

42. Author's interview with Fram Dinshaw.

43. Palakunnathu G. Mathai, 'A Maverick in Politicks', *Business Today*, 22 September 2019, https://www.businesstoday.in/magazine/the-break-out-zone/a-maverick-in-politics/story/376775.html.

44. PTI, 'Jinnah House Row: Bombay HC Allows Nusli Wadia to Replace His Mother as Petitioner', *Economic Times*, 9 August 2018, https://economictimes.indiatimes.com/news/politics-and-nation/jinnah-house-row-bombay-hc-allows-nusli-wadia-to-replace-his-mother-as-petitioner/articleshow/65340133.cms.

45. Baiju Kalesh, 'Tata Sons EGM: Rift between Ratan Tata, Nusli Wadia Widens over Cyrus Mistry Feud', *Economic Times*, 12 November 2016.

Chapter 4: Missing the Midas Touch

1. Ibid.

2. Marzban Jamshedji Giara, *Parsi Statues*, Marzban J. Giara, Mumbai, 2000.

3. Jamsheed Kanga, 'Building for Posterity' in Nawaz B. Mody (ed.), *Enduring Legacy: Parsis of the 20th Century*, published by Nawaz B. Mody, 2005.

4. Ibid.

5. Ratan Karaka, 'Last of the Sethias', *Parsiana*, 1975.

6. Jamsheed Kanga, 'Building for Posterity' in Nawaz B. Mody (ed.), *Enduring Legacy: Parsis of the 20th Century*, published by Nawaz B. Mody, 2005.

7. Aman Nath and Nandini Lakshman, *Changing Skylines: The Shapoorji Pallonji Sesquicentennial, 1865–2015*, Pictor Publishing, Mumbai, 2015.

8. Ratan Karaka, 'Last of the Sethias', *Parsiana*, 1975.

9. Ibid.

10. Aman Nath and Nandini Lakshman, *Changing Skylines: The Shapoorji Pallonji Sesquicentennial, 1865–2015*, Pictor Publishing, Mumbai, 2015.

11. Related to the author by a Time and Talents member who was present at the meeting.

12. Author's interview with Soli Sorabjee.

13. See paragraph 19.16 at p. 223 of Tata Consultancy Services Ltd vs Cyrus Investments Pvt. Ltd, https://main.sci.gov.in/supremecourt/2020/212/212_2020_31_1503_27229_Judgement_26-Mar-2021.pdf.

14. Affdavit submitted by the Tata Trusts to the National Company Law Board Tribunal.

15. Deepak Parekh, 'When the Tatas had No Money to Pay Pallonji Family', https://www.businesstoday.in/current/economy-politics/when-the-tatas-had-no-money-to-pay-pallonji-family/story/238963.html.

16. Jehangir Pocha, 'Tata Sons: Passing the Baton', *Forbes India*, 12 December 2011.

17. Ibid.

18. Mistry family sources.

19. Author's interview with A.K. Bhattacharya.

20. Aman Nath and Nandini Lakshman, *Changing Skylines: The Shapoorji Pallonji Sesquicentennial, 1865–2015*, Pictor Publishing, Mumbai, 2015.

21. Author's interview with Sucheta Dalal.

22. Author's interview with Cyrus Mistry.

23. Reeba Zachariah & Namrata Singh, 'Mistry First Tata Chairman Who Didn't Head the Trusts', *Times of India*, 29 October 2016.

24. Author's interview with Nusli Wadia.

25. Author's interview with Cyrus Mistry.

26. Ibid.

27. Nirmalya Kumar, 'How Cyrus Mistry was Fired as Tata Chairman', blog post, 21 October 2017, https://nirmalyakumar.com/2017/10/21/how-cyrus-mistry-was-fred-as-tata-chairman/.

28. Ibid.

29. Money Life digital team, 'Global Experts Question Harvard Dean Nitin Nohria's Role in Tata Imbroglio', 22 December 2016, https://www.Moneylife.in/article/global-experts-question-harvard-dean-nitin-nohrias-role-in-tata-imbroglio/49242.html.

30. T.T. Ram Mohan, 'A Comprehensive Win for the Tatas', *Business Standard*, 8 April 2021, https://www.business-standard.com/article/opinion/a-comprehensive-win-for-the-tatas-121040801739_1.html.

31. Mukund Rajan, *The Brand Custodian: My Years with the Tatas*, Harper Business, Delhi, 2019.

32. Swaminathan Aiyar, 'Charitable Trusts must Not Exert Corporate Control', *Times of India*, 5 January 2020.

33. Mukund Rajan, *The Brand Custodian: My Years with the Tatas*, Harper Business, Delhi, 2019.

34. Author's interview with Nirmalya Kumar.

35. Author's interview with Ratan Tata.

36. Satish John & Kala Vijayaraghavan, 'We Won't Curtail Investments in Retail Businesses', *Economic Times*, 23 June 2020.

37. Kala Vijayraghavan, Satish John & Arijit Barman, 'Tatas Object to Shapoorji Pallonji Group Plan to Pledge Stake', *Economic Times*, 1 April 2020.

38. Rajat Sethi, 'Tata-Mistry Case: A Bittersweet Victory for the Tata Group', *Bloomberg Quint*, 30 March 2021, https://www.bloomberg quint.com/opinion/tata-mistry-case-a-bittersweet-victory-for-the-tata-group.

Chapter 5: The History of an Entrepreneurial Community

1. Mani P. Kamerkar, 'Parsis in Maritime Trade on the Western Coast of India from the Seventeenth to the Nineteenth Century', Nawaz Mody (ed.), *The Contribution of the Parsi Community to Western India between 1818 and 1920*, Allied Publishers, 1998.

2. Ibid.

3. Jesse Palsetia, 'Early Commerce and the City of Bombay' in Pheroza Godrej and Firoza Mistree (curators of the exhibition catalogue), *Across Oceans, Flowing Silks*, Spenta, Mumbai, 2013.

4. Ibid.

5. Mani P. Kamerkar, 'Parsis in Maritime Trade on the Western Coast of India from the Seventeenth to the Nineteenth Century', Nawaz Mody (ed.), *The Contribution of the Parsi Community to Western India between 1818 and 1920*, Allied Publishers, 1998.

6. Amitav Ghosh, 'The Parsis and the China Trade' in Pheroza Godrej and Firoza Mistree (curators of the exhibition catalogue), *Across Oceans, Flowing Silks*, Spenta, Mumbai, 2013.

7. Jesse S. Palsetia, *Jamsetjee Jejeebhoy of Bombay: Partnership and Public Culture in Empire*, Oxford University Press, Delhi, 2015.

8. Ibid.

9. Thomas Manuel, 'The Opium Trader Who Became Baronet of Bombay', *Hindu Magazine*, 5 May 2019.

10. Jesse Palsetia, 'Early Commerce and the City of Bombay' in Pheroza Godrej and Firoza Mistree (curators of the exhibition catalogue), *Across Oceans, Flowing Silks*, Spenta, Mumbai, 2013.

11. Eckehard Kulke, *The Parsees in India*, Vikas, Delhi, 1978.

12. Rayoman Ilavia, 'Parsi, Thy Name Is Charity', *Times of India* Readers' Blog, 15 September 2019, https://timesofindia.indiatimes.com/readersblog/jiyoparsi/parsi-thy-name-is-charity-5686/.

13. Author's interview with Shernaz Cama.

14. Author's interview with Rustom Jejeebhoy, Eighth Baronet.

15. Ibid.

16. 'Zenobia Shroff, Jeejebhoy Dadabhoy and the Industrialisation of Bombay', in Nawaz Mody (ed.), *The Contribution of the Parsi Community to Western India between 1818 and 1920*, Allied Publishers, 1998.

17. Eckehard Kulke, *The Parsees in India*, Vikas, Delhi, 1978.

18. Ibid.

19. Author's interview with Adi Jehangir.

20. Ibid.

21. Ranjit Hoskote, 'Jehangir Sabavala' in Nawaz B. Mody (ed.), *Enduring Legacy: Parsis of the 20th Century: Vol. II*, published by Nawaz B. Mody, 2005.

22. Piloo Nanavutty, *The Parsees*, National Book Trust, 1977.

23. Ibid.

24. Mani P. Kamerkar, 'Trade Union Movement' in Nawaz B. Mody (ed.), *Enduring Legacy: Parsis of the 20th Century: Vol. II*, published by Nawaz B. Mody, 2005.

25. Ibid.

26. Ibid.

27. Ibid.

Chapter 6: Billionaires, Old and New

1. Sarah Wheaton, 'Meet the Indian Drug Mogul Who's Challenging the West over Vaccines', *Politico*, 16 July 2020.

2. Barkha Dutt's interview with Adar Poonawalla, 'Betting on the Covid Vaccine', *Mojo*, 21 July 2020.

3. Author's interview with Cyrus Poonawalla.

4. AP, 'Covid-19 Vaccine Exports Depend on India Situation: Serum Institute's Adar Poonawalla', *Economic Times*, 7 April 2021, https:// economictimes.indiatimes.com/industry/healthcare/biotech/ pharmaceuticals/covid-19-vaccine-exports-depend-on-india-situation- serum-institutes-adar-poonawalla/articleshow/81935477.cms.

5. Bloomberg Billionaires Index 2020, https://www.bloomberg.com/ billionaires/.

6. PTI report, 'Wealth of Serum's Poonawalla Grows Fastest in India during Pandemic: Hurun Research Report', *Outlook*, 23 June 2020, https:// www.outlookindia.com/newsscroll/wealth-of-serums- poonawalla-grows-fastest-in-india-during-pandemic-hurun-research- report/ 1874844.

7. Author's interview with Cyrus Poonawalla.

8. Ibid.

9. Sarah Wheaton, 'Meet the Indian Drug Mogul Who's Challenging the West over Vaccines', *Politico*, 16 July 2020.

10. Barkha Dutt's interview with Adar Poonawalla, 'Betting on the Covid Vaccine', *Mojo*, 21 July 2020.

11. Ibid.

12. Jamal Shaikh, 'Family over Fashion', *Hindustan Times Brunch*, 9 August 2020.

13. N. Madhavan, 'Serum Institute's Adar Poonawalla is More than Just a Businessman', *Forbes India*, 5 December 2016.

14. Ibid.

15. Rahul Kanwal's interview with Cyrus Poonawalla, 'Jab We Met', India Today TV, 13 July 2019.

16. Author's interview with Cyrus Poonawalla.

17. Ibid.

18. Bakhtiar K. Dadabhoy, *Sugar in Milk: Lives of Eminent Parsis*, Rupa & Co., Delhi, 2008.

19. B.K. Karanjia, *Vijitatma: Founder-pioneer Ardeshir Godrej*, Viking, New Delhi, 2004.

20. Ibid.

21. B.K. Karanjia, 'The Godrej Dynasty' in Nawaz B. Mody (ed.), *Enduring Legacy: Parsis of the 20th Century*, published by Nawaz B. Mody, 2005.

22. Bakhtiar K. Dadabhoy, *Sugar in Milk: Lives of Eminent Parsis*, Rupa & Co., Delhi, 2008.

23. B.K. Karanjia, 'The Godrej Dynasty' in Nawaz B. Mody (ed.), *Enduring Legacy: Parsis of the 20th Century*, published by Nawaz B. Mody, 2005.

24. Sohrab Godrej & B.K. Karanjia, *Abundant Living, Restless Striving: A Memoir*, Penguin, Delhi, 2001.

25. Nadir Godrej interview by Ankit Dey and S. Aijaz, yourstory.com, May 1975.

26. Author's interview with Maneck Davar.

27. Sohrab Godrej & B.K. Karanjia, *Abundant Living, Restless Striving: A Memoir*, Penguin, Delhi, 2001.

28. Author's interview with Maneck Davar.

29. B.K. Karanjia, *Final Victory: The Life and Death of Naval Pirojsha Godrej*, Penguin, Delhi, 2000.

30. Author's interview with Pheroza Godrej.

31. Author's interview with Maneck Davar.

32. Author's interview with Pheroza Godrej.

33. B.K. Karanjia, *Final Victory: The Life and Death of Naval Pirojsha Godrej*, Penguin, Delhi, 2000.

34. Author's interview with Pheroza Godrej.

35. Ibid.

36. TNN, 'Godrej May See Restructuring as Clan Differs on Business Strategy', *Times of India*, 27 June 2019.

Chapter 7: The Community's Backbone

1. Berjis Desai, *Oh! Those Parsis: A to Z of the Parsi Way of Life*, Zero Degree Publishing, Chennai, 2019.

2. Eckehard Kulke, *The Parsees in India: A Minority as Agent of Social Change*, Vikas Publishing House, Delhi, 1975.

3. Robert E. Kennedy, Jr, 'The Protestant Ethic and the Parsis', *American Journal of Sociology*, vol. 68, No. 1, July 1962.

4. Bachi Karkaria, *In Hot Blood: The Nanavati Case that Shook India*, Juggernaut, Delhi, 2017.

5. Abhishek Manu Singhvi, 'Nani Palkhivala: God's Gift to India', *Times of India* blog, 12 May 2019. https://timesofindia.indiatimes.com/blogs/straight-candid/nani-palkhivala-gods-gift-to-india/?source=app&frmapp=yes.

6. Bakhtiar K. Dadabhoy, *Sugar in Milk: Lives of Eminent Parsis*, Rupa, Delhi, 2008.

7. Author's interview with Soli Sorabjee.

8. Homai N. Modi, 'Nani Palkhivala: Exemplary Citizen', in Nawaz B. Mody (ed.), *Enduring Legacy: Parsis of the 20th Century*, published by Nawaz B. Mody, 2005.

9. Author's interview with Subramaniam Ramadorai.

10. Bakhtiar K. Dadabhoy, *Sugar in Milk: Lives of Eminent Parsis*, Rupa, Delhi, 2008.

11. Author's interview with Soli Sorabjee.

12. Fredun E. DeVitre, 'Eminent Lawyers', in Nawaz B. Mody (ed.), *Enduring Legacy: Parsis of the 20th Century*, published by Nawaz B. Mody, 2005.

13. Author's interview with Rohinton Nariman.

14. Author's interview with Fali Nariman.

15. Ibid.

16. Noshir Antia and Behman Daver, 'The Healing Touch' in Nawaz B. Mody (ed.), *Enduring Legacy: Parsis of the 20th Century*, published by Nawaz B. Mody, 2005.

17. Author's interview with Dr Farokh E. Udwadia.

18. Noshir Antia and Behman Daver, 'The Healing Touch' in Nawaz B. Mody (ed.), *Enduring Legacy: Parsis of the 20th Century*, published by Nawaz B. Mody, 2005.

19. Ibid.

20. Author's interview with Jamsheed Kanga.

21. Kersi Meher-Homji, 'Legendary Cricketers' in Nawaz B. Mody (ed.), *Enduring Legacy: Parsis of the 20th Century: Volume IV*, published by Nawaz B. Mody, Mumbai, 2005.

22. Bertil Falk, *Feroze: The Forgotten Gandhi*, Roli Books, Delhi, 2016.

23. Ibid.

24. Ibid.

25. Ibid.

26. Ibid.

27. Ibid.

28. As told to author by the late D.N. Singh, a journalist at the *Indian Express* at the time.

29. Nergesh Charna, 'Parsis in Politics' in Nawaz B. Mody (ed.), *Enduring Legacy: Parsis of the 20th Century: Volume I*, published by Nawaz B. Mody, Mumbai, 2005.

30. Author's interview with Muncherji Cama.

Chapter 8: Trailblazing Women

1. Eckehard Kulke, *The Parsees in India: A Minority as Agent of Social Change,* Vikas Publishing House, Delhi, 1975.

2. Author's interview with Muncherji Cama.

3. Parinaz Madan and Dinyar Patel, 'The Pioneering Lawyer Who Fought for Women's Suffrage in India', *BBC News*, 23 December 2020, https:// www.bbc.com/news/world-asia-india-55134978.

4. Ibid.

5. Ibid.

6. Noshir Antia and Behman Daver, 'The Healing Touch' in Nawaz B. Mody (ed.), *Enduring Legacy: Parsis of the 20th Century: Volume II*, published by Nawaz B. Mody, Mumbai, 2005.

7. Haresh Pandya, 'Homai Vyarawalla, Pioneering Indian Photojournalist, Dies at 98', *The New York Times*, 28 January 2012, https://www.nytimes.com/2012/01/29/world/asia/homai-vyarawalla-india-photojournalist-dies-at-98.html.

8. Nawaz B. Mody and Marzban Giara, 'Through the Lens' in Nawaz B. Mody (ed.), *Enduring Legacy: Parsis of the 20th Century: Volume III*, published by Nawaz B. Mody, Mumbai, 2005.

9. Duncan Fallowell, *How to Disappear: A Memoir for Misfits*, Ditto Press, London, 2011.

10. Ibid.

11. Encyclopaedia Iranica, https://www.iranicaonline.org/articles/pavry-bapsy-cursetji.

12. Author's interview with Adi Jehangir.
13. Usha Thakkar, 'Avabai B Wadia: Visionary Activist' in Nawaz B. Mody (ed.), *Enduring Legacy: Parsis of the 20th Century: Volume II*, published by Nawaz B. Mody, Mumbai, 2005.
14. Author's interview with Anu Aga.
15. Ibid.
16. Kersi Meher-Homji, 'Legendary Cricketers' in Nawaz B. Mody (ed.), *Enduring Legacy: Parsis of the 20th Century: Volume IV*, published by Nawaz B. Mody, Mumbai, 2005.
17. Author's interview with Diana Edulji.

Chapter 9: Pioneers in Cricket, Theatre and Cinema

1. Vasant Raiji, *India's Hambledon Men*, Tyeby Press, 1986.
2. Ibid.
3. Ibid.
4. J.M. Framjee Patel, 'Stray Thoughts on Indian Cricket', *Times of India*, Bombay, 1905.
5. Scyld Berry, *Cricket the Game of Life—Every Reason to Celebrate*, Scyld Berry Hodder and Stoughton, 2015.
6. Vasant Raiji, *India's Hambledon Men*, Tyeby Press, 1986.
7. W.A. Bettersworth, *Chats on the Cricket Field*, Merrit and Hatcher Ltd, 1910.
8. Gulu Ezekiel and Vijay Lokappally, *Speed Merchants: The Story of Indian Pace Bowling 1880s to 2019*, Bloomsbury, 2020.
9. Kersi Meher-Homji, 'A Gentleman's Game', in Nawaz B. Mody, ed., *Enduring Legacy Volume III : Parsis of the 20th Century*, Nawaz B. Mody, Mumbai, 2005.
10. Author's interview with Gulu Ezekiel.
11. Ibid.
12. Rusi Modi, *Some Indian Cricketers*, National Book Trust, 1974.
13. Author's interview with Diana Edulji.
14. Harish Bhatt, 'Sir Dorabji Tata and the Olympic', *The Hindu*, 26 August 2020.
15. Rashna Nicholson interview with *Parsiana*, 'More than a Natak', September 2021.

16. Farrokh Jijina, 'Parsi Theatre's Four Pillars', *Parsiana*, September 2021.
17. Ibid.
18. Rashna Nicholson, 'How Parsi Theatre Gave an Impetus to Hindu Mythological Plays in Victorian India', *Wire*, 2 November 2021.
19. Nicola Pais, *Chalo Natak: The Appeal and Influence of Parsi Theatre*, 16 July 2021, Indian Cinema Heritage Foundation.
20. Farrokh Jijina, 'Underexposed Film Maker', *Parsiana*, 2019.
21. Amrit Gangar, 'Sohrab Modi, Historical Film Maker', in Nawaz B. Mody, ed., *Enduring Legacy*, Volume III, *Parsis of the 20th Century*, Mumbai, 2005.
22. Farokh Jijina, 'Actor Bombay Irani is Taking on New Roles', Parsiana, 2019.
23. Coomi Vevaina, 'Adi Marzban', in Nawaz B. Mody, ed., *Enduring Legacy*, Volume III, *Parsis of the 20th Century*, Mumbai, 2005.
24. Author's interview with Bachi Karkaria.

Chapter 10: The Iconic Four

1. Jessica Steinberg, 'Music Master Digs Freddie Mercury', *The Times of Israel*, 26 December 2012. https://www.timesofsrael.com/a-maestro-who-digs-freddie-mercury/.
2. Chintamani Deshmukh, *Homi Jehangir Bhabha*, National Book Trust, Delhi, 2010.
3. Ibid.
4. Ibid.
5. Jamsheed Kanga, 'Dr Homi Bhabha: Renaissance Man' in Nawaz B. Mody (ed.), *Enduring Legacy: Parsis of the 20th Century: Volume II*, published by Nawaz B. Mody, Mumbai, 2005.
6. Chintamani Deshmukh, *Homi Jehangir Bhabha*, National Book Trust, Delhi, 2010.
7. Ibid.
8. Ibid.
9. Raj Chengappa, *Weapons of Peace: The Secret Story of India's Quest to be a Nuclear Power*, HarperCollins India, Delhi, 2000.
10. Ibid.
11. Ibid.

12. Marzban Jamshedji Giara, 'Prophet of the Atomic Age: Dr. Homi Jehangir Bhabha', *parsikhabar.net*, 29 October 2019. https://parsikhabar.net/science/prophet-of-the-atomic-age-dr-homi-jehangir-bhabha/21284/.

13. Author's interview with Maja Daruwala.

14. Ibid.

15. Maj. Gen. (Retd) Shubhi Sood, *Leadership: Field Marshal Sam Manekshaw*, SDS Publishers, Noida, 2006.

16. Brigadier (Retd) Behram Panthaki and Zenobia Panthaki, *Field Marshal Sam Manekshaw: The Man and His Times*, Niyogi Books, Delhi, 2014.

17. Ibid.

18. Ibid.

19. Lieutenant General Depinder Singh, *Field Marshal Sam Manekshaw: Soldiering with Dignity*, Natraj Publishers, Delhi, 2003.

20. Ibid.

21. Vinod Saighal, 'Field Marshal Sam Manekshaw', *The Guardian*, 30 June 2008, https://www.theguardian.com/world/2008/jun/30/india.

22. Maj. Gen. (Retd) Shubhi Sood, *Leadership: Field Marshal Sam Manekshaw*, SDS Publishers, Noida, 2006.

23. Ibid.

24. Author's interview with Maja Daruwala.

25. Lieutenant General Depinder Singh, *Field Marshal Sam Manekshaw: Soldiering with Dignity*, Natraj Publishers, Delhi, 2003.

26. Vinod Saighal, 'Field Marshal Sam Manekshaw', *The Guardian*, 30 June 2008, https://www.theguardian.com/world/2008/jun/30/india.

27. Zubin Mehta, *The Score of My Life*, Amadeus Press, New York, 2009.

28. Ibid.

29. Ibid.

30. Ibid.

31. Ibid.

32. Bakhtiar K. Dadabhoy, *Sugar in Milk: Lives of Eminent Parsis*, Rupa, Delhi, 2008.

33. Zubin Mehta, *The Score of My Life*, Amadeus Press, New York, 2009.

34. Albin Krebs and Robert Mcg. Thomas Jr, 'Notes on People; Wagnerian Ring Cycle is Once Again Complete', *New York Times*, 21 November

1981,   https://www.nytimes.com/1981/11/21/nyregion/notes-on-people-wagnerian-ring-cycle-is-once-again-complete.html.

35. Anvar Alikhan, '"Freddie Mercury was a Prodigy": Rock Star's Panchgani school bandmates remember "Bucky"', *Scroll.in*, 5 September 2016, https://scroll.in/article/815380/freddie-bucky-mercury-the-12-year-old-rockstar-from-panchgani.

36. Laura Jackson, Freddie *Mercury: The Biography*, revised, updated edition, Piatkus, London, 2011.

37. Sooni Taraporevala, *Parsis: The Zoroastrians of India—A Photographic Journey*, Overlook Books, London, 2004.

38. Ian Chapman and Henry Johnson (eds), *Global Glam and Popular Music: Style and Spectacle from the 1970s to the 2000s*, Routledge, Abingdon, 2016.

39. Matt Richards and Mark Langthorne, *Somebody to Love: The Life, Death and Legacy of Freddie Mercury*, Weldon Owen, London, 2016.

40. Shekhar Bhatia, 'Freddie Mercury's Family Tell of Singer's Pride in His Asian heritage', *The Telegraph* (UK), 16 October 2011.

41. Arzan Sam Wadia, 'Old Relatives from Mumbai Pay Tribute to Jer Bulsara', parsikhabar.net, 24 November 2016. https://parsikhabar.net/news/old-relatives-from-mumbai-pay-tribute-to-jer-bulsara/14692/.

42. Sooni Taraporevala, *Parsis: The Zoroastrians of India—A Photographic Journey*, Overlook Books, London, 2004.

43. Laura Jackson, Freddie *Mercury: The Biography*, revised, updated edition, Piatkus, London, 2011.

44. Ibid.

45. Ibid.

46. Ibid.

47. Lesley-Ann Jones, *Bohemian Rhapsody: The Definitive Biography of Freddie Mercury*, Hodder & Stoughton, London, 2011.

Chapter 11: Two Rebels a Century Apart

1. Rukhsana Shroff and Kerman Mehta, *Joyous Flame: The Parsi Zoroastrians,* Parzor Foundation for Preservation of Vulnerable Human Heritage, Delhi, 2011.

2. K.F. Nariman, 'How Madame Cama Upheld India's Honour', *Bombay Chronicle*, 19 August 1938, https://com.wstub.archive.org/details/dli. Granth.12603/page/14/mode/2up?q=Madame+Cama.
3. Author's interview with Muncherji Cama.
4. Bakhtiar K. Dadabhoy, *Sugar in Milk: Lives of Eminent Parsis*, Rupa, Delhi, 2008.
5. Shirin Darasha, *Madame Cama*, Navneet Publications, Delhi, 1997.
6. Khorshed Adi Sethna, Madame Bhikhaiji Rustom Cama, Publications Division, Ministry of Information and Broadcasting, Govt. of India, Delhi, 2013.
7. Nawaz B. Mody, 'Madame Bhikhaiji Rustom Cama—Sentinel of Liberty', *Parsis in Western India: 1818–1920*, Nawaz B. Mody (ed.), Allied Publishers, Mumbai, 1998.
8. Shirin Darasha, *Madame Cama*, Navneet Publications, Delhi, 1997.
9. Nawaz B. Mody, 'Madame Bhikhaiji Rustom Cama—Sentinel of Liberty', *Parsis in Western India: 1818–1920*, Nawaz B. Mody (ed.), Allied Publishers, Mumbai, 1998.
10. Ibid.
11. Ibid.
12. Ibid.
13. Khorshed Adi Sethna, Madame Bhikhaiji Rustom Cama, Publications Division, Ministry of Information and Broadcasting, Govt. of India, Delhi, 2013.
14. Author's interview with Muncherji Cama.
15. Author's interview with Nawaz B. Mody.
16. Author's interview with Kobad Ghandy.
17. Ibid.
18. Sunetra Choudhury, *Behind Bars: Prison Tales of India's Most Famous*, Roli Books, Delhi, 2017.
19. Author's interview with Kobad Ghandy.
20. Ibid.
21. Sheela Bhatt, 'Kobad Ghandy: The Gentle Revolutionary', *Rediff.com*, 23 September 2009, https://news.rediff.com/special/2009/sep/23/kobad-ghandy-the-gentle-revolutionary.
22. Ibid.

23. Author's interview with Jyoti Punwani.
24. Author's interview with Kobad Ghandy.

Chapter 12: Coda: An Ancient Faith in Modern Times

1. Paramita Ghosh, 'A Daughter Fights: When a Parsi Woman Marries a Non-Parsi Man', *Hindustan Times*, 12 February 2018, https://www.hindustantimes.com/india-news/a-daughter-fights/story-wHATGvGvyRYGaB0UPWNojN.html.
2. Author's interview with Jehangir Patel.
3. Jyoti Shelar, 'Zoroastrianism does Not Discriminate, Say Wadia Brothers', *The Hindu*, 26 March 2018, https://www.thehindu.com/news/cities/mumbai/zoroastrianism-does-not-discriminate/article23350456.ece.
4. Firoza Punthakey Mistree and Cashmira Vatcha Bengalli (eds), *The Collected Scholarly Writings of Dastur Firoze M. Kotwal*, vol. 1, Parzor Foundation for Preservation of Vulnerable Human Heritage, Delhi, 2018.
5. Jesse S. Palsetia, *The Parsis of India: Preservation of Identity in Bombay City*, Brill, Leiden, 2001.
6. Ibid.
7. Rukhsana Shroff & Kerman Mehta, *Joyous Flame: The Parsi Zoroastrians*, Parzor Foundation for Preservation of Vulnerable Human Heritage, Delhi, 2011.
8. Eckehard Kulke, *The Parsees in India: A Minority as Agent of Social Change*, Vikas Publishing House, Delhi, 1975.
9. Author's interview with Rohinton Nariman.
10. Ibid.
11. Rohinton F. Nariman, *The Inner Fire: Faith, Choice, and Modern-Day Living in Zoroastrianism*, Hay House Publishers India Pvt. Ltd., Delhi, 2016.
12. Dasturji Khurshed Dastoor, 'Historical Chronology of Kisseh-i-Sanjan and the Iranshah Atash Behram', a paper delivered at 'Celebrating a Treasure: 140 Years at the First Dastoor Meherjirana Library', a Parzor-Meherjirana Initiative held in Navsari, Gujarat, 12–15 January 2013.
13. Fali Major, 'Reaching for the Light', *Parsiana*, 7 March 2016.

14. Jesse S. Palsetia, *The Parsis of India: Preservation of Identity in Bombay City*, Brill, Leiden, 2001.

15. Author's interview with Noshir Dadrawala.

16. Jesse S. Palsetia, *The Parsis of India: Preservation of Identity in Bombay City*, Brill, Leiden, 2001.

17. Ibid.

18. Fali Nariman, 'Parsi Lore and Law', *Parsiana*, 1994.

19. David Hornsby, 'The Zoroastrian Flame: Khojeste Mistree Talks about One of the World's Oldest Surviving Religions and What We can Learn from it in the Present Day', *Beshara Magazine*, Issue 9, 2018.

20. Author's interview with Bachi Karkaria.

21. Author's interview with Jamsheed Kanga.

22. Author's interview with Khojeste Mistree.

23. Firoza Punthakey Mistree and Cashmira Vatcha Bengalli (eds), *The Collected Scholarly Writings of Dastur Firoze M. Kotwal*, vol. 1, Parzor Foundation for Preservation of Vulnerable Human Heritage, Delhi, 2018.

24. Ibid.

25. Ibid.

26. Ibid.

27. Author's interview with Khojeste Mistree.

28. Eckehard Kulke. *The Parsees in India*, Vikas, Delhi, 1978.

29. Jehan Daruwala, 'The Fourth Estate: Pioneering Journalists', in Nawaz B. Mody (ed.), *Enduring Legacy: Parsis of the 20th Century: Volume 2*, published by Nawaz B. Mody, 2005.

30. Author's interview with Shernaaz Engineer.

31. Coomi Vevaina, Adi Marzban, in Nawaz B. Mody (ed.), *Enduring Legacy: Parsis of the 20th Century: Volume 2*, published by Nawaz B. Mody, 2005.

32. Author's interview with Bachi Karkaria.

33. Bachi Karkaria, *In Hot Blood: The Nanavati Case That Shook India*, Juggernaut, Delhi, 2017.

34. Meher Pestonjee, 'Roots', *The Illustrated Weekly of India*, April 1992, https://archive.org/details/in.ernet.dli.2015.100828/page/n91/mode/2up?q=Meher.

35. Firoza Punthakey Mistree and Cashmira Vatcha Bengalli (eds), *The Collected Scholarly Writings of Dastur Firoze M. Kotwal,* vol. 1, Parzor Foundation for Preservation of Vulnerable Human Heritage, Delhi, 2018.

36. Author's interview with Khojeste Mistree.

37. Author's Interview with Kersi Deboo.

38. Prachi Bari, 'India's First "Open Fire Temple" in Pune Breeds New Hope for Zoroastrianism, Parsis', *Hindustan Times*, 24 May 2018, https://www.hindustantimes.com/india-news/india-s-first-open-fre-temple-in-pune-breeds-new-hope-for-zoroastrianism-parsis/ story-dKPl9W25NF649IAMnxvsXL.html.

39. Lisa Gray, 'Zoroastrian "Fire Temple" Opens in Houston', *Houston Chronicle*, 29 March 2019, https://www.houstonchronicle.com/news/houston-texas/houston/article/Zoroastrian-fre-temple-opens-in-Houston-13726958.php.

Index